A. Rippin
Sept '91
BSOAS review

CHRIST IN ISLAM AND CHRISTIANITY

Christ in Islam and Christianity

The Representation of Jesus in the Qur'ān and the Classical Muslim Commentaries

Neal Robinson

Senior Lecturer in Religious Studies
The Cheltenham and Gloucester College of Higher Education

M
MACMILLAN

First published 1991

Published by
MACMILLAN PRESS LTD
Houndmills, Basingstoke, Hampshire RG21 2XS
and London
Companies and representatives
throughout the world

Printed in Great Britain by
Billing & Sons Ltd, Worcester

British Library Cataloguing in Publication Data
Robinson, Neal
Christ in Islam and Christianity.
1. Jesus Christ
I. Title
232
ISBN 0–333–52209–5

To Danielle

ما رَوْضَةٌ مِنْ رِياضِ الحَزْنِ مُعشبةٌ　　خَضْراءُ جادَ عَلَيها مُسْبِلٌ هَطِلُ

يُضاحِكُ الشمسَ منها كوكَبٌ شَرِقٌ　　مُؤَزَّرٌ بِعَمِيمِ النَّبْتِ مُكْتَهِلُ

يَوْماً بِأَطْيَبَ مِنْهَا نَشْرَ رائِحَةٍ ،　　وَلا بِأَحسَنَ مِنها إذْ دَنا الأُصُلُ

al-A‘shā

Contents

Preface

The invitation to deliver five lectures at Essex University in November 1988 encouraged me to give some shape to research which might otherwise have been put to one side indefinitely. I am indebted to Dr Andrew Linzey, Director of the Centre for the Study of Theology, both for the invitation and for other kindnesses. It also gives me pleasure to thank Drs Peter and Margery Wexler for their stimulating hospitality. In addition I must gratefully acknowledge permission to use extracts from the following preparatory studies:

'Fakhr al'Dîn al-Râzî and the Virginal Conception', *Islamochristiana*, XIV, (1988), pp. 1–16.
'Creating Birds from Clay: A Miracle of Jesus in the Qur'ān and Classical Exegesis', *The Muslim World*, LXXIX, (1989), pp. 1–13.
'Jesus and Mary in the Qur'ān: Some Neglected Affinities', *Religion* (Lancaster) XX (1990), pp. 161–75.

The lectures themselves needed considerable revision and amplification to transform them into a book. While carrying out this work I have appreciated the patience and good will of Sophie Lillington of Macmillan and of Anne Rafique.

I would like to thank the staff of the Bibliothèque Nationale Paris and the Bodleian Library Oxford for their helpfulness and Maggie Wheel of the Library of the College of St. Paul and St. Mary for her cheerful persistence in applying for rare books and articles on inter-library loan.

If I were to mention by name the many friends and acquaintances who have helped and encouraged me the list would be embarrassingly long. I cannot, however, refrain from mentioning Geoffrey Paul. Although he died before the work was begun, I have thought of him throughout.

Quotations from the Qu'rān

Throughout the text quotations from the Qur'ān are enclosed within guillemets (« »), to distinguish them from other quoted matter.

Introduction

In January 1979, as the result of a chance encounter in Tunisia, I became interested in Islam and resolved to devote my spare time to learning Arabic in order to study the Qur'ān. Nine months later, when I had acquired a rudimentary knowledge of the language, I moved to Bradford where I had the privilege of meeting ulama[1] from India and Pakistan and students from all over the Arab world. I soon discovered that there was an enormous gulf between Muslim and non-Muslim Qur'anic interpretation. Indeed on one issue in particular – the Qur'anic representation of Jesus – the gulf was so wide that at times I wondered whether Muslim and non-Muslim scholars were talking and writing about the same Book. The non-Muslim scholars generally gave the impression that their approach was objective and based on sound historical method. They tended to dismiss Muslim interpretation as hide-bound by tradition. The Muslims, for their part, insisted that there was a normative interpretation of the Qur'ān enshrined in ancient commentaries such as the *Tafsīr al-Qur'ān al-'Aẓīm* of Ibn Kathīr. They had no time for people who attempted to understand the Qur'ān in the light of unaided reason for they were aware that the Prophet Muḥammad (God bless him and give him peace!) had solemnly warned that anyone who interprets the Qur'ān without knowledge will take his seat in Hell-fire.

Because of my own background in New Testament studies, I felt a certain amount of sympathy with both parties without being entirely at ease with either of them. On the one hand, the historical-critical approach was second nature to me and I could scarcely believe that the definitive interpretation of the Qur'ān was to be found in a Muslim commentary written over six hundred years ago. On the other hand, I was well aware that modern New Testament critics often make naive assumptions about their own scholarly objectivity and that they all too frequently depreciate the labours of patristic and mediaeval commentators. I therefore made up my mind to investigate the history of non-Muslim responses to the Qur'anic representation of Jesus and also to persevere with Arabic until I reached the stage where I would be able to read the classical Muslim commentaries for myself. This work is the fruit of my labours.

Of the two tasks which I set myself the first quickly began to pall. It was not long before I became aware of the age-old tradition of Christian polemic and apologetic which often colours the writing of even the most well-meaning non-Muslim historians. It was also relatively easy to see that non-Muslim historians differed in their approaches, some emphasising the importance of the Christian environment from which Islam emerged, others stressing the vicissitudes of Muḥammad's relations with Christians and still others attaching more importance to his consciousness of being a prophet like Jesus. Chapters 2, 3, 4 and 5 spell this out in more detail. They are elementary surveys which are not meant to be exhaustive. If they help the newcomer to the field to see his or her way through the maze of secondary literature they will have served their purpose.

The classical Muslim commentaries are a different matter. They have proved an endless source of fascination and excitement. Chapters 6, 7 and 8 provide background information which should help to put them into their historical and cultural context. I confess that it was several years before I could begin to read the commentaries themselves. Then at long last, while my brother-in-law and his friend were crossing the Atlantic in a barge, I found myself sailing alone in uncharted and scarcely navigable seas of a different sort. There is a relatively manageable edition of Ibn Kathīr but some of the earlier commentaries are taxing in the extreme. Punctuation is virtually non-existent, the āyas are not numbered, the gaps between words are inadequate and the print is small, cramped and smudged. In truth these works are not meant for closet reading but to be passed on from generation to generation in a setting like that so vividly described by Taha Hussein in his account of his student days at al-Azhar.[2] I mention this in order to make clear from the outset that, despite my efforts, my researches in this area are of a provisional nature. I have selected four topics – Jesus' return, the crucifixion, the miracles and the virginal conception – for extensive treatment. I have attempted to distil from five classical commentaries everything which is of relevance to their interpretation. Most of this material is presented in Chapters 9 to 15 together with brief accounts of the various non-Muslim approaches to the same subjects. In the case of the miracles and the virginal conception I have, however, been selective and have frequently resorted to summary, not wishing to duplicate work which I had published elsewhere. Finally in Chapters 16 and 17 I have examined the way in which the same four key topics are dealt with in the principal Shīʿite and Ṣūfī commentaries.

1 Jesus in the Qur'ān

INTRODUCTION

The Qur'ān, which is comparable in length to the New Testament, is said to have been revealed piecemeal to the Prophet Muḥammad over a period of about twenty-three years. For ten years after the onset of the revelations Muḥammad continued to live in his native Mecca which was an important commercial centre controlling the caravan route between southern Arabia and Syria. Then, because of mounting opposition, he and his followers emigrated to Yathrib, a large oasis which is about 250 miles to the north and which is now known as Medina. The Emigration or *hijra* took place in 622 CE and marks the beginning of the Muslim era.[1]

According to Muslim tradition, when Muḥammad died the whole of the revelation was available on loose writing materials and had also been committed to memory by the Companions. Within a few years several of the Companions, including the first Caliph Abū Bakr, produced written editions of the Qur'ān for their personal use. A standard edition was promulgated by the fourth Caliph 'Uthmān (d.35/656). Subsequently various orthographic improvements were made but the content, order and divisions of the text have remained unchanged.[2]

In printed editions of the Qur'ān the text is divided into ṣūras and āyas.[3] In order to appreciate Islam's relationship to Judaism and Christianity there is no substitute for reading through all one hundred and fourteen ṣūras. They abound in references to God, creation, the Jewish prophets and the forthcoming judgement and resurrection. The following list is limited in scope. It comprises all the passages which explicitly mention Jesus (*'Īsā*), Christians (*Naṣārā*) or the Gospel (*Injīl*) together with a few others which may allude to them. It does not include all the references to the Jews or to 'the People of the Scripture', an expression which can denote both Jews and Christians:

2:26,62,87,111–141,253 // 3:1–84,113–5 // 4:44–57,142,156–75 // 5:14–18,46–120 // 6:84–90,106 // 7:40–9,156–9,179,186 // 9:29–35,80,111–114 // 10:68 // 16:103 // 18:9–26 // 19:1–40,92f. // 21:74–94 // 22:17 // 23:45–55 // 24:34–40 // 33:7–27 // 36:13–32 // 39:4,29 // 42:13–6 // 43:57–65,81 // 44:14 // 48:29 // 57:12–13,25–29 // 58:7 // 61:1–14 // 66:1–12 // 85:1–9 // 98:1–8 // 105:1–5 // 112.

If we concentrate more narrowly on the references to Jesus and piece them together we will obtain the following composite picture.

THE QUR'ANIC JESUS: A COMPOSITE PICTURE

The story of Jesus is told at some length with particular stress on the background to his birth. Before Mary was born, her mother, the wife of 'Imrān, vowed that the child would be a consecrated offering to God. She was distressed at giving birth to a girl but sought God's protection from Satan for her and her offspring. God accepted her and when she had grown up Zechariah was chosen by lot to be her guardian. Whenever Zechariah went into the sanctuary where Mary lived he found that she had food which she claimed had been supplied by God (3:33–7,44).

There are two accounts of Zechariah's asking God to provide him with an heir and of his incredulity when told that despite his advanced age and his wife's barrenness he would have a son (3:38–41 and 19:2–15). The details about Zechariah and his son John need not concern us. Suffice it to note that in one version it is stated that John would believe in a word from God (3:39) and that in the other version it seems to be implied the name John had not previously been bestowed on anyone (19:7).

The annunciation to Mary is also related twice. It occurred when she had withdrawn in an easterly direction and was concealed by a curtain or screen. Mary was told that God had chosen her and made her pure and preferred her above all the women of creation. She was given good tidings of a word from God whose name was the Messiah Jesus Son of Mary; he would be illustrious in the world and in the hereafter and was one of those brought near. In one version the news is said to have been announced by the angels whereas in the other version there is reference to God's Spirit who took the form of a perfect man and who reassured her that he was only a messenger sent from her Lord in order to bestow on her a pure boy. Mary asked how she could have a son since she had not been unchaste. According to one version she received the reply that God creates what He wills by simply decreeing it. According to the other version she was told that it was easy for God and that he would be made a sign for mankind, a mercy from God and a thing ordained (3:42–47, 19:16–22). In neither account of the annunciation are we told any more about how the conception occurred but elsewhere there are two brief allusions to

God breathing into Mary of His Spirit (21:91, 66:12).

When Mary conceived she withdrew to a distant place. She was driven by the pangs of childbirth to the trunk of a palm tree and she wished that she were dead and forgotten. A voice told her not to grieve but to drink from the rivulet which her Lord had placed beneath there and to eat the ripe dates which would fall upon her when she shook the tree (19:22–25 cf. 23:50). Mary was instructed not to speak to anyone. She then brought the child to her own folk who expressed their stunned amazement addressing her as 'Sister of Aaron' and exclaiming that her father had not been a wicked man nor had her mother been a whore. She pointed to the infant and he spoke to them in her defence asserting that he was God's servant, that God had given him the Scripture and had appointed him a prophet. He said that God had made him blessed wheresoever he was and had enjoined upon him prayer and alms-giving for the duration of his life. Finally he declared that peace was upon him on the day of his birth, the day of his death and the day of his being raised to life (19:26–33).

Little is said about Jesus' teaching although at the annunciation Mary was told that he was destined to speak to mankind in the cradle and also when of mature age (3:46). To perform his task he was strengthened by the Holy Spirit and given signs (5:110, 2:87) and God taught him the Scripture and Wisdom and the Torah and the Gospel (3:48, 5:110). Jesus attested the truth of what was in the Torah (3:50, 5:46, 61:6). He made lawful some of the things that were forbidden to the Children of Israel in his day (3:50 cf. 3:93). He came to them with wisdom and made plain to them some of the things about which they were in disagreement (43:63). He enjoined on them fear of God and obedience to himself and the main thrust of his message was that God was his Lord and their Lord and that to worship God was the straight path (3:50f, cf. 5:72, 117, 19:36, 43:64). He warned them that paradise was forbidden to those who ascribe partners to God (5:72) and he cursed those of the Children of Israel who went astray (5:78). The religion which he was sent to establish was that of Noah, Abraham, Moses and subsequently of Muḥammad himself (33:7, 42:13). The Gospel which was bestowed upon him contained guidance light and admonition (5:46). It compared worshippers to seed which shoots up delighting the sowers (48:29). Like the Torah which it confirmed and the Qur'ān which was revealed after it, it contained God's promise of paradise to those who gave their lives fighting in God's cause (9:111). It also mentioned the coming of an unlettered prophet (7:157). Jesus himself brought good tidings of one whose name would be Aḥmad (or 'more highly praised')[4] (61:6). He summoned his own disciples to be 'helpers' in God's cause and they described themselves as those who were 'submitted' and who 'bore witness' (3:52f., 5:111, 61:14).

The signs which Jesus performed by divine permission are listed twice. First, at the annunciation Mary was told that he would be a messenger to the Children of Israel. As a sign for them from their Lord he would fashion a bird from clay which would become a real bird when he breathed into it, he would heal the blind from birth and the leper, he would raise the dead and he would announce to them what they ate and what they stored in their houses (3:49). The second list is given in retrospect when God reminds Jesus of his favour towards him and his mother. The list is very similar to the first one but it lacks the reference to Jesus' clairvoyance. Moreover in reminding Jesus of his favour God adds that He restained the Children of Israel from him when the unbelievers among them reacted to his coming to them with clear proofs by accusing him of sorcery (5:110, cf. 61:6) Appended to the second list is an account of how the disciples asked Jesus whether his Lord was able to send down a table spread with food for them to eat so that they might know for certain that he had spoken the truth. Jesus asked God to send it down as a feast for the first of them and the last of them and as a sign. God answered that He would send it down and that after that He would punish in an unprecedented way any who disbelieved (5:112–115).

The references to the end of Jesus' earthly existence are some of the most puzzling. The unbelievers schemed and God schemed, and God is the best of schemers. God told Jesus that He purposed to 'receive him' (or 'cause him to die'?), raise him to Himself and purify him from those who disbelieved (3:54f, cf. 5:117). The People of the Scripture, who were guilty of speaking a tremendous calumny against Mary, also said that they slew the Messiah Jesus Son of Mary whereas they did not slay him or crucify him but it appeared so to them. God raised him to Himself and moreover there is not one of them who will not believe in him before his death and on the day of resurrection he will be a witness against them (4:156–9). Finally there may be an oblique reference to Jesus' future return as being indicative of the approaching hour of judgement (43:61).

Jesus' name occurs in lists of prophets whom God inspired (4:163) who were of the righteous (6:85) and with whom God took a solemn covenant (33:7). It is asserted that the Messiah Jesus son of Mary was only a messenger of God, His word which He conveyed to Mary and a spirit from Him (4:171). He was like Adam whom God created from dust and whom God commanded into being (3:59). He was a servant on whom God bestowed his favour and made a pattern for the Children of Israel (43:59, cf. 4:172, 19:30). God constituted him and his mother a sign (23:50). Yet he was only a messenger and there had been messengers who passed away before him. His mother was a saintly woman but they were both mortals who ate food (5:75). If God had wished to destroy him and his mother with everyone else on earth none could have hindered Him (5:17). When challenged by God, Jesus denies that he told mankind to take him and his mother as two additional deities: he pleads that God knows what is in his mind but that he does not know what is in God's mind (5:116). Christians should not exaggerate in their religion nor say anything about God other than the truth. They should cease saying 'three'; they wrongly call Jesus Son of God for God is far above taking a son (4:171, cf. 9:30 etc.) Those who say that God is the Messiah son of Mary or that God is the third of three are indeed disbelievers (5:72f).

DISCUSSION

The above summary is only an initial approximation. It is of limited value for at least four reasons. First, it is inevitably coloured by decisions about the translation and interpretation of the passages on which it draws. Second, although most of the Qur'anic references to Jesus have been taken into account, the material which refers to Christians or has a bearing on their beliefs is much more extensive. Third, no attention has been paid to the order in which the material was revealed and to the possibility that the Qur'anic representation of Jesus developed and changed with the passage of time. Fourth, the summary ignores the form of the revelations and might therefore give the misleading impression that the Qur'ān is little more than a collection of propositional statements.[5] I shall attempt to compensate for these deficiencies in later chapters. Nevertheless the summary as it stands will furnish us with an adequate basis on which to examine the responses of Christian polemicists and apologists.

2 'Īsā Through Christian Eyes: Polemic and Apologetic

The secondary literature about Jesus in the Qur'ān written by non-Muslims is extensive and I cannot undertake a complete survey.[1] My concern is simply to distinguish the different perspectives from which the subject has been approached. In this chapter I will examine two specifically Christian perspectives which both entail the a priori conviction that the truth claims of Christianity are correct and that the Christ of Christendom is the yardstick by which the Qur'anic 'Īsā must be judged. The first of these is the polemical perspective. The second I shall call the apologetic perspective for want of a better name.

THE POLEMICAL PERSPECTIVE

As Islam rapidly overran many of the former Christian territories of the Byzantine Empire, Christian theologians not unnaturally developed a polemical approach to the new religion which they perceived to be inimical to their own faith. Many of the arguments used by the Byzantine polemicists filtered through to Western Christendom and survived the waning of the Middle Ages to become the stock-in-trade of nineteenth-century Protestant missionaries. At the risk of oversystematising, I suggest that there are four principal strands to the polemical response to the portrayal of Jesus in the Qur'ān. First, there is the claim that what the Qur'ān says about Jesus and Christianity is hopelessly distorted. Second, there is the attempt to pinpoint factual errors in the Qur'ān which can be shown to be based on misunderstandings. Third, there is the allegation that Muḥammad derived his information from heretical or Jewish informants and fourth, there is the insistence that there are elements in the Qur'anic representation of Jesus which are more Christian than Muslims suppose. Let us look briefly at each of these strands in turn.

From early times, many Christians have rejected what the Qur'ān says about Jesus and about their own beliefs on the grounds that it is distorted. For instance al-Kindī (died c.204/820) stated that the Qur'ān's insistence that God had never taken a consort or a son and that He was without equal was wide off the mark if aimed against the teaching of the Church.[2] At a slightly later date the Muslim scholar al-Jāḥiẓ was commissioned to write a tract replying to Christian criticisms of Islam. We learn from this that the Christians in his day flatly denied that they had ever believed secretly or publicly in the divinity of Mary. Moreover they ridiculed the Qur'ān's assertion that Jesus spoke to mankind in his infancy insisting that, despite their great number and the diversity of the countries in which they lived, they knew nothing of this miracle and had no record of it in their scriptures.[3] Equally ancient is the Christian rejection of the insinuation that Jesus foretold the coming of Muḥammad.[4]

Potentially more damaging is the polemicists' claim to have pinpointed factual errors in the Qur'ān which they could account for. I shall mention only three of the most famous of these. First, there is the statement that nobody had been called John before Zechariah's son (19:7). Already in al-Jāḥiẓ's day Christians were arguing that this was based on a misunderstanding of *Luke* 1:61 where we read that there was nobody in Zechariah's family who bore that name.[5] Second, a ninth-century Christian theologian called Nicetas of Byzantium noted the oddity of Mary's being greeted as 'Sister of Aaron' (19:28). He concluded that Mary, whose name in Greek and Arabic is Maryam, had been confused with Miriam the sister of Aaron and Moses.[6] Subsequent writers took this a step further by indicating that 'Imrān, the name which the Qur'ān gives to Mary's father, sounds suspiciously like Amram the Old Testament name of the father of Moses, Aaron and Miriam (*Numbers* 26:59). Third, in the seventeenth century Maracci argued that Muḥammad called Jesus *'Īsā* because he confused him with Esau.[7]

If the Qur'ān gives a distorted and inaccurate account of Jesus and of Christian beliefs about him it cannot be of divine origin. Christian polemicists were not slow to point this out and often suggested more mundane sources from which Muḥammad might have gained his information. In so doing they were not without a precedent because we learn from the Qur'ān itself that some of Muḥammad's contemporaries thought that he relied on a human teacher (16:103, 25:4f, 44:13f). Two ancient suggestions which continued in vogue for centuries were that he was instructed by the Arian monk Baḥīrā whom he encountered during his childhood or alternatively that a Nestorian monk called Sergius deliberately set out to use him to corrupt the Arabs.[8] Others have claimed that Muḥammad derived his information from his wife's cousin Waraqa, from a Christian bishop called Quss whose sermons he heard while attending the fair at 'Ukāẓ or from Salmān the Persian who helped him erect siege works to protect Medina.[9] On the whole the polemicists favoured heretical Christian informers rather than Jews. Nevertheless al-Kindī thought that the Qur'ān echoed the false accusations made against Christianity by early Jewish converts to Islam[10] and Maracci assumed that the Jews called Jesus Esau out of hatred and that Muḥammad took the name from them in good faith.[11]

The fourth strand in the polemical response – the insistence that, despite everything, there are elements in the Qur'anic representation of Jesus which are more Christian than Muslims suppose – has had a lasting influence. John of Damascus indicated that the Qur'ān refers to Jesus as 'word' and 'spirit' and argued that since God cannot be separated from His word and His spirit Jesus must be divine.[12] Others, as we shall see in a later chapter, took issue with the Muslim claim that the Qur'ān denies the crucifixion and pointed to texts such as 3:55 and 19:33 which seemed to them to assert the reality of Jesus' death.

CHRISTIAN APOLOGETIC

In the modern period a number of Christian writers have laid maximum stress on the fourth strand of the polemical response while doing their best to ignore the other strands or to explain them away. I have dubbed these writers 'apologists' because they frequently seem to be motivated by the desire to commend the Christian faith to Muslims. Nevertheless other motives may sometimes be present and will be discussed at the end of the chapter.

There are a number of important details on which the Qur'ān and the New Testament appear to be in agreement. These include the blessedness of Mary, the virgin birth of Jesus, the description of him as Messiah, servant and prophet, and the belief that he healed the blind, cleansed lepers and raised the dead to life. Apologists concentrate on this common ground and build upon it by reading in Christian meanings. They argue for instance that virginal conception and the miracles which the Qur'ān attributes to Jesus imply that he was more than human and that the title 'servant' connotes the suffering servant prophesied by Isaiah or the portrayal of Jesus in the Christological hymn of *Philippians* 2:6–11.

The principal plank in the apologists' argument is the Qur'anic reference to Jesus as 'word' and 'spirit'. Charles-J. Ledit does not hesitate to assert that the Qur'ān proclaims the incarnation of the Word of God who was with God from the beginning and assisted Him in the act of creation. He bases this claim on the fact that in one of the Qur'anic accounts of the annunciation Jesus is described as both 'Word' and 'one of those brought near' (3:45). According to his line of reasoning if Jesus were simply called 'one of those brought near' the implication would be that he was an incarnation of one of the spirits who stand in God's presence (cf. 4:172). But since he is also called 'Word' he differs from the other spirits in not being a reality exterior to God but one which proceeds from His ineffable Being just as speech is formed in our mind before it is spoken.[13] Now the problem with this is that the Qur'ān seems not to attach any great significance to the title 'word', for in an āya which specifically warns Christians against exaggerating it says that Jesus was « . .*only* a messenger of God and His word which He cast unto Mary and a spirit from Him . . .» (4:171, my emphasis). Ledit glosses over this problem but R.C. Zaehner tackles it head on. He notes that the same āya includes a denial that God has a son and so he comments:

> What, in fact, is Muhammad denying in this passage? Nothing more, it would appear, than that God was physically the Father of Jesus . . . In this passage he in fact affirms not only the Virgin Birth on which the Qur'ān always lays great emphasis, but also that Christ is 'only' God's messenger and His *Word* (*kalima*) – a spirit from Him, that is to say not carnally conceived, but conceived by the divine afflatus and the divine *fiat* – exactly, then, what orthodox Christianity means by the 'Word made flesh'.[14]

Yet will the Qur'ān go as far as recognising in Jesus that divine character which calls for worship? Ledit suggests that the Qur'ān provides a 'stepping stone' in that direction when it narrates how God commanded the angels to prostrate themselves before a human being whom He created from clay and into whom He breathed some of His spirit (38:71–4). Noting that this passage refers to a 'human being' rather than to Adam, Ledit interprets it as a reference to Christ whom St Paul describes as the second Adam, a spirit who brings life (*1 Corinthians* 15:45)[15]. Once again Ledit has glossed over a serious problem because he fails to mention that there are six other references to this incident in the Qur'ān and that all six explicitly mention Adam. Zaehner is more honest but less cautious. He notes that the Qur'ān compares the creation of Jesus to the creation of Adam (3:59) and so he turns to examine what it says about the latter and remarks:

> it seems clear that Adam is regarded as being a divine being, for it is not lawful to fall down in obeisance to any but God . . . Moreover, in comparing Jesus to Adam, Muhammad was, no doubt, unconsciously reproducing the Christian doctrine of Jesus as the second Adam. It would therefore follow that Jesus who was sinless and presumably on that account raised by God unto Himself, was also worthy of worship from the moment that God breathed His spirit upon Mary, just as Adam was before Him. But whereas Adam lost the divine spirit by sin, Jesus did not and was accordingly raised up to God's own presence where He must remain a legitimate object of worship for all time.[16]

In all this the modern apologists are simply extending arguments which can be found in embryonic form in the writings of the early polemicists. Nevertheless there is an important difference. The polemicists were unperturbed by the apparent tensions in the Qur'ān: if some āyas pointed to the divinity of Christ whereas others flatly denied that he was divine that was not their problem. The apologists, on the other hand, usually treat these tensions more circumspectly. They occasionally admit that such tensions exist but play them down by suggesting that the negative statements in the later ṣūras can be attributed to a growing hostility to Christianity which was historically conditioned.[17] More often, however, they attempt to reduce the tension by attenuating the Qur'ān's negative statements. Take for example the repeated denials that God has a son. Christian apologists suggest that many of the passages in the Qur'ān which contain these denials make no mention of Jesus for the simple reason that they are actually directed against Arab paganism rather than against Christianity. The remaining passages can be accounted for by assuming that Muslims who had recently been converted from Arab paganism inevitably understood the Christian Trinity as an analogue of the pagan triads worshipped in pre-Islamic Arabia, that is to say they supposed that Christians were tritheists who worshipped God, Mary and their son Jesus.[18] In any case, they argue, orthodox Christians agree with the Qur'ān that God is a single Reality who «neither begets nor is begotten» (112:3) and that God is not «the third of three» (5:73). They share the Qur'anic repugnance at the very thought of Mary's being God's consort and of God physically begetting a son.

The apologists' approach to the crucifixion is very similar. Not content, like the polemicists, merely to point to āyas which seem to refer to Jesus' death, they exercise considerable ingenuity in interpreting 4:157 so as to attenuate, or even dispose of, the apparent denial of the crucifixion. Their views on this matter will be examined in detail in Chapter 11.

DISCUSSION

The weaknesses of the polemical perspective are obvious. The polemicists suffer from selective vision; their vested interest in Christianity leads them to focus on certain issues while ignoring others and it prevents them from evaluating their observations impartially. Nevertheless some of their observations are intriguing and have, as we shall see, helped to set the agenda for serious historical investigation.

The apologetic perspective is more difficult to assess. It is undeniable that there are passages in the Qur'ān which speak of Jesus and Mary in terms which are redolent of Christian devotion and which would have appealed to Muḥammad's Christian contempories. There is therefore nothing intrinsically improbable in the apologists' basic assumption that the Qur'ān – at least in part – is less anti-Christian than its Muslim interpreters allege. One looks in vain, however, for a sustained attempt to test this assumption by grappling with the Muslim exegetical tradition. Moreover, despite the apologists' insistence on their own impartiality, their approach probably owes much to extrinsic factors. Three such factors merit consideration. First, – although I doubt that this is true of either Ledit or Zaehner – there may sometimes be an element of bad faith, an underhanded and dishonest attempt to commend Christianity to Muslims by foisting on them a Christian interpretation of the Qur'ān which they know full well does not do justice to all the evidence.[19] Second, there is the influence of that venerable tradition within Christianity which identifies Jesus Christ as the incarnation of the *Logos* or universal cosmic Reason. The implications of that identification are that although the fullness of God's truth is only found in Jesus Christ it is nonetheless present in a piecemeal and partial fashion in the whole human race. Consequently non-Christian religions can be regarded as having an educative role in preparing men and women for the fullness of the Gospel.[20] Third, in some writers there may be a deep-seated psychological need – an urge to reconcile their intuitive recognition of the validity of Muslim experience of the Transcendant with their own continued allegiance to traditional Christian verities.[21]

It seems appropriate at this point to mention the work of Kenneth Cragg and Geoffrey Parrinder neither of whom is easy to categorise. Although a former research student of Zaehner, Cragg differs from him in his apparent readiness to accept that there is a sense in which the Qur'ān does deny both the divinity of Christ and his death on the cross. At any rate, he avoids tackling these denials head on. He attempts instead to bring the Qur'ān and New Testament into dialogue with each other. For instance in one of his recent books he draws attention to the Qur'anic assertion that the Messiah will never scorn (*yastankifa*) to be a servant of God (4:172) and links it with the Christological hymn in *Philippians* which speaks of Jesus emptying himself and taking the form of a servant. Unlike the Qur'anic passage however, the Christological hymn is not juxtaposed with a denial that God could ever have a son. Cragg comments:

> Paul, in Phil. 2 is saying, in line with the Qur'ān, that Jesus as Messiah will never consider servanthood beneath his dignity (this is the sense of *yastankifa*) but gladly embraces it as the self-expanding task of love. He makes no reservation of himself in obedience to the costly will of God. This, as Paul sees it, is the very nature of Christ's Sonship. In Surah 4:172, the same readiness in Jesus for humility is stated and saluted. But the passage sees this servanthood as the very disqualification of the notion that Jesus is 'Son'. Clearly the 'sonship' here in mind is that of pampered 'status' which will not soil a hand, lest the heir be mistaken for a menial slave. Such is not the Sonship of Jesus in the New Testament. The logic by which, for the Qur'ān, Jesus can never be 'Son' to God is precisely the logic by which, for Paul and the New Testament, he is. Both Scriptures affirm his being gladly 'servant' to God. That is their unity. The Qur'ān however, denies his 'Sonship' on the very grounds in which the Christian sees it to consist, namely a loving obedience to God. For the latter there is a quality of service which only the 'Son' can bring.[22]

Parrinder's approach as exemplified in *Jesus in the Qur'ān*[23] is different again and is perhaps best described as eclectic. This book is a mine of valuable information and scholarly reflection. Nevertheless on sensitive issues which divide Muslims and Christians the author tends somewhat cautiously to come down on the side of the apologists.

3 ʿĪsā and the Church Historian

In this chapter two broad areas of historical research will be considered: first, the study of Eastern Christianity and its penetration into Arabia and second, the quest for parallels to the Qur'anic material in ancient Christian writings.

EASTERN CHRISTIANITY AND ITS PENETRATION OF ARABIA[1]

For several centuries before the rise of Islam international affairs in the Near East were dominated by the rivalry of Byzantium and Persia. To a great extent what happened on the ecclesiastical scene was determined by the home and foreign policies of these two great political powers.

The Byzantine Empire was staunchly Christian. The Byzantines' penchant for Greek philosophy and their desire for a united church and state led to an obsession with Christological debates and conflicts. Two of the heresies which they condemned in the fifth century were still influential in Muḥammad's time. The first of these was Nestorianism, named after Nestorius the Patriarch of Constantinople who was deposed by the Council of Ephesus in 431. He was a Syrian by birth and Nestorianism took root in Edessa the intellectual centre of the Syriac Christian world. The second heresy was Monophysitism, the doctrine that after the incarnation Christ had only one nature or *phusis*. Monophysitism was condemned at Chalcedon in 451 but never extirpated. Despite bitter persecution[2] it thrived among Syriac-speaking Christians and amongst the Copts in Egypt whence it spread to neighbouring Abyssinia. Byzantium did not only persecute Christian heretics; she was equally intolerant of Jews and Manichees.

Within the Persian Empire the situation was different. The state religion was Zoroastrianism and heresies including Manichaeism were rigorously supressed but ethnic minorities enjoyed a fair degree of religious freedom. In particular there were large settlements of

Aramaic-speaking Jews and Syriac-speaking Christians of Nestorian persuasion. The Jewish settlements were ancient and well-established, some of them having been in continued existence since the Babylonian exile in the sixth century before Christ. The Nestorian Christians were relative new-comers, refugees who had crossed the border to escape Byzantine persecution. The first wave came in the immediate aftermath of the Council of Ephesus but their numbers were swelled in 489, when the theological school at Edessa was closed by order of the Byzantine Emperor. A few years later the school reopened but in Nisibis and under Persian protection. The Nestorians were active missionaries and spread from Persia following the trade routes as far as Ceylon and China.

Persia and Byzantium courted the favour of the semi-nomadic Arab principalities on their southern frontiers so as to secure themselves from the attacks of the nomads of the Arabian peninsula. Persia's clients, the Lakhmid dynasty of Ḥīra, were officially pagan but many of their subjects were Nestorians or Monophysites. Although in principle Byzantium was intolerant of heresy she was of necessity more lenient in her foreign policy. Her clients, the Ghassanids, were solidly Monophysite. Moreover because of their importance for Byzantine security they were able to further the interests of Syriac- and Arabic-speaking Monophysites on both sides of the frontier. In 542, at the request of the Ghassanid phylarch Ḥārith, the Empress Theodora went as far as arranging for the consecration of two roving bishops to care for the Syro-Arab Monophysite communities.

Even the religious history of the southern part of the Arabian Peninsula was affected by the policies of Persia and Byzantium. The Byzantine Emperor Justinian preferred Monophysitism to Judaism because he associated the latter with Persian interests. He therefore backed the Abyssinians when in 525 they launched a punitive expedition against Dhū Nuwās the Jewish king of Yemen to avenge the deaths of the Monophysite martyrs of Najrān. For a brief period after this Yemen had Abyssinan Monophysite rulers. One such ruler called Abraha constructed a magnificent church in Ṣan'a in the hope of creaming off the lucrative pilgrim traffic from the pagan cult centre in Mecca. Not content with this he marched on Mecca in 570 but was forced to retreat. Persia reacted by invading Yemen, ousting the Abyssinians and installing a regime which was tolerant towards pagans, Jews and Christians but which probably favoured Nestorians rather than Monophysites.

Our information concerning religion in the Arabian heartland is more sketchy. Muslim historians give the impression that, apart from the large settlements of Jews at Khaybar and Yathrib, the population was predominantly pagan. It is possible, however, that they deliberately played down the presence of Christianity for apologetic reasons. Certainly Orthodox Christianity can have had little appeal to the Arabs, for it was associated with Byzantine imperialism, but Monophysitism and Nestorianism were diffused by the Christianised and semi-Christianised tribes in the north and were also actively propagated by missionaries. Moreover, since for centuries Arabia had proved a safe haven for those fleeing from persecution we should probably posit the presence of other heresies including various forms of Jewish Christianity as well of Manichaeism which was a religion in its own right. There is no evidence of organised Christianity in Mecca but the Meccans controlled the trade which passed up and down the Western fringe of Arabia and were thus in direct contact with Christians in Syria and Najrān as well as with Christian towns and monasteries along the caravan route. There were individual Christians who resided there including Abyssinian slaves and Syrian merchants.[3] There were also a handful of indigenous Arabs who were drawn to monotheism apparently without formerly attaching themselves to Judaism or Christianity.[4] The Kaaba is reputed to have contained pictures of Jesus and Mary along with many idols, and a pre-Islamic Christian poet seems to have identified the supreme God of the Kaaba with his own God.[5]

PARALLELS TO THE QUR'ANIC MATERIAL IN ANCIENT CHRISTIAN WRITINGS

It is unlikely that the canonical Christian scriptures or other Christian writings were translated into Arabic before the rise of Islam.[6] Thus we should probably think in terms of an indirect knowledge of Christian sources based on hearsay or *ad hoc* translation rather than on literary borrowing. But what were these sources? In broad terms Syriac Christian literature seems a strong candidate for several reasons. First, Syriac accounts for a large proportion of the borrowed words in the Qur'ān and for the Qur'anic spelling of many Biblical names.[7] The peculiar spelling of *'Īsā* still remains something of an enigma but the most plausible explanation is that it is derived from Isho, the Syriac name for Jesus. This explanation is preferable to the one advocated by the polemicists for there is no evidence that Jews have ever called Jesus Esau. Second, in common with the homilies of Syriac church fathers the Qur'ān repeatedly stresses the horrors of hell-fire and the voluptuous rewards of paradise and cites God's creative power as proof of His ability to resurrect the dead.[8] Third, certain features of the Qur'anic references to Biblical characters are in keeping with the Syrian Church's typological exegesis which saw the Old Testament through the eyes of the New. For instance the description of Mary as 'Sister of Aaron' (19:28), which seemed such a blunder to the polemicists, would surely not have seemed in the least odd to Christians who thought of Mary as having been present on Mount Horeb as the burning bush which was not consumed.[9] Similarly Jesus' summons to his disciples to be 'helpers' in God's cause (61:14), which sounds like a call to jihād, makes admirable sense on the assumption that Jesus was present in Old Testament times as Joshua who led the Children of Israel in the conquest of the Promised Land.[10]

Typological fusion of the New Testament with the Old may also be the key to the curious episode of the table spread (5:112–115). The Qur'ān hints at a special meal shared by Jesus and his disciples, a meal which constitutes a festival, it is therefore natural to look for points of contact with the last supper. In the Qur'ān the disciples make their request in order that their hearts may be put at rest and that they may know that Jesus has spoken the truth. This is reminiscent of words from the supper discourse in John's Gospel, 'Let not your hearts be troubled. You believe in God, believe also in me', (*John* 14:1). In the Qur'ān God threatens that henceforth He will punish in an unprecedented way any who are disobedient. This might be a distant echo of Paul's claim that many of the Corinthians had been punished for participating in the Lord's supper unworthily (*1 Cor.* 11:27–30) or it might be derived from the Old Testament story of how God punished many of the Israelites after feeding them with the manna. These two explanations are not mutually exclusive for Paul interpreted the Old Testament story typologically (*1 Cor.* 10:1–10). Finally the most puzzling feature of the Qur'anic episode, the disciples' request for a table to be sent down for them, could also be based on typological exegesis of the same Old Testament story, for according to the Psalmist the people sinned by saying, 'Can God spread a table in the wilderness?' (*Psalm* 78:19)[11]

A further pointer to the influence of Syriac Christian literature is the Qur'ān's apparent debt to the gospel harmony known as Tatian's

Diatesseron. This was a composite work comprising sections of *Matthew*, *Mark* and *Luke* inserted into John's framework so as to produce a single book. It began with the Johannine prologue about the Word, progressed through Luke's accounts of the angelic annunciations to Zechariah and Mary and followed the latter with Matthew's report of how Mary was found to be with child by the Holy Spirit. This tallies with the Qur'anic reference to 'the Gospel' rather than to the gospels, with the designation of Jesus as God's Word which He cast unto Mary, with the high profile given to Zechariah and Mary, and with the apparent identification of the angel Gabriel with the Holy Spirit.[12] It should further be noted that whereas Luke tells us that Mary queried the angel's good tidings on the grounds that she did not 'know' a man (*Luke* 1:34), in Tatian's version she said that no man had known her. This slight change which makes the male the active partner seems to be reflected in the Qur'ān in Mary's insistence that no man had touched her (3:47 and 19:20)[13]

Some of the features of the Qur'anic representation of Jesus which cannot be traced to the canonical gospels or to the *Diatesseron* are reminiscent of the apocryphal infancy gospels. The *Protoevangelium of James* mentions that as a child Mary received food from an angel, that when she was 12 a guardian was chosen for her by casting lots and that immediately before the annunciation she was occupied making a curtain for the temple.[14] The Latin *Gospel of Pseudo-Matthew* includes the miracle of the palm tree and the stream but in the context of the flight into Egypt.[15] *Pace* the anti-Muslim polemicists, there may have been Christians who believed that Jesus spoke in the cradle for this is mentioned in the *Arabic Infancy Gospel*.[16] Finally the miracle of creating birds from clay is found in the *Infancy Story of Thomas*.[17] Syriac translations of the *Protoevangelium of James* and the *Infancy Story of Thomas* existed in pre-Islamic times. The *Arabic Infancy Gospel* and the *Gospel of Pseudo-Matthew* are later works but both probably drew on pre-Islamic Syriac sources.

Up until now I have spoken in general terms of the influence of Syriac Christian literature. Is it possible to be more specific about the sectarian nature of the influence? Typological exegesis of the Old Testament and eschatological piety were characteristic of Syrian Christianity right across the board. The infancy gospels appealed to the masses more than to the theologians but were doubtless popular with Orthodox and 'heretics' alike. The *Diatesseron* is, however, a somewhat different matter. Originally favoured by all Syrian Christians, it was banned by Rabbula the Orthodox bishop of Edessa in the first half of the fifth century; nevertheless it long continued in vogue amongst Nestorians and Monophysites. Moreover there are other features of the Qur'anic representation of Jesus which arguably point to Nestorian and Monophysite influence. Nestorius objected to calling Mary by the title *Theotokos* – God-bearer or Mother of God. J.N.D. Kelly sums up his attitude as follows:

> God cannot have a mother, he argued, and no creature could have engendered the Godhead; Mary bore a man the vehicle of divinity but not God. The Godhead cannot have been carried for nine months in a woman's womb, or have been wrapped in baby-clothes, or have suffered, died and been buried.[18]

The Qur'ān's insinuation that Christians took Jesus and Mary as deities in addition to God (5:116) may therefore echo Nestorian anti-Orthodox polemic. Furthermore, Schedl has recently drawn attention to a Nestorian text which provides a precedent for the Qur'ān's insistence that those who say God is the Messiah are unbelievers (5:17).[19] Nestorius's real concern seems to have been to safeguard the distinctness of the human and divine natures of Christ and to avoid any suspicion that they were mixed or confused. However his language was often deliberately provocative and to his opponents it seemed that he was splitting Christ into two distinct persons. The Monophysites went to the other extreme and jeopardised Christ's humanity by stating that after the incarnation he had only a single divine nature and that 'the Trinity was one Divinity, one Nature, one Essence'.[20] In the light of all this it is arguable that the Qur'ān sides at times with the Nestorians and at times with the Monophysites but attempts to resolve the difference between them by insisting that neither of them are right about the person of Christ. In agreement with the Nestorians it stresses the full humanity of Jesus and Mary. In agreement with the Monophysites it emphasises that God is One. In opposition to both it rejects all Trinitarian language and all talk of divine Sonship no matter how it is understood.

The above explanation of the Qur'anic representation of Jesus exclusively in terms of Nestorian and Monophysite influence is attractive because it is a neat solution to the problem. It is, however, almost certainly an oversimplification. There are other Christian movements which need to be taken into account. Monophysitism spawned a number of heresies of its own including Tritheism.[21] It is conceivable that the Qur'anic injunction to Christians to cease saying 'three' was a direct appeal to opponents of this particular deviation.

A second off-shoot of Monophysitism was Julianism, the doctrine that from the moment of the incarnation Christ's body was incorruptible. The enigmatic statement in the Qur'ān which appears to deny Christ's death on the cross may be a reflection of this doctrine. Alternatively it may be a reflection of Gnostic teaching about the crucifixion of a substitute.[22] The fourth-century Christian heresiologist Epiphanius mentions the Antideco-Marianites who worshipped Mary as a goddess.[23] It is possibly they who are envisaged in the Qur'anic insinuation that Christians deified both Jesus and his mother. Epiphanius and other church fathers also mention several Jewish Christian sects which were active in Arabia. These included the Ebionites and Elkesaites. Although our knowledge about them is very fragmentary and there is no direct evidence that they were active in Muḥammad's time, there is much in the Qur'ān which is in accord with their beliefs and practices.[24] They were radically anti-Trinitarian, revering Jesus as an angel and prophet but denying that he was divine or that his death had saving significance. They had their own gospel and rejected the epistles of Paul who is significantly never mentioned in the Qur'ān.[25] Moreover, like the Muslims they practised circumcision, abstained from wine and performed elaborate ablutions before their prayers. Closely related to Jewish Christianity was the eclectic religion known as Manichaeism. Mani its founder had at one stage been an Elkesaite. He taught that Jesus was a prophet but denied that he was crucified.[26] More interestingly still, he believed that the Paraclete had not been effectively revealed until he himself experienced his first vision, which provides a precedent for the Qur'ān's apparent identification of Muḥammad with the Paraclete.[27] The fact that the Qur'ān comprises 114 ṣūras may also indicate a link with Manichaeism because there are the same number of logia in the *Gospel of Thomas*, an apocryphal writing which was highly prized by the Manichees.[28]

The situation is further complicated by the known presence of Jews in pre-Islamic Arabia. The influence of Judaism on the ṣūras revealed in Medina is generally recognised.[29] Even here however, it is not always easy to decide whether a given passage owes more to Judaism than to Christianity. A case in point is the angelic prostration before Adam. We have seen that Christian apologists attribute this to Christian speculation about Christ the second Adam. *Prima facie* this seems probable, a Jewish origin being much less likely in view of Jewish opposition to worshipping any but God. But the Qur'ān does not actually say that the angels *worshipped* Adam. Moreover there are Jewish sources which speak of God ordering the angels to offer Adam obeisance.[30] Since Muḥammad broke with the Jews shortly after arriving in Medina it is puzzling that the Medinan ṣūras show such extensive acquaintance with Rabbinic Judaism. One possible explanation is that the information was furnished by Nestorian Christians from Persia where Jews and Nestorians lived in close proximity and engaged in controversy with each other. An alternative suggestion is that, already in the Meccan period, Muḥammad was influenced by sectarian Jews and that he went to Medina armed with their stock objections to Rabbinic Judaism.[31]

DISCUSSION

The sheer complexity of the two issues discussed in this chapter should put us on our guard against attempting to draw anything other than the most general conclusions. Despite our extensive knowledge of Byzantine Orthodoxy and of the principal forms of Christianity which flourished in Syria and Persia, we know all too little about Christianity as practised in Najrān and Abyssinia in the seventh century and even less about Arab tribal Christianity. The external evidence and the evidence of the Qur'ān itself both point to a predominantly heterodox influence on the early environment of Islam. Although the external evidence would favour Nestorianism and Monophysitism, the internal evidence is equally indicative of some form of Jewish Christianity. We should probably think in terms of a variety of rival sects some of which may have vanished without trace.

4 Muḥammad and the Christians

In the last chapter I attempted to view the Qur'anic Jesus material against the broad back-drop of the ecclesiastical situation which contributed to the environment from which Islam emerged. It is now time to look at the same material specifically in terms of Muḥammad's relations with Christians. I shall discuss the extra-Qur'anic evidence and the chronological order of the revelations and then attempt a synthesis.

TRADITIONS ABOUT MUḤAMMAD'S DEALINGS WITH CHRISTIANS

There are a number of traditions about Muḥammad's encounters with individual Christians and I will mention only the most important. The first such encounter was reputedly with the monk Baḥīrā. According to the Muslim versions of this story[1] the meeting took place in Syria while Muḥammad was accompanying his uncle Abū Ṭālib with a merchant caravan. The monk recognised that the boy was a prophet and advised Abū Ṭālib to take special care of him because of Jewish enmity. It is impossible to tell whether or not the story contains a historical kernel. As it stands it is clearly a legend which serves to show that despite Jewish rejection of Muḥammad's claim to prophethood his true nature was recognised by a holy and learned representative of Christianity. In this respect it resembles St Matthew's story of how the wise men from the East paid homage to the infant Jesus whereas the Jewish authorities sought to kill him.[2] There is no evidence that Baḥīrā was an Arian or that he instructed Muḥammad. To claim, as Christian polemicists have done, that he primed him with information about Christianity is almost as disingenuous as arguing that the wise men taught Jesus oriental magic. As for Sergius, the other heretical monk beloved of Christian polemicists, he seems to be entirely a figment of their imagination.

Quss ibn Sā'ida, whose sermons Muḥammad is said to have heard at the fair at 'Ukāẓ in central Arabia, is scarcely a less shadowy figure than Baḥīrā. Blachère suggests that Quss may not be a proper name at all and that the word could be linked with the noun *qissīs* 'a monk'. He dismisses the extant fragments of sermons attributed to Quss as spurious.[3] Trimingham admits that some scholars have doubted Quss's existence but argues that it would be difficult to account for the strength of the legends that have accumulated about him if he were not historical.[4]

We are on more certain ground with reports that when Muḥammad began to experience revelations and lacked self-confidence he received encouragement from Waraqa b. Nawfal. According to the version preserved by Bukhārī, it was Muḥammad's wife Khadīja who took him to see Waraqa. Waraqa was her cousin and had become a Christian in pre-Islamic times. He knew how to write Hebrew letters and had transcribed part of the Gospel in Hebrew although he was now old and blind. When Muḥammad told him of his experience, Waraqa told him that the angel whom he had seen was the Nāmūs whom God had sent to Moses. He continued:

> 'Would to God that I were young now! How I wish that I could be alive when your fellow citizens banish you!' 'So they will drive me out?' cried the Prophet. 'Yes', retorted Waraqa, 'No man has ever brought what you bring without being persecuted. If I am still alive on that day I will help you with all my strength.' Soon after that Waraqa died and the revelation was interrupted.[5]

There is no reason to doubt that this story has an historical core. The general circumstances in which Muḥammad needed encouragement would hardly have been invented. Nor would the reference to the Nāmūs (Greek *nomos* = law) which was later misunderstood as designating the angel of revelation rather than the revelation itself. On the other hand, the insistence on Waraqa's death is suspect: it is contradicted by other reports which assert that he lived for several more years and it conveniently explains why he did not become a Muslim despite his recognition of Muḥammad's mission.[6] Unfortunately we have no reliable evidence concerning the type of Christianity which Waraqa himself espoused nor is there any way of telling how much Khadīja and Muḥammad learned from him about Christianity.

Later on in the Meccan period Muḥammad's opponents hinted that he relied on a human teacher. The Qur'ān does not tell us whom they had in mind, only that this person's speech was foreign or unclear whereas the revelations which Muḥammad received were in pure

Arabic (16:103). Muslim traditions name several possible candidates including a convert called Yā'ish who possessed books and a Byzantine servant called Jabr. The most elaborate explanation is that the reference is to two slaves called Jabr and Yasār who manufactured swords in Mecca; they used to recite the Torah and the Gospel and when Muḥammad passed by he stopped to listen to them.[7] It is difficult to evaluate these traditions. The diversity of the suggestions may indicate the absence of reliable reports concerning the affair.

After the emigration to Medina, Salmān the Persian and Māriya the Copt joined Muḥammad's entourage. Salmān had been born and bred a Zoroastrian but attached himself to Christians in Syria and then went to Medina to find the awaited prophet. He subsequently played an important part in the construction of ditches to defend the city.[8] Māriya was one of two women sent to Muḥammad as a present by the leader of the Copts and was presumably a Monophysite. She became Muḥammad's concubine and bore him a son.[9] Both Salmān and Māriya were undoubtedly close to Muḥammad during the last few years of his life but whether or not either of them added to his store of information about Christianity we simply do not know. In any case they came on the scene too late to have had a decisive influence.

In addition to the traditions about Muḥammad's more or less private encounters with individual Christians we must consider the evidence concerning various incidents which brought the Muslim community into contact with Christianity. The first such incident on record occurred in 615 CE. In that year Muḥammad encouraged 83 of his Companions to avoid persecution by fleeing to Abyssinia. The implication is that he thought that they would be safer in a Monophysite Christian country than they were in Mecca. Some of them returned when false reports reached them that the danger was over but others remained in Abyssinia permanently.[10]

The remaining incidents all took place during the Medinan period. To begin with Muḥammad tried to rally both the Christians and Jews to his support but his relations with the latter soon soured and in 2/624, as a result of a revelation, the *qibla* (direction of prayer) was changed from Jerusalem to Mecca. In 7/628 Muḥammad attempted to enter into diplomatic relations with Persia and with the major Christian powers including Byzantium, Abyssinia and Egypt.[11] The following year his adoptive son Zayd was killed in combat with Byzantine forces when he led an expedition to Mu'ta in Palestine. The details are obscure but it may be conjectured that this episode led to a hardening of Muḥammad's attitude to Byzantine Christianity.[12] Subsequently, when the Emperor Heraclius vanquished the Persians and restored the true cross to Jerusalem, Muḥammad must have realised that he had no chance of winning the Arab tribes to the North unless he could demonstrate that he could exert more authority in the area than the Byzantines. Thus in 8/630 he led his biggest campaign; in a massive show of strength 30,000 men marched northwards as far as Tabūk, concluding treaties with various Christian groups and requiring them to pay poll tax. Muḥammad probably dealt with the Christians in Southern Arabia in much the same way although he may have been slightly more favourably disposed to them because they were not under Byzantine influence. One of the main groups of Christians in the South was those of Najrān. In 10/631 they sent an impressive embassy including Christian scholars to Muḥammad at Medina. They were allowed to use the mosque for prayers but refused to become Muslims preferring instead to pay tribute.[13] Less than a year before Muḥammad died he received a letter from Musaylima of the largely Christian tribe of Ḥanīfa in central Arabia. Musaylima wrote to him as one prophet to another suggesting that they should divide the land between them.[14] Muslim sources describe him as a 'false prophet' but there is no reason to doubt his sincerity. The incident furnishes us with a rare glimpse of Arab tribal Christianity with its charismatic politico-religious leadership.

THE CHRONOLOGY OF THE REVELATIONS

The present order of the ṣūras is not chronological. There is general agreement among Muslims concerning most of them as to whether they were revealed at Mecca or Medina but no such agreement concerning the sequence in which they were revealed. In the standard Egyptian edition each ṣūra is given a heading which names those revealed immediately before and after it. This information is, however, derived from only one of the three rival lists which have been in existence since at least the third/eighth century.[15] The lists were probably based on early material of two kinds. First, there were biographical traditions linking passages from the Qur'ān with incidents in Muḥammad's life.[16] In some cases these may preserve genuine reminiscences but in others they are probably guess-work. Second, there were traditions concerning which of the Qur'anic ordinances had been abrogated by later revelations.[17] For example it was held that 2:219, which speaks of wine as a great sin but also of some usefulness, was abrogated by 5:90 which describes it as an abomination. Several non-Muslim scholars have taken the Muslim traditions as their starting point and have attempted to produce a more accurate sequence using additional criteria such as style and theology on the assumption that there was a gradual development in both. The most widely accepted proposal is that of Nöldeke who adopted the Muslim distinction between Meccan and Medinan revelations but divided the Meccan ṣūras into three periods. I will therefore repeat the list of passages given in Chapter 1, this time putting them in Nöldeke's order and adding a brief description of their content. The numbers in brackets denote the supposed chronological order; for example (9) signifies that according to Nöldeke this was the ninth ṣūra to be revealed.

First Meccan Period

(9)	105:1–5	Abraha's abortive campaign against Mecca.
(22)	85:1–9	Monophysite martyrs of Najrān (?)
(44)	112	Unity of God. He neither begets nor is begotten

Second Meccan Period

(53)	44:14	Accusation that Muḥammad is 'taught'.
(58)	19:1–33	Annunciation and birth. Reference to «the day I die».
(60)	36:13–32	Parable of the godless citizens (cf. legend of Agabus martyred at Antioch (?))
(61)	43:57–65	Jesus an example, servant and knowledge for the hour.
	43:81	«If the Compassionate had a son . . .»
(64)	23:45–55	Mary and Jesus a sign.
(65)	21:74–94	Zechariah and she who was chaste.
(66)	25:2	God has not taken a son.
	25:4–5	Accusation that Muḥammad has fables read to him.
(69)	18:9–27	Folk of the cave (cf. seven sleepers of Ephesus.)

Third Meccan Period

(73)	16:103	Accusation that he has a human teacher.

(80)	39:4	«If God had desired a son . . .»
	39:29	Echo of dominical saying (?) (cf. *Matthew* 6:24)
(83)	42:13–16	Muḥammad's religion is that of Moses and Jesus.
(84)	10:69	They say God has taken a son.
(87)	7:40–49	Echo of dominical sayings (?) (cf. *Matthew* 19:24 and *Luke* 16:24ff.)
	7:179,186	(cf. *Matthew* 13:13 and 24:32)
(89)	6:84–90	Jesus mentioned in list of prophets.
	6:106	Accusation that Muḥammad has studied.

Medinan Period

(91)	2:26	Echo of dominical saying (?) (cf. *Matthew* 23:24)
	2:62	Reward for Christians.
	2:87	Jesus given clear proofs and strengthened with Spirit.
	2:111–13	Difference between Jews and Christians. Establish prayer and poor due. God will judge according to works and not in accordance with Jewish and Christian exclusivism.
	2:120	Tensions between Muḥammad and the Jews and Christians who want him to follow their religion.
	2:135–40	Jews and Christians seek to convert Muslims. Ripost that they follow Abraham the *ḥanīf*, serve the same Lord as Jews and Christians and make no distinction between the prophets. 'Baptism' (?). Change of Qibla.
	2:253	Jesus given clear proofs and strengthened with Spirit. If God had willed, those who followed him would not have fought among themselves.
(92)	98:1–8	People of the Scripture divided.
(97)	3:1–32	Miscellaneous. Doubters cause dissension by concentrating on the ambiguous āyas.
	3:33–64	Annunciation and birth, 'one of those brought near', Mary chosen above all women, miracles, confirming the Torah but making licit

		some of the things which were forbidden. Disciples are 'helpers' who have 'submitted' and 'bear witness'. God 'received Jesus'. Jesus like Adam. Summons to worship none but God and engage in mutual cursing of liars.
	3:65–85	Abraham neither a Jew nor a Christian but a *ḥanīf*. Scripturists vary in trustworthiness. Muslims believe in what was revealed to Moses, Jesus and the prophets and make no distinction between them.
	3:113–15	Not all Scripturists are alike.
(98)	61:1–14	Jesus a messenger confirming Torah, bringing good tidings of Aḥmad. Disciples 'helpers'.
(99)	57:12–13	Echo of dominical saying (?) (cf. *Matthew* 25:1ff.)
	57:25–9	Jesus a messenger; kindness and mercy in the hearts of his disciples.
(100)	4:44–57	Idolatry of the Scripturists.
	4:142	Echo of dominical saying (?) (cf. *Matthew* 6:5)
	4:156–9	Jews speak 'tremendous calumny' against Mary. They wrongly claim to have killed the Messiah. God raised him.
	4:163	Jesus named in list of prophets.
	4:171–2	Jesus only a messenger, word, spirit. Do not say 'three'. God is far above having a son. Like the angels Jesus will not scorn to be a servant of God.
(103)	33:7–27	God's covenant with the prophets.
(105)	24:34–40	God is light.
(106)	58:7	Echo of dominical saying (?) (cf. *Matthew* 18:20).
(108)	48:29	Gospel likens worshippers to seed which shoots up delighting the sower.
(109)	66:1–12	Mary an example for the believers.
(113)	9:29–35	Jihād against Jews and Christians until they pay tribute. 'Uzair and Messiah wrongly called Son of God (*Ibn Allah*). Rabbis and monks wrongly taken as lords; they are avaricious.

	9:80	«Though you ask forgiveness for them seventy times . . .»
	9:111–14	Gospel promises paradise to those who die fighting.
(114)	5:14	Christians have broken their covenant with God. Therefore He has set enmity between them.
	5:17–18	Those who say God is the Messiah are disbelievers. Jews and Christians wrongly say they are God's sons.
	5:46–7	Jesus received Gospel confirming the Torah.
	5:51	Don't take Jews and Christians as friends, they are friends to each other.
	5:63	Failure of priests and rabbis to prohibit usury.
	5:69	Jews, Sabaeans and Christians who believe have no reason to fear.
	5:72	Those who say God is the Messiah are disbelievers. The Messiah said idolaters would be forbidden paradise.
	5:75	The Messiah was a Messenger. Messengers have passed away before. His mother saintly. They both ate.
	5:82–3	Jews and unbelievers contrasted with Christians and their priests and monks. The latter seen favourably.
	5:109–120	God reminds Jesus of His favour to him: strengthening him with Spirit, granting him miracles, submission of disciples, episode of table. Insinuation that Christians have taken Jesus and Mary as deities.
(?)	19:34–40	(Later addition inserted in (58)?) God has not taken a son.
	19:92–3	(Whole of 75–98 a later addition appended to (58)?) God has not taken a son.
(?)	22:17	(1–24 one of several Meccan elements in a predominantly Medinan ṣūra (107)?) God will judge between religions.
(?)	7:156–9	(Late Medinan addition to (87)?) Unlettered prophet described in Gospel.

SYNTHESIS

An attempt must now be made to correlate the Qur'anic material with the extra-Qur'anic traditions. There are four questions which we must try to answer. First, can Muḥammad's alleged informer be identified with any of the individuals with whom he is known to have been in contact? Second, were the revelations about Jesus in any way related to the emigration to Abyssinia or the arrival of the embassy from Najrān? Third, what evidence is there for thinking that the revelations became progressively more hostile to Christianity? Fourth, were the Qur'anic denials that God had ever taken a son originally directed against Christians or against Arab pagans?

The accusation that Muḥammad had a human teacher is mentioned in (53) 44:14, (66) 25:4–5, (73) 16:103 and (89) 6:106, from which we should perhaps infer that it was frequently voiced during the second and third Meccan periods but not before or after. The accusation was probably first made in response to (49) 54, (50) 37 and (51) 71 which are the earliest ṣūras to narrate episodes from the lives of Noah and other Old Testament worthies. The earliest revelations concerning Jesus and Christians occurred slightly later, pride of place going to (58) 19:1–34, an exquisite infancy narrative, and (69) 18:9–27, the Qur'anic version of the sleeper legend, both of which exhibit remarkably detailed knowledge.[19] We are therefore looking for an informer or informers who were well versed in these matters and with whom Muḥammad was in contact during the second and third Meccan periods. Unless we discount the tradition that Waraqa died shortly after hearing about the initial revelations, none of the individuals mentioned at the beginning of this chapter will fit the bill.

Ibn Isḥāq states that the Muslims who emigrated to Abyssinia recited part of ṣūra nineteen (58) in the presence of the Negus and that he responded favourably.[20] It is difficult to know whether to give credence to this tradition. Nöldeke seems not to have questioned it and to have taken it as the basis for ascribing 19:1–33 to the second Meccan period.[21] There are a few Abyssinian loan words in the Qur'anic Jesus material including *al-ḥawāriyyūn* (the disciples, 3:52, 5:111f, 61:14) and *mā'ida* (a table spread, 5:112) which are found only in Medinan ṣūras. It is tempting to suppose that Muḥammad learned them from the Muslims who returned from Abyssinia but it is equally possible that they had already been absorbed into the Arabic language.[22] The traditions concerning Muslim relations with the Christians of Najrān are no less difficult to evaluate. According to Ibn

Isḥāq the first part of ṣūra three (97) was revealed when they sent their embassy to Medina in 10/631 but Nöldeke favours an earlier date for this ṣūra and notes that there is a rival tradition which states that 3:61 was included in the letter which Muḥammad despatched to the Emperor of Byzantium in 7/628.[23]

In tackling the third question I will leave aside the denials that God has ever taken a son since they complicate the issue. Apart from these denials, nothing negative is said about Christianity or Christian beliefs about Jesus in any of the Meccan ṣūras. On the contrary there is much that most Christians would warm to including the infancy narrative and the sleeper legend which have already been mentioned. The gloating reference to Abraha's abhortive attack (9) is hardly an exception and in any case it is counterbalanced by the allusion to the martyrs of Najrān (22) who are depicted in a positive light.[24] From the beginning of the Medinan period the references to Christians are more nuanced and objections are made to some of their beliefs and to their exclusiveness. However, the most adverse statements are all concentrated in ṣūras nine and five which Nöldeke holds were the very last ṣūras to be revealed and which he ascribes to the period after the clash with the Byzantine forces at Mu'ta.

It remains for us to discuss the Qur'anic denials that God has ever taken a son. The evidence is complex and to avoid confusion I will attempt to list the main points which need to be taken into account:

1. These denials are already found in the first Meccan period when the opposition to Muḥammad came from pagans. It is therefore intrinsically probable that in that period they were anti-pagan in intent rather than anti-Christian.
2. In every case except one, the word used to denote a 'son' is *walad*. Since this word is derived from the verb *walada* meaning to beget, it might be better to translate it 'offspring'. Christian apologists sometimes argue that Jesus is not God's *walad* because there is no question of God having begotten him by carnal intercourse with a female consort. This is perfectly true but in view of orthodox credal language about Jesus being 'begotten not made' the argument should not be pressed.
3. The one exception is 9:30 in the last ṣūra to be revealed. There the term used is *Ibn Allah*, Son of God, and it is quite clear that it is Christian belief about the Messiah which is being repudiated.
4. In their present state, all the ṣūras which contain extensive

references to Jesus also include a denial that God has offspring. It is possible that this is because these ṣūras were revised during the Medinan period. For example Nöldeke maintains that ṣūra nineteen originally consisted of 19:1–33, 41–74 since these āyas all rhyme in *-iyyan* whereas āyas 34–40 end in the much more common *-ūna* frequently found in the Medinan period and ayās 75–98 end in *an*.[25] This accords with the Muslim tradition that the emigrants recited *part* of this ṣūra to the Negus of Abyssinia. What they recited was presumably the original nucleus which lacked the strident denials that God had offspring.

DISCUSSION

Nöldeke's chronological reclassification of the ṣūras is a useful historical tool but it is only an approximation. It should be borne in mind that the revelations were recited liturgically during Muḥammad's life-time and that they probably underwent frequent amplification thus making it impossible to reconstruct the stages of development with any accuracy. Muslims have no difficulty in reconciling the gradual and piecemeal nature of the revelation with their belief that the Qur'ān is eternal. They hold that, like everything else, the vicissitudes of Muḥammad's relations with Christians were foreordained and that the revelations were therefore given to him on the appropriate occasions.

In broad outline Nöldeke's scheme is generally accepted by non-Muslims but there have been some dissenting voices. Mention must be made of two scholars who have put forward radical proposals inspired by critical work on the Old Testament. Wansbrough[26] rejects most of the Muslim traditions about the occasions of the revelations and about the collection of the Qur'ān. He argues that after the Prophet's death there was a long period of oral tradition during which the revelations continued to be modified. On this reckoning some of the doublets in the Qur'ān – for example the two infancy narratives in 19:1–33 and 3:35–48 – may be versions of the same revelation which were preserved in different circles. Lüling[27] argues that Muḥammad's theology was from the first very close to that of Jewish Christianity but that this has been obscured by subsequent editing and by the incorrect vocalisation of the consonantal text. For example he tries to show that ṣūra 96, which is generally thought to have been the first revelation, was originally a Christian hymn about the prayer of a pious man to his Creator and that ṣūra 74, also a very early revelation, was a Christological hymn which referred to the descent into hell. Neither Wansbrough nor Lüling has a large following but it is too early to assess the impact of their work.

5 Muḥammad and Jesus

Since many of the non-Muslim scholars who have studied the Qur'anic representation of Jesus have been Christians, it is hardly surprising that they have focused their attention on Muḥammad's knowledge of and contacts with Judaism and Christianity. Judging by Nöldeke's chronological classification of the ṣūras, however, Muḥammad believed in the unity of God and in his own vocation as a warner of the impending judgement before he gained detailed knowledge of Jewish and Christian sacred history. It is therefore arguable that the primary datum is Muḥammad's consciousness of being a prophet and that it is this which ought to provide the interpretative key to the Qur'anic Jesus material. In this chapter I shall examine three facets of the material which seem to bear this out: its integration in the structure of the Qur'anic discourse, the similarity of 'Īsā and Muḥammad and the alleged arithmetical composition of the ṣūras.[1]

THE STRUCTURE OF THE QUR'ANIC DISCOURSE

The structure of the Qur'anic discourse has been analysed by Mohammed Arkoun[2] but its relevance to an assessment of the material about Jesus and Mary is rarely appreciated. This structure implies an Omniscient Magisterial Speaker (God) who employs the first person singular (I, Me, My), the first person plural (We, Us, Our) and the third person singular (He, Him, His) when speaking of Himself.[3] It also implies a privileged individual (Muḥammad) who is addressed by the Speaker and required by Him to relay the message to others. The Speaker knows the innermost thoughts of this individual (e.g. 6:33). He also has detailed knowledge of events which took place in the remote past (e.g. 18:13–18).

Turning now to the material about Jesus and Mary, we should first note that this too is the utterance of the Omniscient Magisterial Speaker who designates Himself 'I' (e.g. 5:110), 'We' (e.g. 5:46) and 'He' (e.g. 4:171). The Speaker knows Jesus' innermost thoughts (5:116). Moreover there is a striking instance where He emphasises His superior knowledge of the events which He narrates:

«This is the tidings of the Unseen which We reveal to you. You were not with them when they cast their reeds [to decide] which of them should have charge of Mary. You were not with them when they disputed.» (3:44)

This oblique reference to the casting of lots to decide who should be Mary's guardian occurs like a cinematographic flash-back in the course of the narration of the annunciation. It has the effect of enhancing the verisimilitude of the story and of giving the impression that the narrator – the Omniscient Magisterial Speaker – observed the events in question.

Like everything else in the Qur'ān this authoritative revelation of the story of Jesus and Mary is addressed in the first place to a privileged individual but is destined for a wider audience. There are three āyas which are of particular interest because they mention Jesus in lists of prophets which also include the privileged individual addressed. Two of these āyas (4:163 and 33:7) are couched exclusively in We-you discourse directed at the individual. The third āya is more complex. It combines We-you discourse addressed to the privileged individual with He-you discourse addressed directly to the wider audience. This is quite clear in Arabic but it is difficult to represent in modern English where 'you' can be either singular or plural. I have therefore included explanatory glosses in square brackets:

«He has appointed for you [Muslims] as religion what He enjoined on Noah and what We have revealed to you [O Prophet] and what We enjoined on Abraham, Moses and Jesus . . .» (42:13)

All three āyas indicate that in the Qur'ān the story of Jesus serves, like the stories of the other prophets, to authenticate the prophetic ministry of Muḥammad and to emphasise the authority of the message of which he is the mediator.

THE SIMILARITY OF 'ĪSĀ AND MUḤAMMAD

It is well known that the Qur'ān depicts Jesus as one of a series of prophets sent by God, a series beginning with Adam and culminating in Muḥammad the privileged individual to whom the Qur'ān itself is addressed. It is hardly surprising, therefore, that the Qur'ān depicts Muḥammad and Jesus as having a number of things in common. Nevertheless the extent of their affinity is not generally appreciated.

Like Muḥammad, the Qur'anic Jesus is called a 'prophet' (*nabī*), a 'messenger' (*rasūl*) and a 'servant' (*'abd*) of God. Like him too he is said to have been sent as a 'mercy' (*raḥma*). He received a revelation called 'the Gospel' just as Muḥammad subsequently received the Qur'ān. Jesus' teaching and the teaching of the Gospel are referred to as 'wisdom', 'right path', 'guidance', 'light' and 'admonition' – terms which recur as descriptions of the Qur'anic message. Jesus declared licit some of the things which were forbidden to the Jews (3:50) just as Muḥammad did, for some of the more detailed food laws were a punishment imposed on the Jews because of their disobedience and thus were relaxed for Muslims (6:146f). Nevertheless the Gospel, like the Qur'ān, was a confirmation of previous Scriptures (3:3). Its central thrust was identical with the central thrust of the Qur'ān – the summons to serve and worship God. Jesus is said to have threatened idolaters with hellfire (5:72) and to have promised paradise to those who died fighting in God's cause (9:111) – threats and promises which correspond to those made in the Qur'ān. Moreover Jesus is said to have practised ritual prayer (*ṣalāt*) and alms–giving (*zakāt*) (19:31), the two fundamental religious obligations of Islam. In view of all this it should come as no surprise that the Qur'ān also states that the revelation addressed to Jesus' disciples urged them to believe in God and His messenger and that they declared that they were 'submitted' (*muslimūn*, i.e. Muslims) (5:111) and wished to be enrolled 'with those who bear witness' (*ma'a al-shāhidīn*, i.e. with those who recite the Muslim confession of faith?) (3:53)[4]

From what has been said so far it should be clear that the Qur'anic representation of Jesus serves to legitimise Muḥammad by giving the impression that he was doing what Jesus had done before him. In one very striking instance this becomes quite explicit:

> O you believers! Be God's helpers as when Jesus Son of Mary said to the disciples 'Who will be my helpers in God's way?' The disciples said, 'We are God's helpers.' A group of the Children of Israel believed and a group disbelieved. We upheld those who believed against their enemies and they gained the victory. (61:14)

Although this passage is very condensed its purport is clear enough. The believers are urged to fight at Muḥammad's side on the grounds that in so doing they will be following the example of Jesus' disciples and that like them they will prove victorious. The word 'helpers' (*anṣār*) is pregnant with meaning. It is the official title given to the people of Medina who rallied to Muḥammad's cause (9:100,107). It also puns with *naṣārā*, the Qur'anic name for Christians.

There would have been no need for a promise of victory if Muḥammad and Jesus had not met with mockery and opposition. Muḥammad's critics mocked him for needing to eat food (25:7). Yet Jesus and his mother had had similar needs (5:75). The 'signs' which Muḥammad brought as proof of his authority – the inimitable revelations of the Qur'ān – led to allegations of sorcery (21:3, 38:4f., 43:31). Yet although Jesus' miraculous 'signs' had been rather different they too had provoked this response (5:110).

THE ALLEGED ARITHMETICAL COMPOSITION OF THE ṢŪRAS

Claus Schedl has written a large monograph on Jesus in the Qur'ān entitled *Muḥammad und Jesus*[5] in which he comments on most of the relevant passages in the 'chronological' order which can be deduced from the headings in the standard Egyptian edition. The most controversial feature of this work is the author's contention that Muḥammad attempted to make the revelations conform to arithmetic models so as to convince his audience that they corresponded to the heavenly archetype of the Qur'ān, the 'Mother of the Book' mentioned in 43:2–4. Two of the most frequently occurring models are the tetraktys and the alphabetic model.[6] The tetraktys (23 + 32 = 55) is the expression of the primitive cosmic formula. There is only 1 (point) + 2 (line) + 3 (arrow) + 4 (space) = 10. If the series 1,2,3,4 is continued up to 10 and written in a triangle the angles and the centre add up to 23 and the other numbers add up to 32:

1
2–3
4–5–6
7–8–9–10

The alphabet model is based on the primitive Arabic alphabet which consisted of only 22 letters like Hebrew. In the Hebrew speculative work called the *Sefer Yeẓirah* (Book of Creation) the letters are put into three groups (3 + 7 + 12 = 22) and these numbers are said to have presided at the creation of time and space and of man who is a microcosm. The way in which Schedl discovers these models in the Qur'ān is best illustrated by a sample analysis and I have chosen for this purpose ṣūra 97 which is generally held to refer to the night when God sent the Qur'ān down to earth in preparation for it to be revealed.[7] The figures on the right denote the number of Arabic words in each āya.

	odd	*even*
1. Behold We sent it down		
on the Night of Power.	5	
2. And what will teach you		
what is the Night of Power?	5	
3. The Night of Power is better		
than a thousand months.		VI
4. The angels and the Spirit descend therein		
by permission of Your Lord with all command.	9	
5. Peace it is until the rising of the dawn.	5	
30 =	24 +	VI

According to Schedl the structure of this ṣūra corresponds to two models which are related to those mentioned above but not identical to them. First, there is what he calls 'the five model'. The primitive cosmic formula consisted of four elements united by a fifth, the quintessence. Here there are four āyas with an odd number of words and one with an even number. The structure also corresponds to 'the Logos model' which is frequently present in the Christian Scriptures. The 24 letters in the Greek alphabet represent the rudiments of the cosmos. To complete and redeem the cosmos it is necessary to add the VI letters of the name *ΙΗΣΟΥΣ* (Jesus) thus obtaining a total of 30 and in Greek 30 is denoted by the letter Lambda which also stands for Logos. Here the 24 words of the 'odd' āyas are completed by the VI words of the 'even' āya. Although the text speaks of the 'command' or 'word' (Arabic *amr*), the equivalent of the Greek *Logos*, the reference is not to Jesus but to the Qur'ān. Thus the Christian belief in Jesus as the incarnate Logos is replaced by the belief in the sending down of the Qur'ān.

DISCUSSION

In the first section we saw that the image of Jesus is mediated by the structure of the Qur'anic discourse and is inseparable from it. It follows that any attempt to translate what the Qur'ān says about Jesus into a series of propositions is likely to reduce the impact of the Qur'anic version of the story and thus to seriously misrepresent it. In its Qur'anic setting there can be little doubt that the story of Jesus serves to authenticate the prophetic ministry of Muḥammad and to emphasise the authority of the message of which he is the mediator.

Let us next consider the resemblance between what the Qur'ān says about Jesus and what it says about Muḥammad. Michaud, who was aware of some of the parallels which I have listed, thought it unneccessary to postulate that Muḥammad had deliberately contrived to produce them. His own explanation had two parts to it. First, following Harnack and Schoeps, he assumed that Muḥammad was influenced by Jewish Christianity and that consequently he initially believed that the religion which he preached closely resembled that of Jesus.[8] Second, Michaud suggested that later on, the traditional data about Jesus which did not fit the image of him as a model prophet were partially harmonised with it by a slow and profound spiritual travail which took place within Muḥammad.[9] I accept the likelihood of both the Jewish Christian influence and the long-term spiritual travail but I question whether they are sufficient to explain all the similarities which we have observed. For example it is surely significant that there is a revelation mentioning how Muḥammad was mocked for eating in the market place (25:7) and another which stresses the mortality of Jesus and Mary and their need to eat food (5:75). In subsequent chapters I shall mention some equally remarkable parallels which have a bearing on the interpretation of what the Qur'ān says about the virginal conception and about Jesus' death.

Schedl's claim that the ṣūras are constructed in accordance with arithmetical models is more problematic. He resorts to too many different models for his analyses to be entirely convincing. Take for instance his reliance on both the symbolism of the alphabet of twenty-two letters and on the tetraktys. These are two distinct arithmetical systems because twenty-two is not in the series of triangular numbers nor is it a factor of a triangular number. Moreover the two systems are drawn from two different streams of Jewish speculation and are never referred to together.[10] Nevertheless the fact that the number of ṣūras in the Qur'ān is the same as the number of logia in the Gospel of Thomas suggests that arithmetic symbolism may have played some part in the final editing of the revelations if not in their initial composition.

6 Currents and Encounters

Our initial surveys of the principal non-Muslim approaches to the Qur'anic Jesus material are now complete and we shall soon turn our attention to the Muslim exegetical tradition. Since the ongoing process of interpreting the Qur'anic references to Jesus did not take place in a cultural vacuum, I propose in this and the next chapter to explain some of the developments within Islam and in Muslim–Christian relations which affected the way in which Jesus was perceived by Muslims during the first seven centuries of the Hijra.

INTERNAL POWER STRUGGLES AND THE EXPANSION OF ISLAM

When Muḥammad died in 11/632 the Muslim community was set for a period of rapid expansion but the Prophet had no male heir nor did he leave clear instructions concerning who should succeed him as leader. There was thus intense competition between various rival factions. The main interest groups were the *muhājirūn* who had emigrated from Mecca with Muḥammad, the *anṣār* who were the Muslims from Medina who had rallied to his cause, and the late Meccan converts mostly from the Banū Umayya clan. There was also a less influential group, often referred to as the 'legitimists', who believed that 'Alī was the divinely designated successor to Muḥammad. The first two Caliphs, Abū Bakr and 'Umar, came from the first group. So too did the third, 'Uthmān, but he also belonged to Banū Umayya clan. With the fourth Caliph the legitimists at last had their turn although like his three predecessors 'Alī was also a *muhājir*. The vehemence of the rivalry may be judged by the fact that, despite all four being revered as the 'Rightly Guided Caliphs', three of them were assassinated.

This rivalry did not prevent Islam's expansion. Within a decade of Muḥammad's death Muslim troops had overrun Syro-Palestine capturing Damascus and Jerusalem and others had completed the conquest of Egypt. The predominantly Monophysite Christian inhabitants of these territories welcomed the invaders who finally delivered them from Byzantine oppression.[1] Some converted to Islam but the majority accepted *dhimmī* status. This gave them freedom to practise their religion unostentatiously and safe-guarded their lives and property but committed them to paying a per capita tax and forgoing the right to bear arms. In the same period the Persian Empire capitulated and *dhimmī* status was extended to the Zoroastrians as well as to the Jewish and Nestorian minorities although the pacification of the former Persian territories proved a long-drawn-out process.

In 41/661, the leadership of the Muslim community passed into the hands of the Umayyad Caliphs. They were members of the Banū Umayya clan, the Meccan aristocracy who had only converted to Islam when Muḥammad's hegemony of Arabia left them no real alternative. They made Damascus their capital, adopted features of Byzantine administration and drew on the expertise of Christian administrators. Umayyad troops soon captured North Africa, once a stronghold of Latin Christianity. In 92/711 they crossed over from Morocco into Spain and eventually penetrated France but were defeated near Tours in 114/732. They also extended the empire to the east entering the Indus valley and capturing Multan.

An uprising which began in Khurāsān saw the Umayyads replaced by the Abbasids in 132/750. They were descendants of the Prophet's uncle al-'Abbās. Twelve years after coming to power they founded Baghdad as their new capital. This was symptomatic of the increasing Persianisation of the Empire. Under the early Abbasids Nestorian Christians rose to positions of influence comparable with those that they had enjoyed at the Persian court. They were greatly valued as physicians and were also employed to translate Greek medical and philosophical texts.

SPECULATIVE THEOLOGY

Damascus, which the Umayyads made their capital, had had a long history as a centre of Graeco-Roman civilisation and of Christian theology. Although the details remain obscure it seems highly probable that contact with Christian scholars in that city stimulated Muslim reflection concerning the status of God's attributes and of the Qur'ān.[2]

Imagine an Orthodox Christian theologian trying to convince a Muslim that God is three persons or hypostases but one substance. He would immediately have been rebuked with a quotation from the Qur'ān: «Do not say "Three". Desist! . . . God is but One God» (4:169). The Christian might have replied that the Qur'ān itself describes God as «Self-Existent» (*qayyūm*, e.g. 2:255), «Knowing» (*'alīm*, e.g. 2:256), «Powerful» (*qadīr*, e.g. 2:20) and «Living» (*ḥayy*, e.g. 25:58) surely thereby implying that 'Self-Existence', 'Knowledge', 'Power' and 'Life' are eternal attributes possessed by Him. Pressing his case further, he might have pointed out that for Trinitarian theologians 'Self-Existence' was the principle of differentiation of the Father whereas 'Knowledge', 'Power' and 'Life' were descriptive of the Son and the Holy Spirit. What were Muslims to do when led into this trap? They seem to have compromised. They admitted that 'Knowledge', 'Power' and 'Life' were three of the many eternal attributes (*ṣifāt*) possessed by God but they insisted that 'Self-Existence' was different because it was descriptive of God in Himself.

The development of Muslim beliefs about the Qur'ān is easier to understand. The Qur'ān clearly purports to be the Word of God addressed to Muḥammad. It also poses the rhetorical question «Are not the creation and the command His?» (7:54) apparently implying thereby that the 'command' is distinct from the 'creation'. When Muslims encountered Christian theologians who asserted that Jesus was the temporal expression of the eternal and uncreated Word of God it was a natural enough step for them to reply that on the contrary this was the status of the Qur'ān.[3]

Not all Muslims were happy with these developments. They were vigorously contested by the Mu'tazilites who perceived them as undermining the central dogma of the Unity of God. Their own position was that God's attributes were not possessed by God but were of His essence. Thus for example God is Powerful by His Power and Power is His essence; He is Knowing by His Knowledge and Knowledge is His essence, and so on and so forth. Some went still further and said that nothing positive could be asserted about God: He is an absolute unity shorn of all qualities. As regards the Qur'ān, the Mu'tazilites accepted that it was the Word of God but insisted that it had been created. For a brief period at the beginning of the third/ninth century Mu'tazilism was the official theological doctrine of the Abbasid Caliphate. Although soon eclipsed by the Ash'arites who regarded their theology as unorthodox, the Mu'tazilites continued to be active in Baghdad and Baṣra for several hundred years.[4]

MUSLIM HISTORIANS

Several Muslims who attempted to write 'universal' histories included material about Jesus in the section on pre-Islamic civilisations. These works give us some indication of the extent to which educated Muslims were familiar with the Christian scriptures.

Ibn Wāḍiḥ al-Ya'qūbī (d.292/905?), who is well known for his geographical treatise, is also the author of a two-volume *History*.[5] In dealing with the story of Mary and Jesus, he follows the Qur'anic outline up to the point where Jesus speaks in the cradle but adds non-Qur'anic and non-Biblical details such as the name of Mary's mother and Jesus' date of birth. He then states that the Gospel writers, for their part, do not mention Jesus' speaking in the cradle. He lists the twelve apostles, refers to the existence of 70 others and informs us that Matthew, Mark, Luke and John wrote the four Gospels. He almost certainly had first-hand knowledge of them for he gives a fairly accurate but incomplete description of their contents. At only two points does he reveal his Muslim bias. First, he changes the wording of Jesus' promise of the Paraclete to include the statement: 'He will be with you as a prophet.' Second, after summarising the Johannine account of the passion and resurrection, he asserts that the authors of the Gospels are in total disagreement and contrasts their words with God's authoritative statement in *Qur'ān* 4:157 which he quotes.

Abū Ja'far al-Ṭabarī (d.310/923) wrote a voluminous *History of the Prophets and Kings* usually simply called his *Annals*.[6] The original was reputedly ten times the length of the 15-volume abridged version which has come down to us. Apart from giving two genealogies of Jesus which closely follow those in *Matthew* and *Luke*, there is no evidence that Ṭabarī had direct or indirect knowledge of the canonical gospels. This is probably the result of deliberate policy because his normal custom is to make almost exclusive use of traditions handed down by Muslims. The traditions which he cites about Jesus abound with folk-tale motifs and are in some ways similar to those in the apocryphal gospels. They need not detain us now for we shall encounter many of them in Ṭabarī's Qur'anic commentary. The use he makes of them is on the whole uncritical although he does indicate the anachronistic nature of a tradition which affirms that Nebuchadnezzar punished the Israelites in order to avenge the death of John the Baptist.

'Alī b. Ḥusayn al-Mas'ūdī (d.345/956) is sometimes nicknamed 'the Herodotus of the Arabs'. His *Murūj al-Dhabab* (Golden Meadows)[7] is an epitome of much larger works. In the opening chapter he mentions the writings of earlier Muslim historians and singles out Ṭabarī's *Annals* as being far superior to all others. Maṣ'ūdī was a notorious globe-trotter and claimed to have visited Nazareth. The account which he gives of Jesus is a strange mixture of material drawn from the Qur'ān, the canonical and apocryphal gospels and Muslim tradition. He states that the Jews spread the rumour that Zechariah had sexual relations with Mary and that he took refuge in the hollow of a tree but was killed when they cut the tree down. Mas'ūdī does not accept the Jews' explanation of Mary's pregnancy. Instead he tells us that God sent the angel Gabriel to her when she was seventeen and that he breathed the spirit into her so that she conceived Jesus. He was born in Bethlehem, several miles from Jerusalem on Wednesday 24th December. Mas'ūdī continues:

> His affair was as God mentioned it in His Book and explained through the mouth of his Prophet Muḥammad (the peace and blessings of God be upon him!) The Christians have alleged that Jesus of Nazareth, that is the Messiah, followed the religion of his people's ancestors and that he read the Torah and the ancient books in the city of Tiberius in the country of Jordan in a synagogue called al-Midras for twenty-nine or thirty years. One day he was reading the book of Isaiah when he saw luminous writing which said 'You are My Son and My Quintessence (*khāliṣtī*). I have chosen you for Myself.' He closed the book, gave it back to the servant of the synagogue and went out saying, 'Now is the word of God accomplished in the Son of Man.'

After narrating the call of the disciples he says that Matthew, Mark, Luke and John were,

> the four disciples who transmitted the Gospel and set forth in it the story of the Messiah and the circumstances of his birth and how John son of Zechariah who is also called John the Baptist baptised him in Lake Tiberius or according to others in the River Jordan which flows from Lake Tiberius into the Dead Sea.

He dismisses the rest of their story with a brief summary:

> [They also mentioned] the marvels which he performed and the miracles which he brought and the treatment which the Jews inflicted on him up until God Most High's raising him to Himself when he was thirty-three years old. The Gospel deals at length with the Messiah, Mary and Joseph the Carpenter but we will leave that out because neither God Most High nor Muḥammad (the peace and blessings of God be upon him) reported anything of it.

MUSLIM POLEMIC

Many Muslim scholars wrote polemical refutations of Christianity. I cannot here do justice to the range and intricacy of their arguments. I will simply attempt to outline how they dealt with one particular problem: the discrepancy between what the Qur'ān said about Jesus and what the Christian Scriptures said about him. It was an unquestioned dogma that the Qur'ān was entirely accurate and trustworthy. Muslim polemicists therefore set out to prove that the Christian Scriptures were at fault.

Jāḥiẓ (d.255/869)[8] denounced the corruption and deviousness of Christians in his own day and then used this as a spring-board for attacking the reliability of those who wrote the gospels. He characterised Christians as arch-sceptics whose own religion had spawned countless heresies and who sowed doubt and dissension among the Muslims. He painted a vivid picture of well-to-do Christians at Baghdad, who possessed fine horses, played polo, wore expensive clothes, had Muslim servants at their beck and call, insulted Islam with impunity and evaded paying the poll-tax. Despite their social advancement and outward prosperity they were, in his opinion, inwardly unclean: they ate pork, rejected circumcision and had sexual relations with women during their periods. Moreover in Byzantium and Abyssinia Christians still practised castration – a cruel and barbaric custom virtually unknown in other countries. The Christian religion was based on the testimony of four men: the authors of the gospels. The Christians themselves admitted that two of them, Mark and Luke, were not apostles but adopted the faith later. None of the four was immune from making errors and omissions. They might even have deliberately lied to further their own ends. In any case the four gospels contradicted each other so frequently that confidence in their reliability was not justified.

Whereas Jāḥiẓ was content to assert that the gospels contained contradictions without going into detail, later polemicists spelled this out with poignant examples. None did so more effectively than Ibn Ḥazm (d.456/1063), who lived in Cordoba in Muslim Spain.[9] He pointed out for instance that John's account of the call of Andrew and Simon differed from the accounts given by Matthew, Mark and Luke[10] in four respects. John said that the call took place before the arrest of the Baptist, the others said that it took place afterwards. John said that it took place by the Jordan, the others said that it took place by the Sea of Galilee. John said that Andrew was called first and then went off to find Simon, the others said they were called together. John said that Andrew was a disciple of the Baptist, the others said that he and Simon were both fishermen. The cumulative effect of Ibn Ḥazm's painstaking analyses is to leave the reader with the impression that the four gospels are a tissue of lies.

For 'Abd al-Jabbār (d.416/1025), Mu'tazilite cadi of Raiy, the principal agents responsible for corrupting Christianity were not the evangelists: they were Paul and the Emperor Constantine.[11] Jesus was a prophet sent to Israel but Paul went to the Gentiles. Jesus obeyed the Mosaic Law but Paul declared it irrelevant. Jesus was a monotheist but Paul introduced alien Greek ideas of incarnation, trinity and redemption. In short he was 'a deceitful liar'. Under Constantine Paul's Greek ideas became full-scale dogmas. The Church set out to convert the Empire but in reality the Empire converted the Church.

MUSLIM APOLOGETICS

A minority of Muslim scholars were prepared to accept the general reliability of the Christian Scriptures. These scholars had to grapple with two problems. First, the Qur'ān implied that the Gospel contained a prophecy of the coming of Muḥammad but the Christians denied this. Second, the Qur'ān said that Jesus was not divine but the Christians alleged that their Scriptures asserted the contrary.

The problem of pin-pointing Jesus' prophecy was tackled by 'Alī b. Rabban al-Ṭabarī, an eminent Christian physician who became a Muslim at the age of seventy. The core of his *Book of Religion and Empire*,[12] which he compiled for the Caliph al-Mutawakkil (232–247/847–861), is a list of proof texts or testimonies from the Old and New Testaments. One of the key texts was Jesus' statement about the Paraclete: 'The Paraclet, the Spirit of truth, whom my Father will send in my name, He shall teach you everything' (cf. *John* 14:26). This promise, he says, cannot refer to Jesus' disciples because they only taught what was already known. It must refer to Muḥammad for in the Qur'ān he taught mankind everything which they did not know. But what about the phrase 'in my name'? The author seems to assume that Paraclet was one of the names attributed both to Jesus (cf. *John* 14:16 'another Paraclete') and to Muḥammad. He further indicates that the numerical value of Paraclet is the same as that of 'Muḥammad son of 'Abdallah the rightly guiding Prophet'. To the objection that he has missed the final letter off 'Paracleta' (the Syriac for Paraclete) he replies that the letter *alif* is a paragogical addition to Syriac nouns but that if it is counted the numerical value of the name will be the same as that of 'Muḥammad is a beloved and good apostle'.[13]

The problem of the New Testament's alleged attribution of divinity to Jesus was first tackled by the Mu'tazilite theologian Ibrahīm al-Naẓẓām (d.231/845). His views are mentioned by Jāḥiẓ who considers them unsatisfactory. Although al-Naẓẓām denied that Jesus was in any sense divine he was apparently prepared to allow that God might have called him 'Son' to indicate his spiritual adoption. He argued that this was no different from God's calling Abraham His 'Friend' (cf. *Qur'ān* 4:125). A much more detailed treatment of the problem is found in a brief work attributed to al-Ghazālī (d.505/1111) but probably written by one of his pupils.[14] The author indicates a number of texts within the New Testament which imply Jesus' humanity and he insists that they must be taken literally. For instance Jesus is on record as experiencing hunger (*Mark* 11:12), confessing ignorance (*Mark* 13:32) and submitting to God's will (*Matthew* 26:39). On the other hand, the texts in which Jesus apparently claims divinity should, he argues, be interpreted figuratively. For instance when Jesus said 'I and the Father are One' (*John* 10:30) the Jews accused him of blasphemy because they thought that he meant it literally. Yet Jesus' reply, in which he pointed out that the Jews themselves were referred to as 'gods' in the Old Testament (*John* 10:34), showed that he was speaking metaphorically.

DISCUSSION

When the Muslims moved out of Arabia into the former territories of the Byzantine and Persian Empires they came into contact with Christians who were far more sophisticated than those whom they had previously encountered. These Christians were familiar with Greek philosophy and logic and thus gave the Muslims an incentive to produce their own rational theology. They also possessed the canonical Scriptures and confronted the Muslims with the Jesus of the four gospels who was so very different from the Qur'anic Jesus with whom they were familiar. Muslim historians, polemicists and apologists reacted to this in a variety of ways all of them made possible by the Qur'ān's rather vague hints that Christians had 'corrupted' the Gospel or 'forgotten' parts of it.[15] The majority view was that the Christian Scriptures were textually corrupt. Within this camp some like Ibn Ḥazm rejected the four gospels as worthless while others like Ya'qūbī accepted that they contained elements of the original Gospel together with extraneous matter added by the evangelists. The minority view, championed by pseudo-Ghazālī, was that the Christians had 'corrupted' the Scriptures by erroneous interpretation rather than by faulty transmission. None the less for all Muslims the Qur'ān continued to be the primary source of information about Jesus even if they were prepared to fill out the picture with information derived from other sources.

7 Shi'ītes and Ṣūfīs

The representation of Jesus in the classical Shi'īte and Ṣūfī commentaries will be discussed in Chapters 16 and 17 respectively. Nevertheless it is impossible to understand the Sunnī commentaries without some basic knowledge of these movements.

SHĪ'ISM[1]

The term Shī'ism is derived from the Arabic expression *Shī'at 'Alī*, 'the Party of 'Alī'. Shī'īte Muslims believe that Muḥammad's divinely-designated successor was his cousin, adopted brother and son-in-law 'Alī b. a. Ṭālib. They hold that after Muḥammad's death, 'Alī and his descendants should by right have been openly recognised as the religious and political leaders of Islam. In actual fact this did not happen. It was not until 'Uthmān was assassinated in 35/656 that 'Alī succeeded him as the fourth Caliph. He was immediately faced with an insurrection in Baṣra but successfully defeated his opponents who included the Prophet's widow 'Ā'isha. This was only the beginning of his troubles because Mu'āwiya, the governor of Syria and a nephew of 'Uthmān, refused to recognise him as Caliph. 'Alī moved his capital to Kūfa in Iraq and marched against the Syrians. After two days of ferocious fighting at Ṣiffin 'Alī's troops began to gain ground. At this point the Syrian cavalry fixed copies of the Qur'ān to their lances and raised the cry 'Let the Word of God decide!' This ruse had the required effect: the fighting ceased and peace was negotiated. Extremists within 'Alī's own camp were, however, dissatisfied and formed a breakaway group known as the Khārijites. One of them assassinated 'Alī outside the mosque in Kūfa in 40/661.

After the death of 'Alī, Mu'āwiya was firmly in control of the Muslim empire which he ruled as the first Umayyad Caliph. 'Alī's elder son Ḥasan, relinquished his claim to the Caliphate and withdrew from political life to live quietly in Medina until his death in 49/669. His brother Ḥusayn, then assumed the leadership of the House of 'Alī. He died in 61/680 while fighting against the Umayyads in the Battle of Karbalā. The Shī'ītes believe that he died as a martyr sacrificing his life in order to remind the Muslim community of the early ideals of Islam which had been largely lost sight of because of the worldliness of Mu'āwiya and his successors.

Members of the principal branch of Shī'ism, the Twelvers, recognise a further nine Imams after 'Alī, Ḥasan and Ḥusayn. The fourth and fifth were political quietists. So too was the sixth Imam, Ja'far al-Ṣādiq but after the Abbasids came to power he was summoned to Kūfa on several occasions and held under arrest. He died in 148/765 probably as a result of being poisoned by Caliph al-Manṣūr. The persecution of the Shī'ītes intensified over the next few decades and the seventh Imam spent the last six years of his life imprisoned in Baghdad until he too was poisoned in 183/799.

The eighth and ninth Imams, 'Alī al-Riḍā and his son Muḥammad al-Taqī, ostensibly fared much better because the Caliph Ma'mūn attempted a *rapprochement* with them. In a surprising move he nominated 'Alī al-Riḍā as his own successor. Then, when 'Alī al-Riḍā died suddenly, he chose al-Taqī to be his son-in-law. These overtures were probably political expedients aimed at quelling Shī'īte rebellions. It is also likely that Ma'mūn was himself responsible for al-Riḍā's untimely death.

From 232/847 the Shī'ītes experienced a period of open persecution; the tenth and eleventh Imams were kept under house arrest in Sāmarrā and access to them was restricted. The eleventh Imam died in 260/873. Shortly after his death his only son Muḥammad, the twelfth and final Imam, mysteriously vanished and was never seen again. Muḥammad was only a child at the time of his disappearance. For the next 69 years, known as the period of his 'Lesser Occultation', he communicated with his followers through four successive agents. The death of the last of these agents in 329/941 marks the beginning of the 'Greater Occultation' which extends to the present day. It is believed that unlike his agents the Imam himself did not die. God has hidden him from sight until the day when he returns as the Mahdī, the Rightly Guided One who will restore religion and justice and will rule before the end of the earth.

THE *GHULĀT* SECTS[2]

The above historical outline mentions only those Imams who are revered by the Twelvers. In reality the early development of Shī'ism was much more complex. After the death of several of the Imams there were disputes about the succession and splinter groups came into existence claiming either that the line of Imams had come to an end or that the Imamate was vested in their candidate. Most of these splinter groups were short-lived. From the viewpoint of later orthodoxy some of their beliefs were patently heretical and those who espoused them were termed *ghulāt* – people whose doctrinal extremism puts them beyond the pale of Islam. Nevertheless their beliefs are pertinent to our study in at least four respects:

1. Some of them alleged that one of the Imams was divine. For instance Ibn Sabā claimed divinity for 'Alī, the Rawandiyya claimed it for al-Manṣūr the second Abbasid Caliph, the Muslimiyya claimed it for Abū Muslim the Abbasid general who led the revolt which toppled the Umayyads, and Abū Khaṭṭāb claimed it for the sixth Imam Ja'far al-Ṣādiq.
2. Around the middle of the second/eighth century Abū Manṣūr al-'Ijlī claimed that he was the piece (*kisf*) of heaven mentioned in *Qur'ān* 52:44, whence his followers earned the name Kisfīyya. He taught that the first two things created by God were Jesus and then 'Alī.
3. Those who believed that the line of Imams had come to an end with a particular Imam often held that he had not really died but would return as the Mahdī to fill the earth with justice. For instance Ibn Sabā is alleged to have claimed that this was the case with 'Alī and that he was alive in the clouds. Similarly the Karibiyya, one of several groups who believed that after the death of Ḥusayn the Imamate passed to Muḥammad ibn al-Ḥanafiyya, claimed that the latter did not die but was concealed on a mountain seven days' journey from Medina.
4. Those who expected the return of a particular Imam as the Mahdī sometimes resorted to bizarre theories in order to explain his apparent death. The Muḥammadiyya believed that a devil took the shape of Nafs Zakiyya (d.145/672) and was killed in his place. The Barkūkiyya held similar beliefs about Abū Muslim who they alleged had inherited the Imamate from the first Abbasid Caliph. In the case of Ḥusayn, the theory was more intricate: it was supposed that his place was taken by a disciple called Ḥanẓala Shibāmī who assumed his likeness although the suffering was transferred to an invisible damned soul called 'Umar.[3]

ṢŪFISM

Ṣūfism is the term used to denote the mystical dimension of Islam. In the Umayyad and early Abbasid periods, however, the Ṣūfis were not so much mystics as ascetics. They reminded men and women of the original ideals of Islam which seemed to have been lost sight of. For them Jesus was a model wayfaring ascetic and they saw in the title the Messiah (*al-masīḥ*) an indication that he used to 'pace through' (*masaḥa*) the earth or that both of his feet were worn flat (*mamsūḥ*) by incessant walking. One of the most famous Ṣūfis in this period was Ḥasan al-Baṣrī (d.728) who was renowned for his scholarship as well as his piety. Abū Bakr al-Kalābādhī (d.380/990), a celebrated theorist of Ṣūfism, mentions how Ḥasan once entered a mosque in Baṣra and discovered a group of Muslims discussing someone and spreading scandal about him. Ḥasan told them to keep silent and related to them traditions on the subject of backbiting which he had heard attributed to Jesus.[4] A letter which Ḥasan addressed to the Caliph illustrates the degree of his asceticism. He warns the Caliph to turn away from whatever delights him in the world which he describes as having 'neither weight nor worth with God'. He depicts the prophets as ascetics: Muḥammad bound a stone around his stomach when he was hungry, Moses' belly was as green as the grass which he ate and Jesus used to say:

> My daily bread is hunger, my badge is fear, my raiment is wool, my mount is my foot, my lantern at night is the moon, my fire by day is the sun, and my fruit and fragrant herbs are such things as the earth brings forth for the wild beasts and the cattle. All the night I have nothing, yet there is none richer than I![5]

There are many more Ṣūfī traditions about Jesus' self-denial.[6] He is said for instance to have possessed only a cup which he threw away when he saw another man drinking from the palms of his hands and a comb which he likewise threw away when he saw another man using his fingers.[7] Some of the Ṣūfis wore a patched frock as an outward sign of their poverty and Jesus was reputedly wearing one of these when he was raised into heaven. Hujwīrī (d.464/1072) relates how a certain sheikh dreamed that he saw Jesus with light flowing from every patch and that he explained to him that because he had sewed on each of the patches out of necessity God had turned all his tribulations into light.[8]

The fear of God so characteristic of the early ascetics was later tempered by an attitude of hope, an attitude which was also ascribed to Jesus. According to one tradition, whereas John the Baptist wept continually from the moment of his birth, Jesus was always smiling. When they met John used to say, 'O Jesus hast thou no fear of being cut off [from God]?' And Jesus would reply: 'O John hast thou no hope of God's mercy? Neither thy decrees nor thy smiles will change the eternal decree of God.'[9]

The first Ṣūfī to stress the need to love God rather than fear him was probably a woman mystic of Baṣra called Rābi'a al-'Adawiyya (d.801) who is credited with this famous prayer:

> O my Lord, if I worship Thee from fear of Hell, burn me in Hell, and if I worship Thee in hope of Paradise exclude me thence, but if I worship Thee for Thine own sake withhold not from me Thine eternal beauty.[10]

Somewhat akin to this is the tradition which cites Jesus as declaring that a person who practises asceticism out of love for God is closer to him than a person who does so out of fear of hell or hope of paradise.[11]

'INTOXICATED ṢŪFĪS' AND THE IMPACT OF AL-ḤALLĀJ

The stress on loving God above all else was one of the factors which led to the development of the doctrine of *fanā'* – extinction or passing away into God. This doctrine was first formulated by Abū Yazīd al-Bistamī (d.875) who was also the first Ṣūfi to take Muḥammad's heavenly ascent (*mi'rāj*) as the theme of his own mystical experience. In a state of ecstasy he declared 'Glory be to me! How great is my majesty!' His explanation of this behaviour was that for a brief moment, after emptying himself of self, he had reached the world of absolute unity where lover, beloved and love are one.[12] This ecstatic utterance was however open to serious misunderstanding and in Baghdad during the course of the ninth and tenth centuries several Ṣūfis who exhibited similar behaviour were executed for blasphemy. The most famous case was that of Manṣūr al-Ḥallāj (d.309/922) who was crucified and decapitated for declaring 'I am the Truth.'[13] One of his disciples alleged that the person who was actually executed was al-Ḥallāj's enemy onto whom his likeness had been projected and some of them claimed that on the day after the execution they saw al-Ḥallāj riding a donkey and heading for Nahrawān. The more widely held view is that, although al-Ḥallāj was crucified, his soul was raised into God's presence in mystic union so that only his body suffered.[14] For this reason, in Turkish and Persian mystical poetry, his execution is often referred to as his *miʿrāj* and he is accordingly depicted as having made his ecstatic utterance while hanging on the gibbet.[15]

The execution of al-Ḥallāj, the activities of the *Malāmatīya* – an extremist antinomian sect which deliberately neglected the requirements of Islamic law – and the tendency of ultra-orthodox Muslims to be suspicious even of more moderate forms of Ṣūfism provided the necessary impetus for Ṣūfi self-definition and apologetics. In the tenth and eleventh centuries Ṣūfism thus crystallised into a recognisable system of co-ordinated doctrines and practices. There were of course many variations but the basic pattern was relatively constant. Ṣūfism was depicted as a spiritual path which could only be followed by those who fulfilled the religious prescriptions of Islam; it was the inner core of the religion and not an alternative to it. The characteristic Ṣūfi practice was *dhikr*, the 'recollection' of God by repeating the divine names. The adept or 'traveller' received spiritual guidance from a sheikh. His journey was mapped out for him as a succession of 'stations' which he could achieve by discipline and perseverance. After the stations would come a series of higher 'states' which would be bestowed on him by God and would not be dependent on his own efforts. The objective was 'extinction' (*fanā'*) conceived of not as an apotheosis but as a dying to self and a temporary union with the Beloved followed by 'continuance' *baqā'* in which the mystic would persist as a conscious individual despite his life having been purified and transformed by God. He should not hope for the final removal of the veil until he took his place in paradise as one of 'those brought near'.

THE BRETHREN OF PURITY[16]

From 297/909 to 567/1171 Egypt was ruled by the Fāṭimid Caliphs. These were Ismāʿīli Shīʿites. That is to say they held that after the death of Jaʿfar al-Ṣādiq, the imamate passed to his son Ismāʿīl. Moreover they themselves claimed descent from Ismāʿīl via a series of hidden Imams. The *Rasā'il* ('Epistles') of the Brethren of Purity constitute a mysterious encyclopaedic work which is an amalgam of religion, esoterism and philosophy. Although this corpus of writings is anonymous it is highly probable that it was produced by Ismāʻīlī propagandists during the period 900 to 981. It propounds an elaborate emanationist cosmology based in part on ideas derived from Pythagorism and Neoplatonism. The Creator is said to be related to the universe via the Universal Intellect beneath which is a hierarchy of being extending down through the Universal Soul, Original Matter and Universal Matter to Determined Bodies. This cosmology is combined with the belief that the history of the universe is a succession of cycles each lasting seven thousand years. The present cycle is sub-divided into millennia each inaugurated by a Messenger of God: Adam, Noah, Abraham, Moses, Jesus, Muḥammad and the *Qā'im* of the Resurrection. Within the first six millennia there were eight series of seven Imams. With the aid of the Messengers and Imams it is possible for human souls to free themselves from the prison of the body and ascend back up through the celestial spheres to the Universal Soul from which they originated.

There are thirty-four passages in this work which mention Jesus or Christianity. Of particular interest is the long summary of Jesus' life in Epistle 44. It depicts him wandering through Palestine preaching renunciation of the world and its delusions and arousing people's desire for the Kingdom of Heaven. Like the other Messengers and Imams he was primarily a 'physician of souls', hence his miracles are understood spiritually. For instance he is said to have healed blindness of heart and raised the Israelites from the death of sin. In the upper room in Jerusalem he told the disciples:

> 'I am about to go away to meet my Father and yours again. Before departing from my human form I am going to leave you a testament and to make a pact and covenant with you. Those who accept my testament and are faithful to my pact will be with me tomorrow; but as for those who do not accept it, I shall not be of them at all nor they of me.' 'What is this testament?' they asked. 'Go and find the kings of all regions', he answered them, 'and transmit to them on my behalf what I have given you and call them to what I have called you, without being in fear or dread of them. For when I have departed from my human form I shall remain in the air at the right hand of the throne of my Father and yours and I shall be with you wherever you go.'

More interesting still is what is said concerning the passion. Jesus' humanity (*nāsūt*) was crucified and his hands were nailed to the cross. He was left there all day, given vinegar to drink, and pierced with a lance. He was taken down from the cross, wrapped in a shroud and laid in the tomb. Three days later he appeared to the disciples and was recognised by them. When the news spread that he had not been killed, the Jews opened up the tomb but did not find his mortal remains (*nāsūt*).

Although the Brethren of Purity rejected Christian claims concerning Christ's divinity they appear to have been reconciled to belief in the reality of the crucifixion. They probably understood his death in terms of their Neoplatonist metaphysics: the soul which constitutes the personality was liberated when the body – the prison of the soul – died on the cross. Apart from the details concerning the crucifixion there is little to suggest that they had first-hand knowledge of Christian sources. Nor is there much overlap with the accounts of Jesus' life given by Muslim historians.

IBN AL-'ARABĪ[17]

Muḥyī al-Dīn Ibn al-'Arabī (d.638/1240), who was born in Spain of Arab stock, was initiated into Ṣūfism in Tunis. The well-known *Bezels of Wisdom* is only one of the four hundred or so extant works attributed to him. Since his writing is not only voluminous but also abstruse, I cannot hope in the space of a few words to do justice either to his theosophical system, which owes much to Neoplatonism, or to his cryptic statements about Jesus.

Ibn al-'Arabī's system is known as *waḥdat al-wujūd* which may loosely be translated as 'Unity of Being'. It is, however, misleading to describe him as a pure pantheist as some Western scholars have done. He believed that God is Absolute Being and that the universe possesses only Relative Being. Before the things in the phenomenal world came into existence they were latent in the mind of God as the archetypes which continue to be the intermediaries between them and the Absolute Reality. On this reckoning the mystic's goal is not to *achieve* union with God but rather to realise that he is already one with Him. Such realisation is facilitated by the prophets and saints to whom divine knowledge has been transmitted by the universal rational principle – also called the 'the Spirit of Muḥammad', 'the Muḥammadan Reality', 'the Perfect Man' and 'the Cosmic Pole' – which roughly corresponds to the *Logos* in Christian Platonism.

In order to grasp the significance which Ibn al-'Arabī attached to Jesus it is necessary to understand how he conceived of the relationship between prophethood and sainthood. Since, according to the Qur'ān, Muḥammad was 'the Seal of the Prophets' (33:40), there could be no prophet after him. Nevertheless there continue to be saints. In every period there is one saint, known as 'the Temporal Pole' or 'Master of the Age', who is the manifestation of the Cosmic Pole for that epoch. Beneath him – or perhaps including him – there are seven *Abdāl* who intercede for humanity. Each of the seven derives his power from one of the prophets in the seven heavens – in descending order these are: Abraham, Moses, Aaron, Idrīs, Joseph, Jesus and Adam. In addition to the seven *Abdāl* – or possibly included in their number – there are four 'Pillars' by whom God preserves the world. The hearts of the four Pillars are conformed to those of Adam, Abraham, Jesus and Muḥammad respectively. In addition each of the four is strengthened by the spiritual nature of one of the archangels and each is allotted one of the four corners of the Kaaba; in the case of the Pillar whose heart is conformed to Jesus the archangel is Gabriel and the corner is the one facing Yemen.

It should by now be obvious that, for Ibn al-'Arabī, Jesus is a trans-historical figure who continues to have an influence on certain types of saints, an honour which he shares with other eminent prophets. There are, however, two further features of Ibn al-'Arabī's description of Jesus which point to the latter's uniqueness – namely the inferences he draws from the virginal conception and his reference to him as 'the Seal of the Saints'. As regards the former he seems to imply that Jesus was able to create birds from clay and raise the dead because he was a spirit from God and it is of the essence of spirits to create life in whatever they touch. He does, however, qualify this:

> The act of giving life was God's and the breathing was Jesus' just as the breathing was Gabriel's and the word was God's. However, the act of giving life to the dead was really Jesus' in as much as it was the outcome of his breathing

Ibn al-'Arabī's references to Jesus as 'the Seal of the Saints' are more perplexing. He cannot simply mean that the succession of saints will come to an end when Jesus returns, because he implies that Jesus *already* has this status. The reason for this is probably the manner in which he was brought into being: other men become saints when they are revivified by the spirit but Jesus was a saint from the beginning because of the part played by the spirit in his conception.

DISCUSSION

For the most part the Sunnī commentaries contain only the vaguest allusions to the matters mentioned in this chapter. Yet this does not mean that they were unimportant or that the Qur'anic exegetes were unaware of them. We shall see later that the Sunni commentaries preserve traditions about Jesus' awaited return and about the crucifixion of a substitute and we shall have to consider whether these traditions were modelled on the *ghulāt* beliefs concerning the Imams or whether the influence was in the opposite direction.

The extent to which Ṣūfism was indebted to Christianity continues to be debated. That there is a measure of indebtedness need hardly be doubted in view of the fact that early Ṣūfism thrived in Syria where it inherited the mantle of Christian asceticism as a movement of protest and counter-culture. Nevertheless the piety of the Ṣūfīs, their technical vocabulary and their reverence for Jesus are all firmly rooted in the Qur'ān.

It is difficult to assess the importance of the writings of the Brethren of Purity, al-Ḥallāj and Ibn al-'Arabī. The *Rasā'il* are a sectarian work and are still cherished by the Isma'īlis. Al-Ḥallāj and Ibn al-'Arabī have both had a profound influence on mainstream Ṣūfism but are viewed with suspicion by those who are concerned with orthodoxy. We shall see too that the commentators are at pains to exclude some of the ideas associated with them although they never name them directly. More representative of the acceptable face of Ṣūfism is a work which I have not yet mentioned: the *Revival of Religious Sciences* by Ghazālī (d.505/1111) which harmonises the mystical interpretation of Islam with the rival claims of legal observance and tradition. The author makes numerous references to Jesus but avoids theosophical speculation and simply portrays him as an itinerant miracle-working ascetic and lover of God.[18]

8 Classical Exegesis

The classical period of Arab civilisation is generally reckoned to have spanned about 350 years beginning at the turn of the fourth/tenth century and drawing to a close with the sacking of Baghdad by the Mongols in 656/1258. The decision to limit the investigation to the representation of Jesus in the classical commentaries needs little justification. Many of the exegetical works written during the formative period of Islam are either no longer extant or have not yet been edited thus making a thorough study of pre-classical exegesis impracticable. On the other hand, the post-classical period is one of cultural decline and its Qur'anic commentaries are scholastic compilations based almost exclusively on classical works. I have, however, allowed myself a generous margin, beginning with Ṭabarī (d.310/923), who stood on the threshold of the classical period, and ending with Ibn Kathīr (d.774/1372) who died over a century after the sacking of Baghdad.

Muslim scholars distinguish between exegesis based on tradition (*tafsīr bi 'l-ma'thūr*) and exegesis based on opinion (*tafsīr bi 'l-ray'*). In theory the former consists exclusively of explanations of the Qur'ān which can be reliably traced back to a sound source whereas the latter makes extensive use of reasoning. In practice, as we shall see, the distinction is not a hard and fast one. I will first discuss some of the types of material encountered in the commentaries wherever possible giving examples which have a bearing on the interpretation of the Qur'anic representation of Jesus. Then I will introduce the five classical commentaries to which I shall be repeatedly referring in subsequent chapters.

THE CHAINS OF GUARANTORS

When citing Muslim traditions it is customary to support them with an *isnād* (pl. *asānid*). This is a chain of names of those who reputedly transmitted the tradition in question and who guaranteed its authenticity. For example, the following isnād occurs 3060 times[1] in Ṭabarī's commentary: 'Bishr b. Mu'āḍ told us. He said Yazīd b. Zuray' told us. He said Sa'īd told us on the authority of Qatāda.'

Experts in tradition pay attention to the words used to denote the manner of transmission. The expression 'He told us' (*ḥadatha-nā*), which occurs three times in this isnād, implies that Ṭabarī heard Bishr when others were present, that Bishr heard Yazīd when others were present and that Yazīd heard Sa'īd when others were present. The much vaguer 'on the authority of' (*'an*) is generally agreed to be allowable if the transmittor is known to be reliable. We shall meet with asānīd in which other terms are used. These include 'he told me' (*ḥadatha-nī*) implying that no one else was present, 'he informed me' (*akhbara-nī*) implying that the speaker submitted traditions to the sheikh and was given oral permission to transmit them and 'he informed us' (*akhbara-nā*) implying that the speaker was present when someone else submitted traditions to the sheikh.[2]

In order to identify the transmitters it is necessary to consult biographical dictionaries compiled for the purpose from the third/ninth century onwards. Unlike many of Ṭabarī's asānīd this one does not pose any problems of identification.[3] The full name of the first transmitter is Bishr b. Mu'āḍ al-Baṣrī (d.245/859) under whom Ṭabarī is known to have studied in Baṣra. The second and third are Yazīd b Zuray' al-Baṣrī (182/798) and Sa'īd b. a. 'Arūba al-Baṣrī (156/773) both of whom were well-known transmitters of traditions. The person at the end of the chain is an early authority on exegesis Qatāda b. Di'āma al-Baṣrī (118/736). Thus the traditions supported by this isnād are ostensibly extracts from Qatāda's commentary as transmitted by an unbroken chain of guarantors in Baṣra.

The biographical dictionaries do not simply include dates and information about who studied under whom. They also record the opinions of various legal scholars concerning the reliability of the named person. These scholars engaged in what was known technically as *al-jarḥ wa 'l-ta'dīl* 'disparaging and declaring trustworthy'. A transmitter might be disparaged on various grounds such as holding heretical views, having a faulty memory or being untruthful.[4] Moreover if some authorities disparaged him and others declared him trustworthy the disparagement would carry more weight. Bishr and Yazīd were universally declared to be trustworthy. So too was Sa'īd although his intellectual faculties were said to have been impaired after 145/763. Both Sa'īd and Qatāda held Qadarite views (that is to say they believed in free will) but since they were discreet and did not try to proselytise this was not deemed sufficient to discredit them.

THE NAMED EARLY AUTHORITIES

Some of the traditions cited in the commentaries are traced back to the Prophet but the majority are attributed to his Companions or their pupils the Successors.

The list of Companions (*Ṣaḥāba*) who concerned themselves with exegesis includes the first four Caliphs as well as Ibn Mas'ūd, 'Ubaiy b. Ka'b, Zayd b. Thābit and a handful of others. Pride of place, however, is given to a young cousin of the Prophet called 'Abd Allah Ibn al-'Abbās (d.68/687). He was reputedly a polymath, expert in such diverse fields as Arabic language, poetry and arithmetic.[5] A high proportion of the material in the classical commentaries is traced back to him by a variety of routes.

The pupils of the Companions are referred to as the Successors (*Tābi'ūn*). Many of them are associated with Qur'anic commentary. The most knowledgeable group of Successors were reputedly the pupils of Ibn al-'Abbās centred at Mecca. This group included Mujāhid (d.103/721), Ikrāma (d.106/724), Sa'īd b. Jubayr (d.95/714), 'Atā' (d.115/733) and many others. A second group comprising the pupils of 'Ubaiy b. Ka'b was centred at Medina. It included Abū al-'Āliya (90/708), Ibn Ka'b al-Qurẓī (117/735) and Zayd b. Aslam (130/747). Also of importance were the pupils of Ibn Mas'ūd who were active in Iraq. This latter group included two people whose names we have already encountered: Qatāda b. Di'ama (d.118/736), who was the named authority in our sample isnād, and the ascetic Ḥasan al-Baṣrī (d.110/728) who was mentioned in connection with Ṣūfism. It also included al-Rābi' b. Anas (d.139/756) and al-Suddī (d.128/745). Finally special mention should be made of the storyteller Wahb b. Munabbih (d.110/728 or 114/732). He was born in the Yemen of Persian stock and is credited with being very knowledgeable about matters relating to the Jews and Christians.

THE *AḤĀDĪTH*

A tradition which is traced back to the Prophet Muḥammad is called a *ḥadīth* (pl. *aḥādīth*). These traditions cover almost every conceivable aspect of the life of the Muslim community and only a very small proportion of them are directly concerned with the exegesis of the Qur'ān. Muslim scholars were well aware that many spurious aḥadīth had been put into circulation by story tellers who pandered to popular taste and by sectarian groups. By the time the classical commentaries were written, however, the wheat had ostensibly been separated from the chaff and six collections had achieved canonical status. The two most important are those compiled by al-Bukhārī (d.256/870) and Muslim b. al-Ḥajjāj (d.261/875). All the aḥadīth in these two collections are regarded as indisputably authentic (*ṣaḥīḥ*) because in every case the text of the saying is supported by one or more unbroken asānīd which reach back to the Prophet and because all the guarantors in the asānīd can be identified and are known to have been reliable, of sound memory and of orthodox belief. The other compilers included many aḥādīth whose asānīd did not quite meet these stringent conditions. Some of them are deemed to be of only 'fair' authority (*ḥasan*) but none the less good enough for establishing points of law. Still others are regarded as 'weak' (*ḍa'īf*); they cannot be used for legal purposes but may none the less be used for exhortation. The two examples which I shall give are both 'authentic'.

From early times Christian polemicists have supposed that the Qur'ān confuses Mary with Miriam. From the perspective of traditional exegesis this matter can be resolved by reference to the following ḥadīth which Ibn Kathīr cites from the collection of Muslim:

> Mughīra b. Shu'ba said, 'The Messenger of God (the peace and blessings of God be upon him!) sent me to the people of Najrān. They said to me, "Do you [Muslims] not recite [in the Qur'ān] «O Sister of Aaron» [19:28]?" I said, "Yes, indeed". They said "And do you know what [period of time elapsed] between Moses and Jesus?"' So I returned to the Messenger of God (peace and blessings be upon him) and informed him. He said "Did you not tell them that [the Jews] used to give [their children] the names of their prophets and of the pious persons who lived before them?"'[6]

Christian apologists frequently emphasise the high esteem which the Qur'ān has for Mary. There can be no denying the Qur'ān's assertion that God preferred her above all the women of creation but this is relativised by another authentic ḥadīth published by Muslim which puts Mary on the same level as Muḥammad's first wife:

> 'Abd Allah b. Ja'far reported that he heard 'Alī say in Kūfa that God's messenger (peace be upon him!) said, 'The best of the women of her [time] was Mary daughter of 'Imrān and the best of the women of her [time] was Khadīja daughter of Khuwaylid'.[7]

THE *ASBĀB AL-NUZŪL*

In addition to the exegetical aḥadīth there are traditions called *asbāb al-nuzūl* or 'causes of the revelation' which record the occasions in the Prophet's life on which various sections of the Qur'ān were revealed. These traditions do not cover the whole Qur'ān and in fact there are very few which have direct relevance to the Jesus material. In Chapter 4 I mentioned the most important one, the tradition which associates the revelation of 3:1–63 with the presence in Medina of the embassy of Christians from Najrān. There are a number of different versions of this tradition, some of them explaining the reason for various details mentioned in this section of the Qur'ān. For instance the Christians reputedly cited the virgin birth as proof of Jesus' divinity whereupon 3:59 was revealed likening Jesus to Adam who was also born by divine fiat.[8]

EXPLANATORY GLOSSES ON RARE WORDS

The Qur'ān contains a number of rare or unusual words. Many of the interpretations traced back to the Companions and Successors are simple glosses which provide a paraphrase or a better known synonym. For instance Jesus is said to have healed 'the blind' (*al-akmah*, 3:49 and 5:110) but the word used occurs nowhere else in the Qur'ān. Al-Suddī and Ḥasan al-Baṣrī glossed it with the similar sounding but more usual word *al-a'mā* which quite definitely means 'the blind.' Others defined it variously as 'born blind in both eyes', 'born blind', 'seeing in the day but not at night', and 'blear-eyed'. Judging by the material presented by Ṭabarī, there seems not only to have been an absence of consensus on what the word meant, but also confusion about what the Companions and Successors said it meant for both Ibn al-'Abbās and Qatāda have two of the above interpretations attributed to them but traced back by different routes.[9]

Let me give another example this time mentioning only the interpretation attributed to Ibn al-'Abbās. We have seen that Christian polemicists frequently allege that the Qur'ān mistakenly states that nobody had been called John before Zechariah's son. Those who make this allegation assume that the āya in question means: «O Zechariah! Behold We bring you good news of a boy whose name is John. We have not before constituted anyone of the same name as him» (19:7).

The word *samīy*, which I have translated 'of the same name', occurs only twice in the Qur'ān – here and at 19:65. In both instances Ibn al-'Abbās took it to mean 'similar'. He said that what is meant is that there had never before been a boy similar to John in the sense of being born to an aged father and a barren mother.[10] Isaac was not like him because although the Qur'ān says that his parents were old it does not say that either of them was infertile.

CITATIONS OF POETRY

When the meaning of a Qur'anic word is disputed the commentators often attempt to define it by quoting a verse of an early poem in which it occurs. This is what Ṭabarī does in the case of *al-akmah*.[11] He states that it means 'the blind' and quotes from Suwayd b. a. Kāhil:

> His eyes became blind (*kamihat*) since they became white
> and he reviled himself when he departed.

Most of the poetic testimonies (*shawāhid*) are furnished by the commentators themselves or plagiarised by them from works on lexicography. However the first person to cite ancient poetry to illustrate the meaning of rare words was reputedly Ibn al-'Abbās. The following example is taken from an opuscule attributed to him entitled *Masā'il Nāfi' b. al-Azraq* (The Questions of Nāfi' b. al-Azraq). When Mary was about to give birth to Jesus, «the birthpangs drove her to the trunk of the palm tree» (19:23). The verb translated 'drove' is *ajā'a*. This is the only place where it occurs in the Qur'ān. Ibn al-'Abbās explained it with a line from Ḥassān b. Thābit:[12]

> When we launched a really fierce attack
> and drove you – (*'ajā'na-kum*) to the foot of the mountain.

The *shawāhid* are not very illuminating unless you are familiar with the poems from which they are drawn. Ḥassān b. Thābit (d.40/659, 50/669 or 54/673) was converted to Islam and put his talents at the service of the Prophet in Medina. The quotation is from a poem which he reputedly uttered after the battle of Uḥud in reply to a taunt by Ibn Ziba'rā. Here is the first part of the poem:[13]

The battle is over, O Ibn Ziba'rā
(Had he been fair he would have admitted our superiority)
You inflicted loss on us and we on you
The fortunes of war often change.
We thrust our swords between your shoulders
Where they drank blood again and again.
We made liquid run from your arses
Like the ordure of camels that have eaten '*aṣal*.[14]
When you took to your heels in the pass
And fled like sheep one behind the other;
When we launched a really fierce attack and drove you to
the foot of the mountain.

Unfortunately not all the *shawāhid* are as easy to track down because commentators frequently omit the name of the poet. When a citation is introduced with the formula 'as the poet said' it is most likely from a well-known poem and it is worth searching the standard anthologies. If, on the other hand, it is attributed to a 'versifier' or 'composer of verse' (*rajāz*) it was probably a stock example used by lexicographers and there is some chance that it will be cited and explained in the great Arabic dictionary of Ibn Manẓūr (d.711/1311).[15]

ANECDOTAL MATERIAL

Much of the material traced back to the Companions and Successors is anecdotal in character. I will give three examples.

The Qur'ān speaks of John «believing in a word from God» (3:39). Ibn al-'Abbās took this to mean that John believed in Jesus whom the Qur'ān elsewhere describes as «a word» (3:45, 4:171). His comment is as follows:

> Jesus and John were cousins. John's mother said to Mary, 'Behold! I find him who is in my belly prostrating himself before him who is in your belly.' So that was his believing in Jesus, his prostration of himself in his mother's belly. He was the first to believe in Jesus and in Jesus' word. And John was older than Jesus.[16]

My second example is a colourful story told by al-Suddī in commenting on Jesus' clairvoyance which is alluded to in 3:49:

> He – meaning Jesus Son of Mary – used to tell the boys who were with him in school what their parents did and what they put aside

for them and what they ate. He said to a boy, 'Hurry off. Your family have put aside such and such for you and they are eating such and such.' So the boy hurried off and cried in front of his family until they gave him that thing. So they said, 'Who informed you about this?' He said, 'Jesus'. That [is the meaning] of the saying of the Majestic and Almighty God: «I declare to you what you eat and what you store up in your houses» [3:49]. So they held back the boys from him and said, 'Do not play with this sorcerer.' And they gathered them together in a house. Jesus came asking for them and they said, 'They are not here.' He said, 'What is in this house then?' They said, 'Pigs'. Jesus said, 'So shall it be!' They opened up and behold they had become pigs. And that is [the meaning of] His saying «[Those of the children of Israel who went astray were cursed] by the tongue of David and Jesus Son of Mary.» (5:115)[17]

Some of the anecdotes are very long. Here is the first part of one which is attributed to Wahb which has a bearing on the virginal conception:

When Mary became pregnant she had with her a close relative called Joseph the carpenter. They had both been taken into service in the mosque which is near Mount Zion. In those days it was one of the biggest mosques. The service of the mosque was highly regarded and it was considered a great honour to work there. Joseph and Mary were personally responsible for servicing it. They swept and they cleaned and they did everything necessary for its upkeep. No one in their time could equal them in zeal and piety.

So the first person to sense that Mary was pregnant was her companion Joseph. When he realised her condition it was an abomination to him. It was stupendous and quite beyond his comprehension. He did not know how he ought to deal with the matter. When he wanted wrongly to suspect her he remembered her goodness and purity and that she had never been absent from him for an hour. When on the other hand he wanted to exonerate her he saw what had happened to her. So when at last he could bear it no longer he spoke to her. The first thing he said to her was, 'Something has crossed my mind concerning you. It is something which I dread. I have struggled to put it out of my mind and to repress it within myself. It has none the less got the better of me. So I thought that talking about it would be the best way of getting it off my chest.'

She said, 'Then speak kindly.'

He said, ‘I was only going to say to you what had crossed my mind. Does a crop grow without seed?’
She answered, ‘Yes.’
He said, ‘And does a tree grow without abundant rain falling on it?’
She said, ‘Yes.’
He said, ‘And can there be a son without a father?’
‘Yes,’ replied Mary. ‘Do you not know that God (Blessed and Exalted be He) when He first created wheat, made it grow without having need of seed? Present day seed is derived ultimately from none other than that wheat which God caused to grow without seed. Or do you not know that God by His omnipotence caused the trees to grow without abundant rain and that by that omnipotence he established the abundant rain as life for the trees after He, of His own accord, had created both of them? Or do you say that God did not have the power to cause the trees to grow until He had made the water to assist Him and that if it were not for the water He would not have had the power to give them growth?
‘No’, replied Joseph, ‘I am not saying that, because I know that God (blessed and exalted be He) can by His omnipotence do whatever He wants. He says to a thing “Be!” and it is.’
‘Do you not know’, continued Mary, ‘that God created Adam and his wife without the help of a father and a mother?’
‘Yes, of course’, replied Joseph. When she had said that Joseph realised that her condition had arisen through God’s will and that it was not for him to question her about the matter and that that was the reason why she had kept it secret. Then he saw to the service of the mosque by himself and took on himself all the work that Mary had previously done.[18]

EXPLANATIONS OF THE QUR’ĀN IN THE LIGHT OF THE QUR’ĀN

Since the Qur’ān in its entirety is considered to be a revelation from God, Muslim interpreters naturally attempt to explain difficulties by referring to other passages whose meaning is undisputed. Sometimes this type of interpretation is traced back to a Companion or a Successor but frequently it is the classical commentator’s own contribution. The two examples which follow are from Ibn Kathīr.

We saw in Chapter 2 that Christian apologists sometimes argue that the command given to the angels to prostrate themselves in front of Adam (2:34, etc.) implies that he was originally divine and is hence a pointer to the divinity of Christ the 'Second Adam'. From a Muslim point of view this type of reasoning is perverse. The central thrust of the Qur'anic message is that God is One, from which it follows that God cannot have expected the angels to worship Adam. Their action can be explained by analogy with Joseph's parents' falling down prostrate in front of their son (12:100). It was a sign of respect, not an act of worship.[19]

My second example concerns the Qur'anic references to Jesus as God's 'word' (3:45 and 4:171). There is no distinction between upper and lower case letters in Arabic and we have seen that Christian polemicists and apologists often argue that these passages should be understood in the light of orthodox Christian teaching about Jesus as the Incarnate Word of God. Ibn Kathīr will have none of this. The Qur'ān warns believers against people who seek dissension by concentrating on ambiguous passages (3:7). In commenting on this āya he says that that is what Christians are doing when they stress that the Qur'ān calls Jesus God's Word but neglect to mention that it also states clearly that he is only a servant on whom God showed his favour (43:59).[20] According to him the child Jesus was a word from God in the sense that he owed his existence to God's command, the creative word transmitted to Mary by the angel Gabriel. That is to say the interpretation of 3:45 is given in 3:47, «God creates what he wills. When he decrees anything He only says to it 'Be!' and it comes into being».[21]

VARIANT READINGS

The first manuscripts of the Qur'ān were written without vowels or other diacritical signs. It was therefore frequently possible to read an āya in more than one way and there grew up a whole series of different systems or schools of reading. Because of a ḥadīth in which the Prophet speaks of the Qur'ān having been revealed in seven *aḥruf*, seven systems came to be accepted as canonical. They were the systems founded by readers in the principal cities: one each in Medina, Mecca, Damascus and Baṣra and three in Kūfa. Each of these seven systems was transmitted in two slightly different forms. The system which is now almost universally adopted is one of the three which originated in Kūfa: the system of 'Āṣīm (d.127/774) as transmitted by Ḥafṣ (d.180/796). In addition to the seven systems there are three which were generally admitted to be orthodox but of less authority. There are also four further systems which were allowed in some circles.[22]

These canonical variants rarely make much difference to the meaning. One example will suffice. At 5:110 and 61:6, two of the seven readers, Ḥamza (d.158/775) and Al-Kisā'ī (d.189/805) whose systems originated in Kūfa, read *sāḥirun*. The other five read *siḥrun*. Thus, whereas according to the majority Jesus was accused of evident *sorcery*, in their view he was accused of being an evident *sorceror*.[23]

The fourteen systems were all based on the consonantal text promulgated by 'Uthmān. However, several of the Companions, including Ibn al-'Abbās, Ibn Mas'ūd and Ubaiy had their own written editions of the Qur'ān which differed from this. No copies of these unauthorised editions have survived[24] but the commentators occasionally mention 'exceptional' readings (*shawādhdh*) which are ostensibly derived from them. The following example is mentioned by Parrinder and Blachère. As far as I can tell it did not find its way into any of the classical commentaries although it is mentioned in a work by Ibn abī Dā'ūd (d.316/928). At 61:6 the Qur'ān has Jesus announce:

> a messenger who will come after me whose name will be Aḥmad.

Ubayy reputedly read:

> a prophet whose community will be the last community and by whom God will put the seal on the prophets and on the messengers.[25]

THE CLASSICAL COMMENTATORS

The earliest commentary which I will make extensive use of is that of Abū Ja'far Muḥammad b. Jarīr al-Ṭabarī (d.310/923)[26] who was born in Āmul in the province of Ṭabaristān. After studying in Raiy and Baghdad he travelled extensively, visiting the principal centres of learning in Iraq, Syria and Egypt before settling in Baghdad where he became a famous teacher. Towards the end of his life he earned the displeasure of the Ḥanbalite extremists, so much so that when he died he had to be interred in his own house because the mob prevented his burial in the cemetery. Nevertheless his profession of faith reveals him to have been a staunchly orthodox Sunnī Muslim.[27] Ṭabarī's written output was enormous and included a number of books on jurisprudence most of which are no longer extant. The two important works of his which have survived are the *Annals*, mentioned in an earlier Chapter, and his Qur'anic commentary: *Jāmi' al-Bayān fī Tafsīr al-Qur'ān* (Collection of Explanations for the Interpretation of the Qur'ān) which he read to his students in 270/884 and dictated to them from 283/896 to 290/903. For several centuries this commentary enjoyed unrivalled prestige with one Baghdad jurist claiming that it would be worth travelling to China to obtain a copy.[28] From the view-point of later orthodoxy, however, the work is mystifying because of the author's inclusion of so much material with faulty asānīd; frequently one of the links in the chain is missing, or is alluded to without being named, or is named but is known to have been disparaged. Ṭabarī comments on the whole Qur'ān in sequence dividing each ṣūra into subsections which vary in length from a single phrase to several āyas. He introduces each subsection with a formula which reminds the reader that it is God's word. Then he gives the text, provides a paraphrase and quotes other passages in the Qur'ān which help elucidate the meaning. If there are any canonical variants he usually discusses them at this point, mentioning the cities in which the readings were favoured rather than the names of the readers. Next he gives a comprehensive collection of traditional comments complete with asānīd. When Ṭabarī knows of several conflicting interpretations he summarises these one at a time, following each summary with the traditional comments on which it is based. He also quotes early poetry in order to throw light on difficult words or constructions and he sometimes reports the opinions of the grammarians of Baṣra and Kūfa. Finally he often mentions exceptional readings but making clear that he rejects them.

Zamakhsharī (d.537/1144),[29] the second commentator whom I have selected, was born in the small town of Zamakhshar in Khwārazm. The whole province was dominated by Mu'tazilism and he studied under the leading Mu'tazilite scholar of his day Abū Mūḍar Maḥmūd b. Jarīr al-Ḍabbī. He travelled widely visiting Bukhāra, Khurāsān, Iṣfahān, Baghdad and Mecca. It was during his second stay in Mecca that the Mu'tazilites living there persuaded him to write his famous commentary on the Qur'ān, *al-Kashshāf 'an Ḥaqā'iq al-Tanzīl* (The Unveiler of the Realities of the Revelation).[30] It took him just under two years and was completed in 528/1138. It is an outstanding example of *tafsīr bi 'l-ray'*. Zamakhsharī sits light on the traditions sometimes mentioning them but almost as an afterthought without asānīd and often without naming the authorities. He excels as a grammarian and gives eloquent and succinct grammatical explanations. He also includes valuable information concerning variants and a wealth of poetic citations. Despite the author's 'heretical' beliefs the work is valued by Sunnī Muslims and is available in a printed edition with orthodox glosses at the foot of the page.

My third commentator, Fakr al-Dīn al-Rāzī (d.606/1210)[31] was born in Raiy where his father was the public preacher. Rāzī junior was something of a polymath: he taught Arabic, Persian, jurisprudence, history, theology and philosophy but also studied medicine and alchemy and was acquainted with astronomy, physiognomy, geometry and mineralogy. After a journey to Khwārazm, where he held public disputes with the Mu'tazilites, and another to Transoxania, where he debated with orthodox theologians and lawyers, he settled down in Herāt. He was a contentious and controversial figure who liked nothing more than to expose the shallowness of other people's scholarship. An Ash'arite in theology and a Shāfi'ite in jurisprudence he none the less differed with both schools on numerous points without deviating from Sunnī orthodoxy. His commentary *Mafātiḥ al-Ghayb* (The Keys to the Unseen)[32] was completed by his pupils after his death although most of the sections which concern us were probably composed by Rāzī himself.[33] His approach is philosophical and analytical; he enumerates the 'questions' or 'problems' which are raised by each āya or group of āyas and then tackles them one at a time listing the various solutions which have been proposed regardless of the generation or doctrinal persuasion of the persons who proposed them. He gives the views of the Companions and Successors but in a less thorough fashion than Ṭabarī and usually without asānīd. On the other hand he cites two early commentaries which were not used by Ṭabarī; those of al-Kalbī (d.146/763–4) and Muqātil b. Sulaymān (d.150/767). Of the classical commentators he occasionally mentions al-Qaffāl (d.365/976) and Ṭabarī (d.310/923) but he draws much more frequently on Ṭabarī's pupil al-Wāḥidī (d.468/1075). He gives extensive references to the views of the grammarians, philologists and the founders of the legal schools. Finally he is an important source of information about Mu'tazilite exegesis for he cites Abū Muslim (d.322/934) and 'Abd al-Jabbār (d.415/1024) as well as drawing extensively on the commentary of Zamakhsharī.[34]

Continuing in chronological order the next commentary of importance is that of Nāṣir al-Dīn Abū Sa'īd 'Abd-Allāh b. 'Umar b. Muḥammad al-Shīrāzī al-Bayḍāwī (d. between 683/1284 and 716/1316?)[35] who was born in the small town of al-Bayḍā' in the province of Fārs north of the capital Shīrāz at a time when the province was at the height of its glory. The population were Sunnites and not surprisingly he grew up to be a staunch Shāfi'ite in jurisprudence and Ash'arite in theology and a bitter opponent of Shī'ites and Mu'tazilites. He studied under his father and succeeded him as Chief Justice of Fārs. After being temporarily dismissed from this post Bayḍāwī travelled to Tabrīz where he composed his famous commentary *Anwār al-Tanzīl wa-Asrār al-Ta'wīl* (The Lights of Inspiration and the Secrets of Interpretation).[36] He followed the *Kashshāf* of Zamakhsharī closely but eliminated all traces of Mu'tazilism. He also incorporated material from other sources to cover those passages of the Qur'ān which Zamakhsharī had passed over in silence. The result is a handy compendium which has proved popular among Muslims and orientalists alike.

Finally, I shall make extensive reference to 'Imād al-Dīn Ismā'īl ibn 'Umar ibn Kathīr (d.774/1373).[37] Unlike his four predecessors he hailed not from Persia but from Syria. He was born in Boṣrā, the sight of Muḥammad's alleged encounter with the monk Baḥīrā. Orphaned at the age of six, he moved to Damascus as the ward of his brother. There he had the opportunity of studying under some of the best Sunnī teachers of his day and proved to be an outstanding student of ḥadīth and jurisprudence. Although a Shāfi'ite, he was deeply influenced by the renowned Ḥanbalite theologian and jurist Ibn Taymīya (d.728/1328) near whose tomb he is buried. He became an eminent teacher and preacher in his own right and his *Tafsīr al-Qur'ān al-'Aẓīm* (Commentary on the Sublime Qur'ān) is, as I have mentioned before, still highly esteemed by Muslim traditionalists. It is a particularly rigid example of *tafsīr bi 'l-ma'thūr*. In the introduction the author discusses the method which should be employed by any commentator. First, he should attempt to interpret the āya by reference to other āyas. Second, he should take into account the Sunna – the words and deeds of the Prophet. Third, he should turn to the transmitted sayings of the Companions. These are the only three sound sources. Moreover the interpretations reliably traced back to the Companions should be distinguished from reports which the Companions themselves received from the People of the Scripture. The latter should only be used as supplementary attestation and should not be relied upon to establish an interpretation.

These reports, known technically as *isrā'īlīyāt*, contain some things which are true because they are attested in the Qur'ān, others which are false because they conflict with the Qur'ān and still others which fall into neither category. After examining the Qur'ān, the Sunna and the interpretations of the Companions, the commentator may draw on the interpretations traced back to the Successors but he is under no obligation to do so. Furthermore if the Successors disagreed over the correct interpretation then none of them should be treated as authoritative. Ibn Kathīr relied on these principles in composing his commentary which is essentially a radically revised version of the work of Ṭabarī. He gave more space to the interpretation of the Qur'ān in the light of the Qur'ān and Sunna, weeded out many of the interpretations which Ṭabarī traced back to the Companions by faulty asānīd and drastically reduced the amount of material derived from the Successors.

DISCUSSION

I have mentioned only some of the components of the classical commentaries. We shall encounter other types of material including grammatical and philosophical discussions which I will do my best to explain as and when they arise. It should also be borne in mind that I have been providing illustrations and not giving exhaustive accounts of how the various exegetical problems were tackled by the commentators. To have done that would have required much more space as will be obvious when I begin my analyses of the four key topics referred to in the Introduction. I must also stress that the five classical commentaries which I have selected are not the only ones although taken together they give a fairly comprehensive picture of classical Sunnī exegesis.

In order to understand the mentality of the classical commentators it is necessary to know something about Islamic jurisprudence. The second/eighth century saw the growth of a number of 'schools' of law in the various centres of learning. These were groups of scholars who sought to elaborate an ideal code of Islamic conduct which combined local custom law with the dictates of the Qur'ān. Within these schools there emerged an opposition movement which pressed for greater attention to be paid to the legal precedents set by the Prophet. Their cause was championed by Muḥammad b. Idrīs al-Shāfi'ī (d.204/820), the father of Islamic jurisprudence and founder of the Shāfi'ite

School. In his *Risāla*, Shāfi'ī firmly establishes the Sunna as the second most important source of law almost on a par with the Qur'ān itself. For him Muḥammad was not simply the most authoritative interpreter of the Qur'ān, his legal decisions were divinely inspired. Thus the aḥādīth were the only authentic Islamic tradition and were not to be overridden by other factors. In addition to the Qur'ān and the Sunna, Shāfi'ī recognised two further sources of law: consensus (defined as the agreement of all Muslims) and analogy. The later school founded by Aḥmad Ibn Ḥanbal (d.241/855) put even more stress on tradition, rejecting human reason in any form and making the Qur'ān and Sunna the sole bases of law. Ibn Ḥanbal himself is reputed never to have eaten water melon because he knew of no prophetic precedent on the matter. The Shāfi'ite and Ḥanbalite Schools fostered the traditional vision of Islam which has been dominant among Muslims since the ninth century. It is a vision of an authentic Islam already existing as a complete and all-embracing system in the time of the Prophet, perfectly understood by the Companions and scrupulously transmitted from generation to generation by an uninterrupted succession of irreproachable witnesses.[38] The method of commenting advocated by Ibn Kathīr accords with his unquestioning acceptance of this vision, an acceptance which is hardly surprising in view of his training as a Shāfi'ite lawyer and his reverence for the Ḥanbalite scholar Ibn Taymīya.

From some of the things which were said in Chapters 6 and 7 it should be obvious that it is not easy to reconcile the traditional vision of Islam with the reconstruction of Islamic history proposed by non-Muslim scholars. Furthermore, on the specific issue of the authenticity of the aḥādīth and the traditions traced back to the Companions, non-Muslim historians frequently follow Goldziher and Schacht in adopting a position of almost total scepticism. I do not wish to enter into technicalities and will merely offer some very simple observations about the traditional material in the classical commentaries. Since the comments attributed to the Successors were considered less authoritative than those attributed to the Companions there is a *prima facie* case for thinking that the former are less likely to be spurious than the latter because there would have been less incentive to invent them. For the same reason the comments attributed to the Companions are in turn less likely to be spurious than the aḥādīth. That this is actually the case cannot of course be proved but there are other grounds for suspicion. Would the Successors have proposed novel solutions to exegetical problems if they had known the authoritative pronouncements of the Companions? And would the Companions and Successors have proposed interpretations which differed from those given by the Prophet? Surely not. Yet this is the impression given by the material recorded in Ṭabarī if we take it at face value. For example in addition to the ḥadīth explaining the appelation 'Sister of Aaron' (19:28) he includes a number of other interpretations such as al-Suddī's statement that Mary was a descendant of Aaron the brother of Moses.[39] Similarly in addition to Ibn al-'Abbās's comment on *samīy* (19:7) he mentions that Ibn Jurayj and Qatāda understood the āya in accordance with how I have translated it.[40] It thus appears that the hierarchy of authorities favoured by Ibn Kathīr to some extent obscures the historical development of exegesis and that in weeding out many of the comments of the Successors he has deprived his readers of precisely those traditions which are most likely to be authentic.

I do not intend to say much about the earlier commentaries at this juncture except to mention that the earliest of them – the one compiled by Ṭabarī – is strictly speaking pre-classical in date and in spirit. Ṭabarī wrote in an age when the traditional vision of Islam was already widespread but was still not completely dominant. In comparison with Ibn Kathīr, Ṭabarī is less rigid and seems more open to the possibility of a plurality of interpretations.

Finally let me make a few brief remarks about some of the components of the classical commentaries. Mention has already been made of the abundance of material attributed to Ibn al-'Abbās. His father, the Prophet's uncle, was the eponymous ancestor of the Abbasid Caliphs. This helps to explain his popularity with commentators who lived in the Abbasid period. There is no reason to doubt that some of the traditions traced back to him are authentic but it seems highly unlikely that he was the first person to cite poetic testimonies in order to explain rare words. Ṭabarī knows nothing of the *Masā'il Nāfiq b. al-Azraq* but he quotes some of the *shawāhid* which it contains without citing the precedent of a Companion or a Successor. It is highly probable that the practice of citing poetic proof texts originated in Iraq in circles where reason was valued more highly than tradition and that it has been fathered on Ibn al-'Abbās to give it a respectable pedigree. The extent to which the supposedly pre-Islamic and early Islamic poetry is genuine is another question altogether and not one which I can tackle here. Concerning the anecdotal material let me simply note that it is quite diverse. Of the three examples which I gave, the first is clearly derived from a

Christian source similar to *Luke* 1:39ff. The second was possibly elaborated by a storyteller to give substance to the somewhat laconic statement in the Qur'ān. The third is different again and might be from a Christian apocryphon either oral or written.

9 Jesus' Return: Qur'ān 4:159

The first generation of Christians were convinced that Jesus would shortly return in glory. Despite the fact that this did not happen in their lifetime, the belief that he would return for the final judgement lingered on and became enshrined in the creeds. Throughout the history of the church this belief has been the subject of renewed speculation during times of social and political upheaval. Such speculation was probably current among Arab Christians in Muḥammad's day although somewhat surprisingly it is not mentioned by Ibn Isḥāq in his account of the beliefs of the Christians of Najrān.[1] The Qur'ān itself does not explicitly refer to Jesus' return but the classical commentators detected allusions to it in 4:159 and 43:61 and occasionally elsewhere. In this chapter I will concentrate on their interpretation of the first of these passages.

The āya occurs in the course of an invective against the People of the Scripture who in this context seem to be the Jews. After a rebuttal of their claim to have killed Jesus it is asserted that God raised him into His presence. Then we are told:

> And [there is] not [one] of the People of the Scripture except [he] will most certainly believe in him before his death, and on the Day of Resurrection he will be a witness against them. (4:159).

The third person singular masculine pronouns – 'him', 'he' and 'his' – are ambiguous. It is not entirely clear who will be believed in, before whose death this will take place and who it is who will be a witness against the Jews on the Day of Resurrection. Let us see how the classical commentators attempt to resolve these difficulties.

ṬABARĪ[2]

Ṭabarī begins by stating that the early interpreters differed over the meaning of this āya. He attributes three lines of interpretation to them:

[A] Some said that «believe in him» means believe in Jesus and «before his death» means before Jesus' death. They took this to be a reference to all of the People of the Scripture believing in Jesus when he comes back down to kill the Antichrist and when all religious communities will become one, namely the true religious community of Islam, the religion of Abraham.

Ṭabarī traces this type of interpretation to five early authorities:

1. Ibn al-'Abbās as reported by Sa'īd b. Jubayr by two routes,[3]
2. Abū Mālik as reported by Ḥuṣayn by three routes,
3. al-Ḥasan al-Baṣrī by five routes,[4]
4. Qatāda as reported by Sa'īd [b. a. 'Arūba] and Ma'mar,
5. Ibn Zayd by one route.

Most of the comments which are cited are very brief; the one thing they have in common is the interpretation of «before his death» as meaning before Jesus' death. 'Awf reported Ḥasan al-Baṣrī as saying 'he has not yet died' and Abū Rajā' reported him as saying 'He is indeed now alive with God.' Several of the comments refer to Jesus' return but (contrary to what Ṭabarī leads us to expect) none actually says that all religious communities will become one. The nearest to this is Qatāda's comment, as reported by Ma'mar [d.154/770], that all religions will believe in Jesus when he returns. Only Ibn Zayd [d.182/798], the most recent of the five, is credited with referring to the killing of the Antichrist. Ibn Zayd is also credited with stating that the belief of the Jews will be of no avail to them at that time.

[B] Others said that it means that the People of the Scripture will come to believe in Jesus before they die because at the moment of death, before the soul leaves the body, every individual is faced with the truth and is able to distinguish it from falsehood.

Ṭabarī traces this type of interpretation to seven authorities:

1. Ibn al-'Abbās as reported by 'Alī b. abī Ṭalḥa, by 'Ikrāma (by three routes), by Sa'īd b. Jubayr (by two routes) and by al-Suddī.
2. Mujāhid as reported by Manṣūr, by Ibn abī Najīḥ (by two routes), by Abū Hashīm al-Ramānī and by Layth.
3. 'Ikrāma (by two routes),
4. al-Ḥasan al-Baṣrī as reported by Farrāt al-Qazzāz (by two routes),
5. al-Ḍaḥḥāk as reported by Juwaybir and 'Abīd b. Sulaymān,
6. Muḥammad b. Sīrīn by one route.
7. Juwaybir [pupil of the Successor al-Ḍaḥḥāk] by one route.

The simplest comment included under this heading is the paraphrastic gloss 'before the death of the Scripturist' which is attributed to Mujāhid and Muḥammad b. Sīrīn. Other relatively undeveloped comments include Juwaybir's statement that Ubaiy read «before their death» and Ibn al-'Abbās's comment, as reported by 'Ali b. abī Ṭalḥa, that no Jew will die until he believes in Jesus. The two versions of the comment attributed to al-Ḥasan al-Baṣrī are: 'Not one of them will die until he believes in Jesus. It means the Jews and Christians', and, 'Not one of them will die until he believes in Jesus before he dies' (*qabla an yamūta*). Tabarī does not remark on the possible ambiguity of the latter.

A number of comments, including all of those attributed to Ibn al-'Abbās except the version reported by 'Alī b. abi Ṭalḥa, give assurances that even if a Jew suffers a sudden and violent death he will none the less believe in Jesus before he dies.[5] Ibn al-Abbās as reported by Sa'īd b. Jubayr[6] is said to have mentioned Ubaiy's reading. Ibn al-'Abbās as reported by 'Ikrāma and al-Dahhāk as reported by Juwaybir are said to have indicated that believing in Jesus means testifying that he is a servant and messenger of God.

[C] A third school of thought was that the People of the Scripture would believe in Muḥammad before they died. Ṭabarī names only 'Ikrāma as reported by Ḥumayd as an alleged authority for this interpretation.

We should note that in Ṭabarī's time there was evidently disagreement concerning what the early interpreters actually said. One of the most revered authorities, the Companion Ibn al-'Abbās, is cited as having been in support of both [A] and [B]![7] So too is al-Ḥasan al-Baṣrī. Moreover one of Ibn al-'Abbās's pupils, 'Ikrāma, is cited as having been in support of both [B] and [C]. Ṭabarī does not draw attention to this. Instead he proceeds to discuss the relative merits of the three interpretations. He eliminates [B] on legal grounds. His argument is as follows. Believing in Jesus is not simply a matter of acknowledging him as a prophet, it involves accepting as true and binding everything which he brought from God. Since Jesus brought attestation to the veracity of Muḥammad, believing in Jesus involves believing in Muḥammad as well. Now God has ruled that every person who believes in Muḥammad is to be treated as one of the faithful. So if it were the case that all the People of the Scripture believed in Jesus before they died then they would have to be treated as Muslims. They would receive Muslim funeral rites, their young children would be accepted into the Muslim community and only Muslims would be entitled to inherit from them. People of the Scripture who died without young children and without mature offspring who professed Islam would thus die heirless. Ṭabarī rejects interpretation [C] on the basis of syntax. The pronoun «him» in the expression «believe in him» must refer back to someone mentioned shortly before. Jesus fits the bill, Muḥammad does not. One would only be justified in supposing that the pronoun referred to Muḥammad if there were another passage from the Qur'ān or in the aḥādīth which supported such an interpretation. Thus by a process of elimination Ṭabarī reaches the conclusion that interpretation [A] is correct – there is not one of the People of the Scripture who will not believe in Jesus before Jesus' death. He states that this refers exclusively to the People of the Scripture who will be alive at the time of Jesus' return. In further support of this interpretation he cites a ḥadīth. The isnād which he gives is identical with one of the isnād already given for Qatāda but is extended back to the Prophet:[8]

> Bishr b. Mu'ādh told us saying Yazīd told me. He said Sa'īd told us on the authority of Qatāda on the authority of 'Abd al-Raḥmān b. Ādam on the authority of Abū Hurayra that the Prophet of God (the peace and blessings of God be upon him!) said:
> 'The prophets are brothers. They are of different mothers but their religion is one. I am the closest of mankind to Jesus son of Mary because there was no prophet between us. He is going to descend so recognise him when you see him. He is a man of average build, of reddish white complexion and with lank hair. His head flows with moisture although it only sheds a drip at a time. He will be wearing two light yellow garments. He will break the crucifixes, kill the pigs and abolish the poll tax. Wealth will abound and people will fight one another because of Islam until God destroys all the religious communities in his time with the exception of Islam. In his time God will also destroy the deceitful false messiah the Antichrist. There will be such security on the earth in his time that lions will lie down with camels, leopards with cattle and wolves with sheep. Youths and boys will play with snakes without harming them or being harmed by them. Then he will tarry on the earth for as long as God wills – perhaps for forty years. Then he will die and the Muslims will pray over him and bury him.'

Ṭabarī's comments on «and on the Day of Resurrection he will be a witness against them» form a separate section. They are however quite brief. He states that what is meant is that Jesus will be a witness against the People of the Scripture. He cites Ibn Jurayj and Qatāda as authorities for this interpretation.

ZAMAKHSHARĪ, RĀZĪ AND BAYḌĀWĪ[9]

Zamakhsharī begins by stating that «will most certainly believe in him» is a qualificative juratory clause occurring after a curtailed statement of what it qualifies and that the word «one» has to be understood. He indicates two other passages in the Qur'ān where a similar construction is employed:
«And [there is] not [one] of us except he has his known position.» (37:164)
«And [there is] not [one] of you except he shall approach it [i.e. hell.] (19:71)

It is clear that Zamakhsharī assumes the correctness of the second of the three traditional lines of interpretation which we encountered in Ṭabarī for he states that the meaning of the āya is that:

> There is not one Jew or Christian who will not believe in Jesus and believe that he is the servant of God and the messenger of God. That will happen when he sees with his eyes just before he gives up the ghost.

To this he adds an all-important rider:

> His believing then will be of no avail because the time of the imposition of religious duties will have ended.

Although he does not mention Ṭabarī he probably has him in mind for the rider nullifies Ṭabarī's objection to this line of interpretation.[10]

Then Zamakhsharī gives the following report on the authority of Shahr b. Ḥawshab:

> Al-Ḥajjāj said to me, 'It is an āya which I have never read without something about it troubling me. If I were to be brought a Jewish or Christian prisoner and I were to chop off his head I would not hear him say that.' So I said, 'When death comes upon a Jew the angels smite his back and his face and they say, "O enemy of God Jesus came to you as a prophet and you called him a liar." Then the Jew says, "I believe that he is a servant, a prophet." In the case of a Christian the angels say, "Jesus came to you as a prophet and you alleged that he was God or the Son of God!" Then the Christian believes that Jesus is God's servant and messenger but his belief is of no avail.' He was suspicious so he sat up, looked at me and said, 'Whom [did you get that] from?' I said, 'Muḥammad b. 'Alī b.

al-Ḥanafiyya told me'. So he began to scratch the ground with a stick. Then he said, 'You have taken it from a pure source or from its place of origin.'

Al-Kalbī said, 'So I said to him [i.e. to Shahr b. Ḥawshab] "What was your intention in telling him that Muḥammad b.'Alī b. al-Ḥanafiyya told you?" He said "My intention was to infuriate him", meaning by adding the name 'Alī since he was known [simply] as Ibn al-Ḥanafiyya.'

This requires some elucidation. Shahr b. Ḥawshab [d.110/728] is a well known traditionist although opinions about his trustworthiness varied because he was accused of embezzling religious funds.[11] Al-Ḥajjāj is the notoriously bloodthirsty Umayyad general who when he was made governor of Kūfa in 695 mounted the pulpit and declared to the congregation that he could see before him heads ripe to be cut off, the blood spurting from beneath their beards.[12] Muḥammad b. al-Ḥanafiyya [d.81/700] was the son of 'Alī b. abī Tālib. Unlike his half-brothers Ḥasan and Ḥusayn, whose mother was the Prophet's daughter Fāṭima, he was born to 'Alī by a woman from the Ḥanīfa tribe. Nevertheless some Shia hailed him as the Madhī who would rid them of Umayyad oppression and after his death they claimed that he had gone into occultation and would return.[13] Al-Ḥajjāj would understandably not have appreciated his being mentioned, even less his being honoured as son of 'Alī. The whole quotation is presumably an extract from the Qur'anic commentary composed by al-Kalbī [d.763], a commentary which was widely viewed with suspicion because of al-Kalbī's Shī'ite sympathies.[14]

As additional support for understanding the āya as an announcement that the People of the Scripture will believe in Jesus before their death, Zamakhsharī cites Ibn al-'Abbās on the authority of 'Ikrāma but without an isnād.[15] He also cites the variant reading of Ubaiy giving the additional information that Ubaiy vocalised the verb «believe» as a plural.

It might be objected that if coming to believe in Jesus *in extremis* will be of no avail then it is pointless for the Qur'ān to mention it. Zamakhsharī forestalls this objection by saying that the Qur'anic announcement serves as a threat. The statement that «he will be a witness against them» is likewise a threat. Zamakhsharī assumes without question that it is Jesus who will be the witness. He will testify against the Jews that they denied him and against the Christians that they called him Son of God.

Zamakhsharī then mentions three other lines of interpretation but without naming authorities. He simply introduces each of them with the words 'and it has been said' (*wa-qīla*). First he refers to the interpretation which links the āya with the ḥadīth about Jesus' return. Whereas Ṭabarī states that only the People of the Scripture who are alive at that time will believe in Jesus, Zamakhsharī says that it is possible that what is meant is that all of them will believe when God brings them to life in their graves and informs them about Jesus' return. His treatment of the other two lines of interpretation is extremely brief:

> And it has been said that the pronoun in «in him» refers back to God Most High. It has also been said [that it refers back] to Muḥammad, the peace and blessings of God be upon him.

The latter interpretation was, as we have seen, mentioned by Ṭabarī who rejected it on grounds of syntax.

Rāzī seems to be largely dependent on Zamakhsharī to whom he refers at one point. He retains only the two principal lines of interpretation and does not state which of them he prefers. He presents them as alternative solutions to the problem caused by our observation that most Jews die without believing in Jesus. He reproduces Zamakhsharī's citation of Shahr b. Ḥawshab but stopping at the words 'pure source.'[16]

In some quarters theological objections were raised against the interpretation which linked the āya with Jesus' return. Rāzī informs us that one theologian said that when Jesus returns either religious obligations will already have been abolished or alternatively he will not be recognisable as Jesus. The rationale behind this is that Muḥammad is the last of the prophets and there can be no prophet after him. Rāzī dismisses this argument as weak. He says that the period of the prophets culminated in the mission of Muḥammad and that when Jesus returns he will be a follower of Muḥammad.[17]

Bayḍawī adds nothing to our knowledge. He plagiarises Zamakhsharī following him in broad outline but condensing his comments and omitting the citation of Shahr b. Ḥawshab.

IBN KATHĪR[18]

Ibn Kathīr's starting point is Ṭabarī's statement that the early interpreters differed. He appropriates Ṭabarī's summaries of the three lines of interpretation together with most of the traditional material preserved by him.

He adds little to Ṭabarī's treatment of interpretation [A] apart from mentioning that, according to Ibn abī Ḥātim, al-Ḥasan al-Baṣrī said that in this context the «People of the Scripture» are the Negus[19] and his subjects.

His presentation of interpretation [B] is subtly different from Ṭabarī's although it is largely dependent on it. Of the versions of the comment traced back to Ibn al-'Abbās he drops the one reported on the authority of al-Suddī. He also drops one of the two versions reported on the authority of Sa'īd b. Jubayr – the version which mentions Ubaiy's reading. He gives all the other versions of Ibn al-'Abbās' comment in full complete with their asānīd which he declares sound. Then he states in summary fashion that this interpretation can likewise be traced by sound asānīd to Mujāhid, 'Ikrāma and Muḥammad b. Sīrīn and that al-Ḍaḥḥāk and Juwaybir spoke in its favour. Note the silence about Ubaiy's reading and about Juwaybir's knowledge of it. Note also the absence of any reference to al-Ḥasan al-Baṣri in all this. Ibn Kathīr has purposely postponed mentioning Ubaiy's reading and al-Ḥasan al-Baṣri's interpretation because he wants to play down the former in order to allow him to use the latter as his trump card. He introduces Ubaiy's reading as reported by al-Suddī on the authority of Ibn al-'Abbās. By postponing the mention of this reading, by not giving it a complete isnād and by giving the impression that the sole evidence for it is al-Suddī's commentary, he effectively devalues it. Finally he at last refers to al-Ḥasan al-Baṣri. Of the two versions of al-Ḥasan's comment which Ṭabarī cited under this heading Ibn Kathīr retains only the ambiguous version which he evidently understands to mean that not one of them will die until he believes in Jesus before Jesus dies. He further states that it is likely that this is what al-Ḥasan intended and that it is likely that it is what the others intended as well! Thus at a stroke Ibn Kathīr eliminates the problem caused by the existence of conflicting traditions by treating interpretations [A] and [B] as complementary rather than as mutually exclusive.

Ibn Kathīr's presentation of interpretation [C] is virtually identical to Ṭabarī's. He does not comment on the fact that 'Ikrāma, the alleged authority for this interpretation, is also said to have advocated [B]. But as we shall see, he has a way of circumventing this problem as well.

In assessing the respective merits of the three traditional interpretations, Ibn Kathīr begins by stating that Ṭabarī was undoubtedly correct in advocating interpretation [A]. The reason he gives for this has two components:

1. The āya marks the culminating point of the sequence of thought which began with the reference to the People of the Scripture claiming that they killed the Messiah. They killed the semblance of Jesus without realising what they were doing. God raised Jesus into His presence and he is still alive.
2. Jesus will return, as is said in multiply-attested aḥādīth, and all the People of the Scripture will believe in him at that time.

Then Ibn Kathīr continues:

> As for those who interpret this āya as meaning that no Scripturist will die before believing in Jesus or Muḥammad (upon them both be blessings and peace), that is actually the case. That is because at death everyone has revealed to him what he was ignorant of and he believes in it.

Now of course Ṭabarī objected to this on the grounds that if it were true it would mean that everyone would die a Muslim and would have to be treated as such. Ibn Kathīr counters this objection by insisting that faith at the moment of death is of no avail. As grounds for saying this he quotes two passages from the Qur'ān, the first of which is taken from the same ṣūra:

> «There is no repentance for those who do ill deeds until at last death presents itself to one of them and he says, 'I repent now'. It does not exist [either] for those who die unbelievers. For those We have prepared a cruel torment.» [4:18]
> «Then when they saw Our violence they said, 'We believe in God alone. We disbelieve in what we used to associate with Him.' Their belief after they had seen Our violence did not avail them in conformity with God's custom which He has applied to his servants. Lost are these unbelievers.» [40.84f.]

Finally Ibn Kathīr gives a comprehensive collection of aḥadīth concerning the return of Jesus. The principal ḥadīth is that published by Bukhārī and Muslīm on authority of Abū Hurayra,

> 'By Him in whose hand is my soul, it will suddenly happen that Jesus Son of Mary will descend amongst you as a just judge. He will break the crucifixes, cause the pigs to perish, suppress the poll

> tax and make wealth so abundant that no one will desire any more. One prostration will be preferable to him to the whole world and all that is in it. Abū Hurayra said: Recite if you like: «And [there is] not [one] of the People of the Scripture except [he] will most certainly believe in him before his death, and on the Day of Resurrection he will be a witness against them.»

To this he adds a host of variants drawn from the *Musnad* of Ibn Ḥanbal and the canonical ḥadīth collections of Abū Da'ūd, Ibn Māja and al-Tirmidhī. He clinches his case by remarking:

> These are multiply attested aḥādīth from the Prophet according to the transmission of Abū Hurayra, Ibn Mas'ūd, 'Uthman b. abī al-'Āṣ, Abū Umāma [al-Bāhilī], al-Nawwās b. Sim'ān [al-Ansārī], 'Abd Allah b. 'Amr b. al-'Āṣ, Majma' b. Jārīya, Abū Shurayḥa and Ḥudhayfa b. Usayd, may God be pleased with them.

Like the earlier classical commentators Ibn Kathīr assumes that «and on the Day of Resurrection he will be a witness against them» refers to Jesus. He attributes this interpretation to Ibn Jurayj whom he credits with linking this passage with 5:116–8 in which Jesus is depicted as being questioned by God and denying that he told mankind to treat him and his mother as deities.

DISCUSSION

The classical commentaries contain such a wealth of detail about this āya that it is not easy to see the wood for the trees. I will attempt to clarify the picture by listing a number of observations and suggestions as follows.

(1) The commentators are unanimous in stating that it is Jesus who will be a witness against the People of the Scripture. Although this gives Jesus an eschatological role it would be wrong to infer that it makes him unique. For according to the Qur'ān God has sent messengers to all peoples and at the resurrection every people will be accompanied by one such messenger who will act as a witness against them.[20]

(2) The commentators mention three possibilities concerning who it is that the People of the Scripture will come to believe in. It may be Jesus, Muḥammad or God. Ṭabarī is surely correct in ruling out Muḥammad on the grounds that «him» must refer back to someone mentioned shortly before. The possibility that the reference is to God

is mentioned only by Zamakhsharī although he seems not to have favoured it. If it is Jesus who will be a witness then it is most probably Jesus who will be believed in. Nevertheless belief in Jesus should be understood in Muslim terms: it is belief that he is a prophet and messenger of God.

(3) More perplexing is the expression «before his death» which could on the face of it mean (a) before Jesus' death or (b) before the death of the Scripturist. I shall refer to (a) and (b) as the core interpretations in order to distinguish them from the full-blown interpretations in Ṭabarī which I have designated [A] and [B].

(4) Both core interpretations have the support of tradition. This is less obviously the case with the full-blown interpretations. Ṭabarī's accounts of [A] and [B] seem to go beyond the evidence of the traditional comments cited by him. In particular [A] reads more like a summary of the ḥadīth which he later brings into the discussion. The core interpretations probably preceded the full-blown ones. However, one cannot be certain about this because traditional interpretations were sometimes transmitted in summary form and one should not therefore automatically assume that the shortest version of a traditional interpretation is necessarily the most original.[21]

(5) Grammatical considerations tip the balance in favour of core interpretation (b). Zamakhsharī correctly perceived that the sentence is an oath used as a threat and that it is elliptical. The words 'there is', 'one' and 'he' are not expressed but have to be understood by the reader. Thus the 'he' referred back to in 'his death' has not actually been mentioned. Moreover to make matters still more complicated the āya ends with a reference to 'them' rather than to 'him'. Failure to understand this construction was probably one of the factors which led to the emergence of the two rival core interpretations.

(6) The reading attributed to Ubaiy – «except [they] will most certainly believe in him before their death» – is a rather clumsy attempt to overcome the difficulty presented by the unfamiliar grammatical construction. Although not to be preferred to the standard text it provides evidence of the antiquity of core interpretation (b).

(7) Once interpreters lost sight of the fact that this āya was a threat rather than a statement, core interpretation (b) would have been open to criticism from literalists on the grounds that in actual fact most Jews die without believing in Jesus. This criticism probably provoked the development of full-blown interpretation [B] as a way of countering it.[22]

(8) Ṭabarī was evidently at pains to prove the correctness of interpretation [A] and to discredit interpretation [B]. He was probably motivated solely by legal considerations. He was an eminent lawyer and founded his own school of jurisprudence.

(9) Ṭabarī was in no doubt that interpretations [A] and [B] were rival interpretations. Ibn Kathīr's attempt to suggest that they are complementary rather than mutually exclusive is hardly convincing. It necessitates severing the connection between interpretation [B] and Ubaiy's reading, for the latter is of course totally incompatible with interpretation [A].

(10) As is so often the case, conflicting interpretations were traced back to the same early interpreters. This does not mean that the traditional material is entirely worthless. We have to reckon with the fact that many of the transmitters whose names occur in Ṭabarī's asānīd were interpreters in their own right and subsequent generations could not always distinguish between what a scholar transmitted and what he himself said or wrote.[23]

(11) It is particularly noteworthy that Mujāhid [d.103/721] is alleged to have favoured interpretation [B]. For when we come to deal with the crucifixion we shall see that in commenting on 4:157 Ṭabarī cites him by the same two routes as having held that a substitute was crucified instead of Jesus. Thus, *pace* Ibn Kathīr, the interpretation of 4:157 need not necessarily determine the interpretation 4:159 and probably did not do so in the early period.

(12) The report of the encounter between Ibn Ḥawshab and al-Hajjāj which is mentioned by Zamakhsharī suggests that early in the second/eighth century this āya was the subject of sectarian controversy. Unfortunately the details are unclear because in Chapter 16 we shall see that the Shī'ite commentaries interpret the incident very differently.

In the next chapter I shall examine the other Qur'anic passages which Muslim exegetes sometimes interpret in the light of the aḥādīth about Jesus' descent to kill the Antichrist. I shall then make some tentative suggestions about the way in which these aḥadīth may have developed.

10 Jesus' Return – continued

The second key passage in which the commentators detected an allusion to Jesus' return is 43:61 which speaks of «knowledge for the Hour». In addition they sometimes broached the subject when commenting on the Prophet's night journey (17:1), the references to Gog and Magog (18:21 and 21:96), Islam's triumph over other religions (9:33) and Jesus' speaking to mankind in his maturity (3:46 and 5:110).

KNOWLEDGE FOR THE HOUR

> «(57) When the Son of Mary is proposed as an example your people cry out loud. (58) They say, 'Are our gods better or is he?' They only mention him to you for the sake of argument. Nay! They are a contentious people. (59) He is nought save a servant on whom We showed favour and whom We set as an example for the Children of Israel. (60) Had We wished We would have set among you angels to act as deputies. (61) He (*or* it) is indeed knowledge for the Hour. Do not be in doubt about it but follow me. This is the straight path. (62) Do not let Satan turn you aside. He is an open enemy of you. (63) When Jesus came with clear proofs he said, 'I have come to you with wisdom and to make plain some of the things concerning which you differ . . .'» (43:57–63)

The sequence of thought in this revelation is by no means clear. We are concerned primarily with the first part of 43:61 «He (*or* it) is indeed knowledge for the Hour.» (*inna-hu la-'ilmun li 'l-sā'ati*).

Ṭabarī[1] states that the interpreters differed over the meaning of the third person singular masculine suffix *-hu*. He reports two interpretations:

[A] Some said it referred back to Jesus. Jesus' appearing is knowledge by which one will know the coming of the Hour for his appearing is one of its portents. His coming back down to earth is an indication of the vanishing of this world and the arrival of the world to come. Ṭabarī gives traditions which attribute this interpretation to eight authorities: Ibn al-'Abbās by four routes, Qatāda by two routes, al-Ḥasan al-Baṣrī, Mujāhid, al-Suddī, al-Daḥḥāk, Abū Mālik and Ibn Zayd by one root each.

[B] Others said *-hu* refers to the Qur'ān. The meaning of the sentence is that this Qur'ān is knowledge pertaining to the Hour for it gives information about the resurrection and judgement. Ṭabarī cites only two traditions which support this. The first traces the interpretation back to al-Ḥasan al-Baṣrī who has already had interpretation [A] accredited to him. The second traces it back to the time of Qatāda without attributing it to him personally. It reports him as having said: 'People used to say the Qur'ān is knowledge pertaining to the hour.'

Ṭabarī does not choose between the two interpretations. He does, however, add some interesting information concerning variant readings which clearly have a bearing on the decision. He knew of three distinct readings:

1. *'ilmun* (knowledge). This was how the readers of the great cities vocalised the word. He regarded it as the correct reading because of their unanimity on this point.
2. *'alamun* (sign, token, distinguishing mark). This was how Ibn al-'Abbās, Qatāda and al-Ḍaḥḥāk vocalised it. Although he does not say so, this obviously fits in well with their contention that the āya refers to Jesus' return.
3. *dhikrun* (recollection, mention, reminder). This is a different word altogether and not simply an alternative vocalisation. It is the reading attributed to Ubaiy. Ṭabarī states somewhat cryptically that it proves the correctness of the vocalisation *'ilmun* (knowledge). I assume that what he means by this is that Ubaiy's reading is an interpretative gloss and that it must be a gloss on *'ilmun* rather than on *'alamun*.[2] In as far as the Qur'ān itself is often referred to as a *dhikrun*[3] Ubaiy's reading seems to lend weight to interpretation [B].

The way in which Zamakhsharī[4] paraphrases the āya suggests that he favours interpretation [A]:

> «He» Jesus on him be peace «is indeed knowledge for the Hour» that is, one of its conditions by which it is known. The condition is called «knowledge» because of the attaining of knowledge by it.

After giving this paraphrase he mentions the variant readings of Ibn al-'Abbās and Ubaiy and cites the following ḥadīth without an isnād:

> Jesus (on him be peace) will descend on a narrow pass in the holy land called Afīq wearing two light yellow garments,[5] the hair of his head lank, in his hand a lance with which he will kill the

> Antichrist. Then he will go to Jerusalem when the people are at dawn prayer led by the imam. The imam will move back but Jesus will give him precedence and pray behind him in accordance with the sharīʻa of Muḥammad (the peace and blessings of God be upon him). Then he will kill the pigs, break the cross, demolish oratories and churches and kill Christians except those who believe in him.

Finally he briefly mentions interpretation [B] which he attributes to Ḥasan al-Baṣrī.

Rāzī[6] follows Zamakhsharī closely. So too does Bayḍāwī[7] but he makes two significant alterations. First, he omits all reference to what I have called interpretation [B]. Second, he mentions a third interpretation:

[C] Jesus is also «knowledge for the Hour» because his bringing the dead to life [during his ministry] indicates God's power to do so [on the Day of Resurrection].[8]

Ibn Kathīr[9] first gives us more information about what I have called interpretation [C]. He mentions that according to Ibn Isḥāq the «knowledge for the hour» is what Jesus brought, by his reviving the dead and curing leprosy, blindness and other illnesses. Ibn Kathīr considers this interpretation dubious.[10] Next he mentions what I have called interpretation [B], which he states was related by Qatāda on the authority of Ḥasan al-Baṣrī and Saʻīd b. Jubayr. He considers this even more improbable. According to him the correct interpretation is interpretation [A], namely that the reference is to Jesus' future return. In support of this he makes five points:

1. Jesus has been mentioned just before and the attached pronoun refers back to him.
2. The return is referred to in 4:159 where «before his death» means before Jesus' death.
3. The variant reading *ʻalamun* supports this interpretation.
4. The interpretation was supported by Mujāhid, Abū Hurayra, Ibn al-ʻAbbās, Abū ʻĀliya, Abū Mālik, Ikrāma, al-Ḥasan, Qatāda, al-Ḍaḥḥāk and others.
5. According to multiply-attested aḥādīth Muḥammad spoke of the return of Jesus as a just judge before the Day of Resurrection.

Ibn Kathīr's case is far from proven. Each of his points calls for comment:

1. It is arguable that the attached pronoun refers back not to Jesus himself but to the Qur'anic statement that he is only a servant. The statement is «knowledge for the Hour» in the sense that

when the hour of judgement comes the statement will be vindicated and all will know that Muḥammad was right in his estimate of Jesus.

2. As we saw in the last chapter, the interpretation of 4:159 is by no means as clear cut as Ibn Kathīr would have us believe.
3. His treatment of the uncanonical variants is one-sided. He mentions the reading *'alamun* as if it furnished independent evidence in favour of his interpretation but he does not mention Ubaiy's reading (*dhikrun*) which is independent evidence against it.
4. He drops two of the eight authorities whom Ṭabarī brings forward in support of interpretation [A] but adds three more. The two whom he drops are the Iraqi Successors al-Suddī and Ibn Zayd. The three whom he adds are Abū Hurayra, Abū 'Āliya, and 'Ikrāma. The first of these is a famous Companion of the Prophet and the other two are well-known pupils of Ibn al-'Abbās. Thus the credentials of interpretation [A] are improved. Nevertheless, by eliminating the names of al-Suddī and Ibn Zayd, Ibn Kathīr deprives his readers of valuable historical evidence concerning the milieu in which this interpretation thrived.
5. Ṭabarī was aware that Jesus' return was mentioned in ḥadīth but unlike Ibn Kathīr he did not insist that the ḥadīth had a bearing on the interpretation of this āya.

MUḤAMMAD'S ENCOUNTER WITH JESUS

> «Glory be to Him who carried His servant by night from the Holy Mosque to the Further Mosque, the surroundings of which We have blessed, that We might show him some of Our signs.» (17:1)

The seventeenth ṣūra is sometimes called 'The Night Journey' because it begins with these words. According to tradition, the reference is to Muḥammad's experience of being taken in a single night from Mecca to Jerusalem whence he was caught up through the seven heavens into the very presence of God.[11]

Ṭabarī devotes twelve and a half pages to this āya which is a fair indication of the importance of the episode for Muslims.[12] Some of the aḥadīth which he cites mention that while Muḥammad passed through the heavens, he met several of the famous prophets of old who greeted him as a fellow prophet. According to a ḥadīth reported on the authority of Ibn al-Musayyib when he returned he gave the following description of Moses, Jesus and Abraham:

> As for Moses his head was like those of the men of the Shanū'a. As for Jesus he was ruddy as though he had just come out of the bath (*dīmās*) and the person whom I have seen who most resembles him is 'Urwa b. Mas'ūd al-Thaqafī. As for Abraham, of all his children it is I who most resemble him.[13]

Ṭabarī also cites a slightly longer version of this ḥadīth on the authority of Abū Hurayra. In this version we are told:

> Jesus was a ruddy man of medium height who had lank hair and freckles on his face. His head seemed to be dripping with water as if he had just come out of the bath.[14]

Most of the aḥādīth cited by Ṭabarī situate Jesus and his cousin John in the second or third heaven, above Adam but below Joseph, Idris, Aaron, Moses and Abraham.

Zamakhsharī,[15] Rāzī[16] and Bayḍāwī[17] briefly mention the tradition that Muḥammad met the prophets but do not refer to Jesus by name.

Ibn Kathīr's treatment of this āya must be well nigh exhaustive.[18] Some of the many aḥādīth which he cites give slightly different details about Jesus' appearance. For instance in one of the traditions reported on the authority of Anas Ibn Mālik he is said to have looked as though pearls flowed from his hair[19] and in versions reported on the authority of Ibn al-'Abbās and Umm Hānī' he is described as between white and red rather than ruddy.[20] Jesus is usually in the second or third heaven but according to some accounts Muḥammad did not stipulate precisely where each prophet was situated.[21] There are also reports that on the way from Mecca to Jerusalem Gabriel made Muḥammad alight to pray over Jesus' birthplace at Bethlehem although Ibn Kathīr states that this detail is objectionable.[22]

The above-mentioned aḥadīth which refer to Muḥammad's encounter with Jesus effectively put the latter's ascent into perspective making it less remarkable than Muḥammad's experience. The concern with the details of Jesus' appearance may in part be explained by a concern to help the faithful recognise him when he returns as a sign of the Hour.

JESUS' RETURN AND THE RELEASE OF GOG AND MAGOG

Gog and Magog are stock figures of Jewish and Christian apocalyptic writing. According to *Ezekiel* 38 and 39:9–20 they are enemies of God who will invade the Holy Land and perish on the mountainside devoured by beasts and birds of prey. *Revelation* 20:7 mentions them in the context of the supreme battle between Satan and the Christian Church. They also figure twice in the Qur'ān. In 18:95–99 reference is made to a barrier constructed by Dhū al-Qarnayn to prevent Gog and Magog spoiling the land. Although they cannot now pass that barrier God will eventually lay it low and they will surge forth. At 21:96 it is said that Gog and Magog will hasten forth from every mound.

In the course of his comments on the 18:99 Ṭabarī cites a hadīth which he traces back to 'Abd Allah b. Mas'ūd:

> 'The Messenger of God (the peace and blessings of God be upon him) said:
> 'On the night of the night journey, I met Abraham, Moses and Jesus. They were conferring with each other concerning the Hour. They submitted the matter to Abraham and Abraham said, "I have no knowledge of it". So they submitted the matter to Moses and Moses said, "I have no knowledge of it". So they submitted the matter to Jesus. He said, "Regarding the arising of the Hour, no one has knowledge of it apart from God. But my Lord has confided in me everything about it except the time of its occurrence. He has confided in me that the Antichrist will come out and that He will cause me to alight to meet him – and it is mentioned that he will have two streams with him[23] – When he sees me God will destroy him and he will melt as lead melts. Even the rocks and the trees will say, 'O Muslim, here is an unbeliever. Kill him!' Hence God will cause the unbelievers to perish. Men will return to their home towns and native lands and Gog and Magog will confront them «and will hasten forth from every mound». They will not come upon anything without eating it and they will not pass by water without drinking it. So mankind will turn to me and will complain about them. I will petition God concerning them and He will cause them to die so that the earth flows with the stench of their odour. He will send down the rain which will wash their corpses away and cause them to flow into the sea. Then He will pulverise the mountains until the earth becomes like tanned leather. My Lord has confided to me that that is how it will be. For them the Hour will be like a pregnant woman who has reached full term and whose family do not know when she will suddenly give birth, whether it will be by night or by day." '[24]

Ṭabarī cites another ḥadith in his comments on 21:96. He traces it back to Ḥudhayfa b. al-Yamān:

The Messenger of God (the peace and blessings of God be upon him!) said:
'The principal signs will be the Antichrist, the descent of Jesus, a fire which will come from the depths of Aden and drive mankind to the gathering place where they will be told all that they said. Then there will be the Smoke [cf. 44:10], the Beast, and after that Gog and Magog.' Ḥudhayfa said, 'O Messenger of God what are Gog and Magog?' He said, 'God and Magog are peoples each numbering 400,000. Not one of them will die before he has put a thousand eyes out of their sockets. They are sons of Adam who will overrun the world and their vanguard will be in Palestine when their rearguard is still in Iraq. They will pass by the rivers of the world drinking the Tigris, the Euphrates and Lake Tiberius before arriving at Jerusalem. Then they will say, "We have killed the people of this world so now let us wage war on those in heaven." They will fire their arrows into the sky and when they return to them tinged with blood they will say, "We have killed heaven's inhabitants." Jesus and the Muslims will be on Mount Sinai and God (Majestic is His Majesty) will reveal to Jesus: "Keep my servants safe on the mountain and in proximity to Aelia."[25] Jesus will raise his head to heaven and the Muslims will believe. So God will send upon Gog and Magog vermin called *naghaf*[26] which will get into their nostrils with the result that from the extremity of Palestine to the extremity of Iraq they will be struck dead. The earth will stink because of their corpses but God will command heaven and there will be torrents of rain which will wash their corpses and the stench of them from the surface of the earth. When that happens the sunrise will occur in the west.'[27]

Of the other four commentators, only Ibn Kathīr cites aḥadīth which mention Jesus at this point. Here is an extract from one of them:

> God will send the Messiah Son of Mary and he will descend at the white minaret on the eastern side of Damascus wearing garments lightly coloured with saffron (*bayna mahrūdatayn*) and placing his hands on the wings of two angels. Then he will pursue him (i.e. the Antichrist) and overtake him and kill him by the eastern gate of Lod.[28]

The version cited by Ibn Kathīr is from the *Musnad* of Ibn Ḥanbal and is traced back to al-Nawwās but virtually the same details are found in a ḥadith in the *Ṣaḥīḥ* of Muslim.

The aḥādīth which mention Jesus and which Ṭabarī and Ibn Kathīr cite in connection with the Qur'anic references to Gog and Magog all presuppose that Jesus' return will be a sign of the Hour. The one which Ṭabarī gives on the authority of 'Abd Allah b. Mas'ūd represents, among other things, an attempt to reconcile that interpretation of 43:61 with the Qur'anic insistence that God alone has knowledge of the Hour (cf.7:187). Like the one which he cites on the authority of Ḥudhayfa b. al-Yamān it puts Jesus' return into perspective by making it one sign among many.

ISLAM WILL PREVAIL OVER ALL OTHER RELIGIONS

> «He it is who has sent His messenger with guidance and the true religion that He may grant it (*or* him) victory over all religions no matter how much the polytheists disapprove.» (9:33)

The first part of this āya does not present any difficulties. The reference is obviously to God's sending Muḥammad with the message of Islam. In the next clause the only real grammatical problem is the ambiguity of the attached pronoun *-hu* which could mean either 'it' or 'him' but some exegetes also made heavy weather of the verb.

Ṭabarī[29] paraphrases 'that He may exalt Islam above all religions', but he states that the early intepreters disagreed about what is meant. There were two schools of thought:

[A] Some said that it is a reference to what will happen when Jesus returns and all religions become one. Ṭabarī traces this view back to two Companions of the Prophet, Abū Hurayra who said 'At the time of the appearance of Jesus Son of Mary' and Abū Ja'far who said 'When Jesus appears the people of every religion will follow him.' In both cases the isnād which Ṭabarī gives *munqaṭi'*.[30]

[B] Others apparently thought that the antecedent of the attached pronoun *-hu* was not 'religion' but 'messenger' and said that what was meant was that God would teach Muḥammad the revealed laws of all religions. Ṭabarī traces this back by a single route to Ibn al-'Abbās.

Ṭabarī does not state which of the two interpretations he prefers but only the first one tallies with his initial paraphrase.

Zamakhsharī[31] does not refer to either of the traditional interpretations. He merely mentions that the clause may be construed to mean either 'that He may grant Muḥammad victory over the peoples of all religions' or 'that He may grant the true religion victory over all religions'.

Rāzī[32] helps us to grasp the issue which gave rise to the two traditional interpretations and to others not mentioned by Ṭabarī. The problem was a theological one: contrary to what the Qur'ān might have led Muslims to expect, Islam had not been completely victorious over other religions in India, China, Byzantium and the rest of the disbelieving lands. Rāzī mentions five different answers to this objection:

1. There is no religion which has been opposed to Islam which Muslims have not triumphed over in some of its territories if not in all. Muslims vanquished the Jews and drove them out of the Arab lands. They vanquished the Christians in Syro-Palestine and the West. They conquered the Zoroastrian Persian Empire. They were victorious against idolaters in some of the lands of the Indians and Turks. Thus what is promised in this āya has been achieved. When it was originally spoken it was a miraculous report concerning the Unseen.
2. According to Abū Hurayra it is a promise which will be fulfilled in the future when Jesus comes. We have already encountered this interpretation in Ṭabarī where it was attributed to the same authority. Rāzī adds that al-Suddī (d.128/745) said that when the Mahdī comes none will remain who has not entered Islam or paid the tax.
3. It is a promise that Islam will prevail over all other religions in the Arabian Peninsula. That has already happened. God has not left any unbelievers there.
4. It means that God will acquaint Muḥammad with the revealed laws of all other religions so that nothing to do with them remains hidden from him. This was the second traditional interpretation mentioned by Ṭabarī.
5. Islam will prevail over all other religions in terms of having better and clearer proof of authenticity than they have. Rāzī dismisses this as weak because Islam already had better and clearer proof than other religions in the very beginning.

Ibn Kathīr[33] does not mention either of the traditional interpretations found in Ṭabarī nor does he hint that there is a theological problem. He simply cites a number of relevant aḥādīth none of which mention the return of Jesus. It is difficult to follow his train of thought but it seems that as regards their content the aḥādīth which he cites fall into three categories as follows.

(1) Aḥādīth in which Muḥammad predicts the triumph of Islam. For instance there is this one from the *Ṣaḥīḥ* of Bukhārī:

> God has collected together the eastern parts and western parts of the earth for me. He will make the dominion of my people reach what He has collected together for me.

And this one from the *Musnad* of Ibn Ḥanbal:

> There will not remain on the face of the earth a bedouin tent or a city house which the word of Islam has not entered.

(2) Another ḥadīth from the *Musnad* in which Muḥammad shows superior knowledge of other religions and also predicts the triumph of Islam:

> 'Adī b. Hātim said, 'I entered the Messenger of God's presence (the peace and blessing of God be upon him!) and he said, "O 'Adī become a Muslim and you will be safe". I said, "I have my own religion". He replied "I am more knowledgeable about your religion than you are." I said, "Are you really more knowledgeable about my religion than I am?" To which he said, "Yes, are you not a *rakūsī*[34] and you devour a quarter of your people's livestock?" I replied, "Yes, that is correct." He said, "You are not permitted to do that in your religion . . . As I am more knowledgeable than you are, what prevents you from becoming a Muslim?"'

The ḥadīth continues with Muḥammad explaining to 'Adī, that although at present Muslims are poor and weak, women in camel-borne sedans will shortly come from Ḥīra to visit the Kaaba and the treasures of the Persian emperor Chosroes will be laid open.

(3) A ḥadīth from the *Ṣaḥīḥ* of Muslim in which Muḥammad expresses his expectation of Arab apostasy:

> 'Ā'isha (may God be pleased with her) reported, 'I heard the messenger of God say, "Night and day will not end until [the people] have taken to the worship of al-Lāt and al-'Uzza." I said, "O Messenger of God, I thought that when God revealed this āya: «He it is who has sent His messenger with guidance and the true religion that He may grant it (*or* him) victory over all religions no matter how much the polytheists disapprove.» [9:33] it implied that it would be fulfilled." He said, "It will happen as God wishes. Then God will send the sweet fragrant air and everyone in whose heart there is as much as a grain of mustard seed of faith will die. Those

who have no goodness in them will survive and will revert to the religion of their forefathers."

Both of the traditional interpretations mentioned by Ṭabarī seem forced. It is surely more natural to understand the āya, in accordance with my translation, as a promise to be fulfilled in the near future. During the first century after Muḥammad's death, with the frontiers forever being pushed back, it must indeed have looked as if Islam was destined to triumph over all other religions. I suggest that the two traditional interpretations preserved by Ṭabarī most probably originated at a later date when the frontiers had become static and the Qur'anic promise had begun to seem problematic. I further suggest that some of the aḥādīth cited by Ibn Kathīr may have been put into circulation for apologetic purposes at around the same time.

JESUS WILL SPEAK TO MANKIND WHEN OF MATURE AGE

«He will speak to mankind while in the cradle and when of mature age and [he will be one] of the righteous.» (3:46)
«I strengthened you with the Holy Spirit so that you spoke to mankind while in the cradle and when of mature age» (5:110)

The word *kahlan*, which I have translated 'when of mature age', occurs in the Qur'ān only in these two āyas and the classical commentators discuss its meaning at considerable length.

Ṭabarī[35] states that it means when fully mature or experienced (*muḥtanakan*), no longer a youth but not yet aged. Then he says that one speaks of a man as *kahl* and of a woman as *kahla* and he cites a line of poetry in which the feminine form occurs:

After sleeping with her I shall not again
pursue any mature woman or young girl.[36]

He explains that Jesus spoke to mankind in his infancy in defence of his mother and as a proof of his prophethood and that he spoke to them as an adult when he received revelation. He goes on to say that the double reference was meant to show that he was like other human beings in as much as he developed from one state to another which would have been impossible had he been divine as the Christians of Najrān alleged. In support of this he cites a number of traditions all of which are attributed to Successors. The first which is traced back to Muḥammad b. Ja'far b. al-Zubayr (d. between 110/728 and 120/738) via Ibn Isḥāq is in line with this interpretation although it does not mention the Christians of Najrān. The others are brief paraphrastic glosses. Qatāda, Rabi' and Ibn Jurayj said he would speak 'when small and when grown up' (*saghīran wa-kabīran*). Mujāhid said that *kahl* meant 'having arrived at the age of reason' (*ḥalīm*). Al-Ḥasan al-Baṣrī said that he would speak 'as a boy and when grown up' (*ṣabiyyan wa-kabīran*). This is not the end of the matter, however, because according to Ṭabarī there were others who said that what was meant was that Jesus would speak to mankind when he reappeared. In particular he cites Ibn Zayd who said: 'Jesus has spoken to them in the cradle and he will speak to them when he kills the Antichrist. When he does that he will be mature.'

Zamakhsharī,[37] does not mention Ibn Zayd's interpretation. After a brief discussion of the grammatical construction he says that the meaning is that:

> He will speak to mankind in these two states in the speech of the prophets without variation between the state of childhood and the state of maturity, the latter being the state in which the reason is well-established and in which prophets prophesy.

Rāzī's discussion is more illuminating.[38] For him the passage poses three problems:

First, what is meant by *kahl*? The answer to this is furnished by philology. It is a combination of strength and the completion of youth. This definition is derived from the expression used by the desert Arabs *iktahala 'l-nabāt* to indicate that a plant has become strong and full-grown. The poet al-A'shā [d.6/627] used the cognate word (*muktahil*) to describe a plant of extreme beauty and perfection when he said:

> where the lofty blooms of the luscious plants
> in their perfection smile back at the sun.[39]

Second, what is the point of mentioning his speaking when mature since unlike his speaking in the cradle this was not miraculous? Rāzī gives four possible answers:

1. It is made clear that he changed from one state to another and was therefore not divine as the embassy from Najrān alleged.
2. What is intended by it is that he will speak on a single occasion

when he is in the cradle in order to vindicate his mother's purity. Then when he is in a state of maturity he will speak by revelation as a prophet.

3. Abū Muslim [d.332/934][40] said that it means that he will speak in the cradle and in maturity in the one manner and one capacity and that there is no doubt that this is a surpassing miracle.
4. Al-Aṣamm [d.200 or 201/815–17][41] said that it means that he will reach the age of maturity.

Third, Jesus' age was reputedly 33 years and six months when he was raised up into God's presence. On this reckoning he had not reached maturity. Rāzī gives two possible solutions to this problem:

1. The root meaning of the word is full-grown and accomplished, i.e. in the case of human beings between 30 and 40. This fits Jesus.
2. The saying of Ḥusayn b. al-Faḍl al-Bajlī[42] that he will be mature after he comes down from heaven at the close of the age and speaks to mankind and kills the Antichrist.

Bayḍāwī[43] adds nothing to our knowledge. His brief comment includes a reference to the interpretation which Ṭabarī attributed to Ibn Zayd and which Rāzī attributed to al-Bajlī:

> It is said that he was raised into heaven while still a youth and that «when of mature age» means after his descent.

Ibn Kathīr makes no reference to Jesus' return. Commenting on 3:46 he paraphrases *kahlan* as 'in his mature state when God reveals to him.'[44] Commenting on 5:110 he says:

> That is, 'you summoned mankind to God when you were small and when you were grown up'. For his speaking included summoning because his speaking to mankind when mature was not in any way miraculous.[45]

I suggest that the key to understanding the debate about the meaning of *kahlan* is furnished by Rāzī's reference to the problem caused by Jesus' age at the time of the ascension. According to the Qur'ān man reaches his full strength when he is forty[46] and according to tradition that was Muḥammad's age when he received his first revelation.[47] Therefore when Muslims learned from Christians that Jesus' life on earth lasted for only 33 years it must have seemed to them that he had not attained maturity. When did they first encounter this information? The historians Ya'qūbī and Mas'ūdī (d.956) certainly knew the Biblical chronology[48] but there is no reason why it should not have reached Muslim ears long before. I suggest that the exegetes who linked Jesus' speaking «in maturity» with his future return did so in response to Christian polemic. This was also probably the motive behind the exegetical use of poetic proof texts. The obvious inference from the verse cited by Ṭabarī is that since the poet once considered 'mature' women worth chasing, the word can be used to describe people who are still comparatively young. The verse cited by Rāzī is also from a famous erotic poem which was probably well known to his readers. The verse in question is printed in Arabic along with the preceding and following verses as part of the dedication of this book. My translation is but a pale imitation of the original:

> Amongst the gardens of the rugged earth
> by abundant rains made green,
> where the lofty blooms of luscious plants
> in their perfection smile back at the sun,
> not a single verdant garden exhales such fragrance by day
> or equals her in loveliness at eventide[49]

DISCUSSION

It remains for me to draw some general conclusions from this and the previous chapter and to make some suggestions about the progressive elaboration of the aḥādīth about Jesus' return.

The following points are I think beyond dispute:

1. It is by no means certain that the Qur'ān itself even alludes to Jesus' return. There are only two āyas which merit serious consideration in connection with this: 4:159 and 43:61. In both instances there are grammatical reasons for questioning this interpretation. Moreover in both instances there is an alternative interpretation which is traced back to Companions and Successors and is supported by a variant reading attributed to Ubaiy.
2. The belief that Jesus will return is nevertheless well established in Islam. The commentators refer to it in connection with seven passages from the Qur'ān. There are a number of aḥādīth which mention it including some which have the highest possible authority because they were judged 'authentic' by both Bukhāri and Muslīm and included in their collections.

3. The aḥādīth give greater place to Christian eschatological beliefs than the Qur'ān does but they also fit them into a Muslim framework. Thus although Jesus will descend and kill the Antichrist his descent will be only one of the signs of the Hour. Although he will descend to earth as a just judge this will be before the resurrection; he will not be God's agent at the last judgement. Moreover what is expected is Jesus' 'descent' rather than his 'return'. This underlies the fact that he will not have a prophetic mission in the last days.
4. The aḥādīth which refer to Muḥammad's encounter with Jesus make Muḥammad's nocturnal ascent the equivalent of Jesus' ascension. In this context we should note that the marks on the rock inside the Dome of the Rock, which are reputedly the footprints left by Muḥammad on the night of the ascent, recall the marks on the rock beneath the Dome of the Ascension on the Mount of Olives which are reputedly Jesus' footprints.[50] As mentioned above, by situating Jesus in the second or third heaven the aḥādīth imply Muḥammad's superiority to Jesus.
5. Some early exegetes, including Ibn Zayd, used the belief in Jesus' future descent as an apologetic device for explaining difficult passages in the Qur'ān possibly in the face of Christian polemic.

As regards the progressive elaboration of the aḥādīth about Jesus' descent, we are on much more difficult ground because of the lack of reliable data. The following suggestions are extremely tentative. I shall concentrate on trying to account for some of the details in the principal ḥadīth mentioned in the last chapter:

1. Before the end of the first/seventh century unrest in the Muslim community caused by civil war led to popular expectations of the Mahdī. In Chapter 7 we saw that the various Shī'ite groups identified him with their own imams. It is well known that there were other Muslims who were not Shī'ites but who none the less fostered similar hopes and expected a Mahdī who would be a descendant of Muḥammad.
2. At about the same time a ḥādīth mentioning Jesus' descent was also put into circulation. It too owed its popularity to the widespread unrest but also to the influence of Christian eschatological beliefs. Some of the non-Shī'ites believed that Jesus

would be subordinate to the Mahdī whereas others claimed that there would be no Mahdī apart from him.

3. The ḥadīth about Jesus' future descent was linked with 43:61 and descriptions of him were incorporated to explain how he could be a sign of the Hour.
4. The ḥadīth was subsequently linked with 4:159 and a clause was inserted which referred to Jesus' death as still lying in the future.
5. The difficulty of reconciling 3:46 with the Christian tradition that Jesus' ministry ended when he was only thirty-three led to the insertion of yet another clause this time referring to Jesus' tarrying a number of years before dying.
6. The failure of Islam to expand its frontiers indefinitely and the resulting perplexity caused by 9:33 led to a further development in some versions of the ḥadīth. This was the addition of the statement 'People will fight one another because of Islam until God destroys all the religious communities in his time with the exception of Islam.'
7. The details derived from the Christian tradition such as the killing of the Antichrist and the Messianic peace could have been incorporated at any time.
8. Equally difficult to date are the references to Jesus' killing pigs, smashing crucifixes and abolishing the poll tax. Although they are found in aḥādīth reported on the authority of Abū Hurayra there is little evidence that they were known to the Successors who specialised in Qur'anic commentary. Early Christian sources testify to Muslim hatred of crucifixes[51] and the notion that Jesus would kill pigs might have been derived from the gospel story of the Gaderene demoniac. On the other hand, these details could have been introduced much later – even as late as the early Abbasid period when Christians rose to senior positions in the court at Baghdad and their success caused much resentment as witnessed by Jāḥiẓ. During that period all Christians were forbidden to carry crucifixes in public processions or to keep pigs openly but some of them were so well placed socially that they infringed these regulations with impunity and occasionally even avoided paying the poll tax.[52] What could be more natural than for their detractors to circulate aḥadith asserting that when Jesus returned the Christians would not get off so lightly?

11 The Crucifixion – Non-Muslim Approaches

The Qur'ān contains only one explicit reference to the alleged crucifixion of Jesus. This occurs in the course of an invective against the People of the Scripture:

> «(156) And for their unbelief and for their speaking a tremendous calumny against Mary. (157) And for their saying "We indeed killed the Messiah Jesus Son of Mary, God's messenger." They did not kill him and they did not crucify him but a semblance was made to them. Those who differ over it are indeed in doubt about it. They have no knowledge about it apart from pursuit of a conjecture. They did not kill him for certain. (158) But God raised him into His presence – God is Mighty, Wise. (159) And [there is] not [one] of the People of the Scripture except [he] will most certainly believe in him before his death, and on the Day of Resurrection he will be a witness against them.» (4:156–9)

The last of these āyas, 4:159, has already been discussed in Chapter 9, where we saw that the majority of the classical commentators held that it referred to the still future death of Jesus, who had been raised alive into heaven and would return to kill the Antichrist. Muslim exegesis of 4:157 will be examined in detail in Chapter 13. For the time being suffice it to note that the words *shubbiha la-hum*, which I have translated «a semblance was made to them», are usually held to mean that it was not Jesus who was crucified but a person who was made to resemble him.

CHRISTIAN POLEMIC

One of the earliest extant Christian writings to contain a reference to Muslim teaching about the crucifixion is the *De Haeresibus* of John of Damascus. John stated that, according to Muḥammad or 'Mamed' as he called him:

> the Jews, having themselves violated the Law, wanted to crucify him and after they arrested him they crucified his shadow, but Christ himself, they say, was not crucified nor did he die; for God took him up to himself into heaven because he loved him.[1]

How accurately this reflects Qur'anic interpretation in John's day is impossible to tell. What is clear is that he knew that Muslims denied that Jesus had been crucified. Moreover in this instance he made no attempt to argue with them about the meaning of the Qur'ān. For him Islam was a heresy. He simply dismissed what the Qur'ān said about this and most other matters as absurd and worthy of laughter.

John of Damascus could afford to ridicule his opponents because he was writing for his fellow Christians and he was writing in Greek, a language which few Muslims could understand. Some thirty years after John's death the Catholicos Timothy I, the leader of the Nestorian Church, faced the much more daunting task of replying in person to a series of questions which were put to him by the Caliph al-Mahdī. One of the subjects which they discussed was whether or not Jesus died on the cross. The Caliph opened the discussion by asking Timothy whether God could die. In his answer Timothy drew on the traditional Christian distinction between Jesus' divine and human natures and indicated that it was the latter which died. Then the Caliph cited *Qur'ān* 4:157 which he evidently understood as a denial of Jesus' death. Timothy replied by quoting the words which the Qur'ān elsewhere attributed to the infant Jesus:

> «'Peace be on me the day I was born, the day I die and the day I am resurrected.'» (19:33)

He also quoted part of another āya:

> «God said 'O Jesus, I am going to receive you [i.e. cause you to die] and raise you to myself.'» (3:55)

He regarded these as clear proof that Jesus had died and been raised. The Caliph answered that Jesus' death still lay in the future. Timothy retorted that Jesus could not have been raised to heaven if he had not died beforehand and that Jesus did in fact die in fulfilment of Old Testament prophecies. The Caliph once again mentioned the key text, *Qur'ān* 4:157, and affirmed that all that was only an illusion for them (*tashbiyyan la-hum*). To this Timothy objected that God would not delude mankind in such a way and that if it were legitimate to describe the crucifixion as an illusion one would have to say the same about the ascension and the other miracles. The Caliph then explained that the reason why God had not allowed the Jews to crucify the Messiah was that He esteemed him highly. Timothy replied that God had not prevented the Jews from murdering the prophets despite His high esteem for them. He pointed out, however, that unlike the prophets, Jesus went voluntarily to his death for St John's Gospel records him as saying that nobody could take his life unless he laid it down on his own accord (cf. *John* 10:17f.)[2]

CHRISTIAN APOLOGETIC

Timothy's position – although he was careful not to say so too bluntly – seems to have been that the Qur'ān is inconsistent: it contains one passage which denies Jesus' death and two others which affirm it. Some Christian apologists have claimed that, on the contrary, the Qur'ān is consistent and that it does not in fact deny the crucifixion. They have based this claim on three types of argument all of which owe something to Timothy's dialogue although he himself did not develop them in the following way.

First, Timothy indicated that *Qur'ān* 19:33 and 3:55 referred to Jesus' death. There are several other āyas which he could have mentioned in this connection:

> «Say, 'Who could avail ought against God if He wanted to destroy Jesus the Son of Mary and his mother...?'» (5:17)
> «The Messiah Jesus son of Mary [was] only a messenger. Messengers have passed away before him.» (5:75)
> «Then when You received me [i.e. caused me to die], You were the watcher over them.» (5:117)

The cumulative effect of these āyas is to establish Jesus' mortality. This is the primary datum and 4:157 ought, according to the apologists, to be interpreted in the light of it.[3]

Second, Timothy mentioned the traditional Christian belief in Christ's two natures. It is arguable that *Qur'ān* 4:157 affirms the indestructibility of the divine nature without actually denying that the man Jesus died on the cross. Thus for example in the twelfth century Paul of Antioch wrote:

> By this statement the Qur'ān gives evidence for the divine nature of Christ which is the Word of God which neither pain nor scorn can touch.[4]

A slightly different argument, and one which is more likely to appeal to Muslims, puts the stress on Jesus' soul rather than on his divine nature. Jesus died a martyr's death and according to the Qur'ān martyrs are alive with God:

> «Do not reckon those who are killed in God's way as dead. No! Alive with their Lord, provided for» (3:169)

Admittedly this āya states that the martyrs have been «killed» whereas 4:157 says that the Jews «did not kill» Jesus. However, the denial is subsequently qualified with the rider:

> «They did not kill him for certain. But God raised him into His presence.» (4:157f)

They did not kill him for certain; in other words they did not *really* kill him because although they crucified his body God raised his soul up to heaven.[5]

Third, Timothy mentioned that, according to *John* 10:17f, Jesus laid down his life of his own accord. In the light of this and other passages from the New Testament, it is arguable that *Qur'ān* 4:157 does not actually deny that Jesus was killed and crucified: it merely denies the Jews' arrogant claim that *they* killed and crucified him. This denial is well founded historically because it was the Romans who carried out the execution (cf. *Mark* 15:15). It is also theologically sound because the real reason for Jesus' death was that it was in accordance with God's will (cf. *Mark* 8:31). If one follows this line of argument the words *shubbiha la-hum* have to be translated «it appeared to them as such»,[6] that is to say it appeared to the Jews that they were solely responsible for Jesus' death because they were not aware of the deeper significance of the event. The alternative is to follow Zaehner in detecting here a distant echo of *Philippians* 2:7ff which speaks of Jesus being 'made in the likeness of men' and refers to God's having 'exalted him' after he had become 'obedient unto death, even death on a cross.'[7]

Not all Christian apologists employ arguments like those just mentioned. Charles Ledit[8] concedes that at one level the Qur'ān does deny that Jesus was crucified. He attributes this denial to Muḥammad's conviction that the machinations of the Jews could not escape God's notice and his belief that God inevitably outwitted them. He also suggests that, like Peter, Muḥammad loved Jesus too much to admit the triumph of his enemies. Nevertheless Ledit believes that at another level – the level of unconscious symbolism – the Qur'ān announces Jesus' passage from death to resurrection. He bases this claim on the strange story of the fish which Moses and his servant carried with them for food. When they reached the confluence of the two seas the servant forgot the fish and it came back to life and swam away (18:71–75). In early Christian symbolism the fish signified Christ who had been sacrificed. Here then the Mosaic Law brings along Christ who died because of it, but it cannot retain him and at the confluence of the two Testaments the risen Christ freely swims abroad in the mission of his apostles!

Kenneth Cragg's approach is more subtle.[9] In the last analysis he admits that the Qur'ān denies the crucifixion's 'real and actual occurrence as a complete event'. Yet he none the less insists that it is an oversimplification to say that it denies the crucifixion. In the Christian understanding there are three elements to the Cross: 'the act of men in wrong, the act of Jesus in love and the act of God in grace'. The Qur'ān clearly asserts man's evil intention of crucifying Jesus. Moreover Jesus was prepared to die and cannot have known in advance that God was going to rescue him. Thus the Qur'ān affirms the first two elements. It is only the third, the act of God in grace, which it denies because on the Qur'anic reckoning, 'God was *not* in Christ reconciling the world to himself': he was with Jesus withdrawing him to heaven.'

SECTARIAN CHRISTIAN PARALLELS

There have been numerous attempts at explaining 4:156–9 in terms of sectarian Christian influences. Three suggestions merit serious consideration. First, Bowman thought that this passage was intended to settle the argument between Nestorians and Monophysites. The Nestorians held that the human nature of Jesus died but that his divine nature returned to God. The Monophysites held that Jesus was but one nature, divine and human conjoined, and that the divine therefore suffered with the human on the cross. The Qur'ān here insists that they are both wrong: Jesus was only human but he did not die.[10] A second possibility, which has been championed by Grégoire, is that the Qur'ān here reflects the teaching of Monophysite extremists who followed Julian of Halicarnassus. About a century before the rise of Islam, Julian pushed the doctrine of one nature after the Incarnation to its logical conclusion and taught that from the moment of union Christ's body was incorruptible. This led him to deny the reality of Christ's suffering.[11] A third possibility, which we must now explore in greater depth, is that Muḥammad held out an olive branch to Christian Gnostics who denied that Jesus was crucified.

According to Irenaeus, a second-century Gnostic called Basilides taught that Jesus:

> did not himself suffer death, but Simon, a certain man of Cyrene, being compelled bore the cross in his stead; so that this latter being transfigured by him, that he might be thought to be Jesus, was crucified, through ignorance and error, while Jesus himself received the form of Simon, and, standing by, laughed at them. For since he was an incorporeal power, and the Nous (mind) of the unborn father, he transfigured himself as he pleased, and thus ascended to him who sent him.[12]

The same doctrine is found in *The Second Treatise of the Great Seth* which is allegedly a revelation delivered by Jesus to an audience of 'perfect and incorruptible ones':

> I did not succumb to them as they had planned. But I was not afflicted at all. Those who were there punished me. And I did not die in reality but in appearance . . . For my death which they think happened, (happened) to them in their error and blindness, since they nailed their man unto their death . . . Yes they saw me; they punished me. It was another, their father, who drank the gall and the vinegar; it was not I. They struck me with the reed; it was another, Simon who bore the cross on his shoulder. It was another on whom they placed the crown of thorns. But I was rejoicing in the height.[13]

The Gnostic *Apocalypse of Peter* seems to imply something slightly different – the crucifixion of a look-alike substitute for the 'living Jesus' which was brought into existence specially for the occasion:

> this one into whose hands and feet they drive the nails is his fleshy part, which is the substitute being put to shame, the one who came into being in his likeness.[14]

The doctrine of the *First Apocalypse of James* is different again. This writing distinguishes between the body which was crucified and the true Jesus who had been within it but who never suffered.[15]

MUḤAMMAD AND THE CHRISTIANS

Whatever the nature of the sectarian influence on 4:156–9, it is difficult to reconcile these āyas with others which seem to affirm the reality of Jesus' death. Some light may be thrown on this problem by considering the various statements in chronological order and in connection with the vicissitudes of Muḥammad's relations with Christians.

According to Nöldeke's chronological scheme the earliest statement is 19:33, the infant Jesus' reference to the day of his death and the day of his being raised. In the original version of the revelation – the version recited to the Abyssinians by the Muslim refugees from Mecca – this was probably the culmination of the story. The Abyssinians may well have understood it as referring to the crucifixion and the resurrection on the third day. The statement itself is, however, much less precise. It does not specify how and when Jesus was to die nor how and when he was to be raised. In view of 19:15, where similar things are said about John, it is perhaps the general resurrection on the day of judgement which is envisaged. In any case the very fact that similar things are said about John detracts from the uniqueness of Jesus. In short the statement sounds more Christian than it is. This is in character with the general tenor of 19:1–33 where the aim seems to be that of appealing to Christian sentiment without making too many concessions to Christian belief.

The other statements all occur in Medinan revelations. Whatever the historical context of ṣūra three, it evidently involved a dialogue between Muslims and Christians in which the principal bone of contention was the unity of God. On that occasion Jesus' death was a secondary matter and for this reason 3:55 is perhaps deliberately imprecise. It seems to refer to God's receiving Jesus in death but as we shall see in the next chapter the verb also has other associations. Moreover the reality of the crucifixion is neither asserted nor denied.

Nöldeke reckons that most of ṣūra four originated between the end of the third year and the end of the fifth year of the Hijra, that is to say some time after the Muslims had broken with the sizeable Jewish community in Medina. 4:156–9 reads like an attempt to referee between rival Christian groups and rally their support in the face of Jewish opposition. Here for once the crucifixion is very much in the forefront of the debate because the Christians disagreed about it among themselves although as we have seen it is not entirely clear what position the Qur'ān espouses.

Despite the later date of ṣūra five it presupposes a situation similar to that of ṣūra three. That is to say it is once again the disagreement between Muslims and Christians about the unity of God which is the central issue. 5:117 is virtually a doublet of 3:55. The statements in

5:17 and 5:75 neither assert nor deny the crucifixion; their purpose is to emphasise the mortality of Jesus in order to counter exaggerated Christian claims concerning his divinity.

MUḤAMMAD AND JESUS

What the Qur'ān says about Muḥammad's fate is in some ways tantalisingly similar to what it says about the fate of Jesus.

First, there are three āyās in which the verb *tawaffā* occurs with God as the subject and Muḥammad as the object of the action:

> «Whether We cause you to see something of what We have promised them or whether We receive you (*natawaffayanna-ka*), unto Us they will be returned (*yurja'una*).» (40:77)
>
> «Whether We cause you to see something of what We have promised them or whether We receive you (*natawaffayanna-ka*), unto Us is their return (*marji'u-hum*) and God is witness (*shahīdun*) over what they do.» (10:46)
>
> «Whether We cause you to see something of what We have promised them or whether We receive you (*natawaffayanna-ka*), on you is incumbent only the preaching and on Us the reckoning.» (13:40)

These are all late Meccan revelations. Thus they are earlier than the two Medinan āyas where the same verb is used with reference to Jesus:

> «[Remember] when God said, 'O Jesus I am going to receive you (*mutawaffī-ka*) and raise you to myself and purify you from those who disbelieve. I am setting those who follow you above those who disbelieve until the Day of Resurrection. Then to Me shall be your return (*marji'u-kum* [all of you].» (3:55)
>
> «[Jesus said], I was a witness against them as long as I remained with them. Then when You received me (*tawaffayta-nī*) You were the watcher over them, You are witness (*shahīdun*) of everything'.» (5:117)

The three āyas about Muḥammad and the two about Jesus are the only ones where the verb is used in the active voice with God as the subject and with one of his prophets as the object. Moreover in both sets of āyas there is a similar emphasis on God's witnessing man's actions and on man's return to Him for judgement. This is too much to be a coincidence; the statements about Jesus must surely have been modelled on the earlier statements about Muḥammad. What is less clear is the bearing that this has on the interpretation of 3:55 and 5:117. In Muḥammad's case, what seems to have been envisaged was that God might cause him to die prematurely, presumably by allowing him to be killed by his persecutors. We are not, however, justified in jumping to the conclusion that this was precisely what did happen in the case of Jesus and that *tawaffā* simply means 'cause to die' or 'receive in death'. To do so would be to ignore the fact that 3:55 contains an additional statement in which God speaks of raising him or causing him to ascend into His presence. The similarity between the fate envisaged for Muḥammad and Jesus' actual fate is I suggest limited to two points: the humanly-speaking premature end to the prophetic ministry and the fact that it was God who brought it to an end. This will be discussed at greater length in the next chapter.

Second, Muḥammad's opponents schemed against him but God was also scheming:

> «When those who disbelieve plot to keep you in bonds or kill you or drive you out, they are scheming and God is scheming. God is the best of schemers.» (8:30)

This is a late Meccan or possibly an early Medinan revelation. Similar things are said about the opposition to other prophets including Abraham (14:47) and Ṣāliḥ (27:50) but the phrase «God is the best of schemers» occurs elsewhere only in a subsequent revelation about Jesus:

> «They schemed and God schemed. God is the best of schemers.» (3:54)

Again it is difficult to know how to interpret the similarities. God's scheming on behalf of Muḥammad is traditionally explained as a reference to the Prophet's escape from Mecca to Medina when 'Alī slept in his bed and acted as a decoy.[16] God's plotting on behalf of Jesus is usually linked with 4:157 and understood as a reference to the crucifixion of a substitute. One might therefore argue that, having himself been delivered from death by a close Companion taking his place, Muḥammad subsequently came to believe that Jesus was delivered in a similar way. The analogy would not, however, be very close because 'Alī was not killed and Muḥammad was not raised into God's presence. If we leave aside the traditional material all that can be said with any certainty is that 8:30 refers to an unspecified deliverance from death in the course of Muḥammad's ministry. In which case 3:54 may refer to a similar deliverance from death *in the course of Jesus' ministry*: for instance after his sermon at Nazareth (cp. *Luke* 4:29).

Third, Muḥammad's status as a messenger of God was no guarantee that he would not die or be killed:

> «Muḥammad [is] only a messenger. Messengers have passed away before him. If he dies or is killed will you turn upon your heels...?» (3:144)

This is a Medinan revelation. The phrase «have passed away before» (*qad khalat min qabli*) occurs a number of times in the Qur'ān with reference to past generations and vanished peoples but the closest parallel to this particular āya is in a subsequent revelation about Jesus:

> «The Messiah Jesus son of Mary [was] only a messenger. Messengers have passed away before him» (5:75).

By the time 3:144 was revealed, Muḥammad was evidently aware of the likelihood of his death in the near future. How then should we interpret the fact that 5:75, a subsequent revelation about Jesus, apparently echoes this āya? I suggest that it is intended to counterbalance the reference to Muḥammad's forthcoming death by stressing Jesus' mortality but without actually gainsaying 4:156–9 which denied that Jesus was killed or crucified.

DISCUSSION

The attempt of some Christian apologists to circumvent the Qur'anic denial of the crucifixion is disingenuous in the extreme. If the intention of 4:157–9 had been to indicate that it was God or the Romans and not the Jews who crucified Jesus this would surely have been stated explicitly. Zaehner's suggestion that 4:157–9 echoes the hymn in *Philippians* 2:7ff is implausible because of the dearth of references to the Pauline Epistles in the Qur'ān. On the other hand Cragg is quite correct to insist that the Qur'ān asserts man's evil intention of killing Jesus.

As regards the alleged sectarian Christian influence on 4:156–9 there are strengths and weaknesses in all three proposals. Bowman's suggestion is a neat one but it is questionable whether you can settle an argument between Nestorians and Monophysites by disagreeing with both parties. Grégoire has made out a good case for thinking that Julianism was widespread in the period which interests us but the Qur'anic text seems to imply rather more than the mere denial of Christ's suffering. In favour of the Gnostic solution we should note that the Qur'ān agrees with Gnostic teaching in three respects: it denies that the Jews killed Christ, it acknowledges that it appeared to them that they did kill him and it asserts that he ascended into God's presence. On the other hand, it may be objected that there is no hard and fast evidence that Gnostic ideas were current in seventh century Arabia[17] and that other statements in the Qur'ān which stress Christ's humanity tell against the influence of Gnosticism. These two objections will be reconsidered in Chapters 13 and 15 respectively.

When the Qur'anic references to Jesus' death and mortality are taken in chronological order and examined in the light of Muḥammad's relations with Christians and of his self-understanding it is less difficult to reconcile them with the literal meaning of 4:157–9 than Christian polemicists and apologists generally suppose. All the same the use of the verb *tawaffā* in connection with both Jesus and Muḥammad is puzzling and calls for more detailed consideration.

12 The Meaning of the Verb *tawaffā*

In the course of the last chapter we encountered two āyas in which God is the subject and Jesus is the object of the verb *tawaffā* which I provisionally translated 'receive':

> «God said, 'O Jesus I am going to receive you (*inn-ī mutawaffī-ka*) and raise you to Myself (*wa-rāfi'u-ka ilay-ya*)'.» (3:55)
> «[Jesus said], 'when You received me (*tawaffaytan-ī*) You were the watcher over them'.» (5:117)

We must now discuss this matter in more detail. I will examine the Qur'anic usage of the various derived forms of the triliteral verb *wafā*[1] and then I will attempt to give an exhaustive analysis of the relevant sections of the classical Muslim commentaries.[2]

QUR'ANIC USAGE

Most Arabic verbs have a root form with three consonants and several derived forms produced by adding letters before or between the three radicals. These derived forms, which European grammarians number II to XV, modify the meaning of the root form in various ways.

The root form *wafā*, with the three consonants *w*, *f* and *y*[3] is not found in the Qur'ān. We do, however, find two instances of the elative of the corresponding adjective (9:111 and 53:41) which suggest that the meaning of the root form is 'to fulfil (a promise)' or 'to be complete'.

Form II, *waffā*, occurs eighteen times as a finite verb and once as a participle:

1. In one instance, where Abraham is the subject and the object is not expressed, the meaning seems to be close to that of the root form, 'to fulfil [a promise]' (53:37).
2. In every other instance the meaning is 'to pay/repay in full' and the context is the last judgement when God will recompense people for their actions in this life (active: 3:57, 4:173, 11:15,111, 24:25,39, 35:30, 46:19, passive: 2:272,281, 3:25,

3:161,185, 8:60, 16:111, 39:10,70, active participle: 11:109)

Form IV, *awfā*, also occurs eighteen times as a finite verb and once as a participle:

1. Frequently it means 'to fulfil (a covenant, vow, promise or obligation)' (with human subject: 2:40, 3:76, 5:1, 6:152, 13:20, 16:91, 17:34, 22:29, 48:10, 76:7, active participle 2:177. With God as subject 2:40).
2. It can also mean 'to give full (measure)' (with human subject: 6:152, 7:85, 11:85, 12:59,88, 17:35, 26:181).

Form X, *istawaffā*, occurs only once where it has the meaning 'demand full payment', 'exact in full' (83:2).

Form VI, *tawaffā*, occurs 25 times as a finite verb and once as an active participle:

1. With angels or angelic messengers as the subject it means 'receive' or 'gather' [at death] (4:97, 6:61, 7:37, 8:50, 16:28,32, 32:11, 47:27). Cf. one instance where death itself is the subject (4:15).
2. With God as the subject it seems to mean:
   (a) 'to receive in death' or cause to die' (10:104, 16:70, 39:42),
   (b) 'to receive in death' or 'to cause to die' *prematurely* (Muḥammad 10:46, 13:40, 40:77, the pious 3:193, 7:126, 12:101),
   (c) 'to receive' souls in sleep, which is likened to death (6:60, 39:42),
   (d) 'to receive' Jesus (5:117, participle 3:55).
3. In the passive it is a euphemism for death, particularly a premature death (2:234, 240, 22:5, 40:67).

THE THREE TRADITIONAL INTERPRETATIONS

Between them the five classical commentators give no less than ten different interpretations of the problematic *inn-ī mutawaffī-ka wa-rāfi'u-ka ilay-ya* in 3:55. Three of these are traced back to early authorities.

[A] It means, 'I am going to cause you to sleep and raise you to myself while you are asleep.' This interpretation corresponds to the usage of the verb in two other Qur'anic passages:

> «God receives (*yatawaffā*) souls at the moment of their death as well as those which do not die during their sleep. He retains the

one for which He has decreed death and sends back the other until a stated term.» (39:42)

«It is He who receives you (*yatawaffā-kum*) at night and He knows what you work by day. Then He resurrects you in it that a stated term may be completed.» (6:60)

This is the first interpretation mentioned by Ṭabarī. He attributes it to a single authority, al-Rābi' b. Anas (Iraqi Successor d.139/756). He records that in connection with this al-Rābi' quoted a ḥadīth on the authority of al-Ḥasan al-Baṣri [d.110/728]:

> The Messenger of God (the peace and blessings of God be upon him!) said to the Jews, 'Jesus did not die. He will return to you before the Day of Resurrection.'

We should note that this ḥadīth is *munqaṭi'* for Ḥasan was born several years after the Prophet's death yet no Companion is named as his authority.

Zamakhsharī, and Bayḍāwī mention this interpretation without naming an authority. Rāzī appears not to mention it although it may have dropped out accidentally because there is no 'third' interpretation in his list which runs from 'first' to 'ninth'. He does, however, mentions Rābi' b. Anas' comment which, as we shall see, he understands differently.

Ibn Kathīr mentions this interpretation fourth but it seems to be the one which he favours. He states that it is the majority view although he offers no evidence to back up his claim. He presents Ṭabarī's material slightly differently so that al-Rābi''s comment is traced back to Ḥasan along with the ḥadīth. He also gives another ḥadīth without an isnād:

> The Messenger of God (the peace and blessings of God be upon him!) used to say when he rose from sleep, 'Praise be to God who brought us to life after causing us to die (*ba'da an amāta-nā*)'.

Finally he refers to Qur'ān 4:156f stating that «before his death» means before Jesus' death which will occur when he returns before the Day of Resurrection.

[B] It means, 'I am going to grasp you from the earth and raise you to Myself'. This interpretation corresponds to the commercial usage of the verb to denote grasping hold of and receiving in full a sum of money which you are owed. Once again the implication is that Jesus was taken up alive without experiencing death.

This is the second interpretation mentioned by Ṭabarī. He attributes it to six early authorities: Maṭar al-Warrāq, al-Ḥasan al-Baṣrī, Ibn Jurayj, Ka'b al-Aḥbar [Yemeni Jewish convert d.32/652], Muḥammad b. Ja'far b. al-Zubayr and Ibn Zayd. It is the interpretation which Ṭabarī himself favours because of the well-attested ḥadīth in which the Prophet is said to have stated that Jesus would die after returning and killing the Antichrist. I fail to follow his reasoning on this point for it seems to me that all four interpretations are compatible with the ḥadīth.

Zamakhsharī, Rāzī and Bayḍāwī mention this interpretation without naming an authority. Rāzī, who mentions it eighth, foresees a possible objection to it: namely God's grasping Jesus from the earth would amount to the same thing as raising him into His presence, hence the words «and raise you to Myself» would be pleonastic. Rāzī's reply is that since God 'receives' [human beings] in one of two ways – by death or by causing them to ascend to heaven – He says «and raise you to Myself» in order to specify which type of 'reception' will be involved.

Ibn Kathīr attributes this interpretation to Maṭar al-Warrāq and makes no mention of the other five authorities named by Ṭabarī.

[C] It means, 'I am going to cause you to die and raise you to Myself.'

This is the third interpretation mentioned by Ṭabarī. He traces it back to three authorities. As this section of his commentary is of particular interest, I shall translate it verbatim:

> Others said the meaning of that is 'I am going to receive you (*mutawaffī-ka*) by the reception (*waffāt*) of death. Mention of those who said that:
> Muthannā told me. He said 'Abd Allah b. Ṣāliḥ told us. He said Mu'āwiya told me on the authority of 'Alī [b. a. Ṭālḥa] on the authority of Ibn 'Abbās, '[God]'s saying «I am going to receive you» means I am going to cause you to die.'
> Ibn Ḥumayd told us. He said Salma told us on the authority of Ibn Isḥāq on the authority of one who is not suspect on the authority of Wahb b. Munabbih the Yemenite that he said, 'God received (*tawaffā*) Jesus for three hours of the day until He raised him to Himself.'
> Ibn Ḥumayd told us. He said Salma told us on the authority of Ibn Isḥāq, 'The Christians allege that He received him (*tawaffā-hu*) for seven hours of the day then God brought him to life.'

It is difficult to evaluate this material. The first isnād is defective for 'Alī b. a. Ṭālḥa cannot have transmitted directly from Ibn 'Abbās. So too is the second because of the substitution of the phrase 'one who is not suspect' for the name of the traditionist. From the standpoint of later orthodoxy the reports from Wahb and Ibn Ishāq are of questionable value because both of them relied on Christian informers. It is almost certainly wrong to deduce from any of these reports that God caused Jesus to die *on the cross* for we shall see in the next chapter that Wahb, Ibn Isḥāq and Ibn al-'Abbās are all credited with teaching that a substitute was crucified.

Ṭabarī does not comment on the asānīd. He simply dismisses this interpretation on the grounds that if God had caused Jesus to die before raising him to Himself it would have necessitated Jesus' dying twice because according to aḥādīth he will die after returning to kill the Antichrist. Yet a second death is out of the question because in the Qur'ān God informs His servants only that He creates them, then causes them to die then brings them to life at the resurrection [30:40]. Once again, I fail to follow Ṭabarī's reasoning for the Qur'ān also mentions that Jesus raised the dead to life by God's permission [3:49, 5:110] and presumably the dead whom he raised had to face death a second time.

Zamakhsharī does not mention this interpretation.

Rāzī lists this interpretation second and presents it slightly differently:

> «receive you» that is cause you to die. It has been transmitted on the authority of Ibn 'Abbās and Muḥammad Ibn Isḥāq. [Those who transmitted it] said what was intended was that his enemies from amongst the Jews should not succeed in killing him. Then after that God honoured him by raising him to heaven. They disagreed concerning the three ways [in which this could have happened]:
>
> Firstly, Wahb said he was received [in death] for three hours then raised.
>
> Secondly, Ibn Isḥāq said he was received [in death] for seven hours. Then God brought him back to life and raised him.
>
> Thirdly, al-Rābi' b. Anas said that God most High received him [in death] when He raised him to heaven. God Most High has said, «God receives (*yatawaffā*) souls at the moment of their death as well as those which do not die during their sleep» [39:42].

Bayḍāwī simply says:

'And it is said, God caused him to die for seven hours, then he raised him to heaven. That is what the Christians held.'

Ibn Kathīr gives the same information as Ṭabarī in a slightly abbreviated form and adds:

Isḥāq b. Bishr said on the authority of Idris on the authority of Wahb, 'God caused him to die for three days, then resurrected him, then raised him.'

A SUPPOSED EXAMPLE OF *AL-TAQDĪM WA 'L-TA'KHĪR*

After listing the three traditional interpretations Ṭabarī mentions a fourth.

[D] It means, 'I am going to raise you to myself and purify you from those who disbelieve and cause you to die after sending you [back] down to the world.' This of course involves reversing the word order. It has to be assumed that the āya comprises an example of what is known technically as *al-taqdīm wa 'l-tal-ta'khīr* – 'putting in advance and putting later'. Ṭabarī does not name any early authority who espoused this interpretation nor does he discuss it but from his comments on 5:116f it appears that he had grounds for rejecting it.[4] This latter passage, which describes God's interrogation of Jesus, begins with the words «And when God said» (*wa-idh qāla Allah*). Moreover in the course of Jesus' reply he says to God «when you received me» (*fa-lammā tawaffayta-nī*). Despite the perfect tenses Qatāda and others argued that the interrogation still lies in the future and will only take place after the resurrection. They thought that *wa-idh qāla Allah* here meant the same as *wa-idhā qāla Allah* 'And when God will say'. In support of this they cited two early poets, Abū 'l-Najm and al-Aswad, who used *wa-idh* as the equivalent of *wa-idhā*. Ṭabarī rejected this as contrary to normal usage and followed al-Suddī in holding that the interrogation of Jesus has already taken place.

Zamakhsharī briefly mentions this interpretation of 3:55.

Rāzī deals with it last. He states that the Qur'ān contains many similar cases of *al-taqdīm wa 'l-ta'khīr*. However in the present instance, in view of the numerous other possible interpretations, he sees no reason to depart from the obvious word order, although God knows best.

Bayḍāwī does not mention this interpretation.

Ibn Kathīr states that this interpretation was advocated by Qatāda and others.

THE INTERPRETATION FAVOURED BY ZAMAKHSHARĪ, RĀZĪ AND BAYDĀWĪ

Zamakhsharī puts forward an interpretation not found in Ṭabarī. It is probably his own suggestion.

[E] It means 'I am holding you back from being killed by the unbelievers and causing you to tarry until the term I have decreed for you and causing you to die by natural causes not by being killed at their hands.'

Rāzī expresses this slightly differently:

> [It means] 'I am going to complete your life and then I will receive you [in death]. But I will not let them kill you. No, I will raise you to heaven and bring you near with the angels and I will preserve you so that they are unable to kill you.'

He seems to favour this because he gives it first and remarks that it is a good interpretation.

Bayḍāwī also favours it and quotes Zamakhsharī almost verbatim.

Ibn Kathīr ignores this interpretation presumably because it does not have the support of tradition.

FIVE FURTHER INTERPRETATIONS

Rāzī mentions five further interpretations. With the exception of the second one, which is also given by Bayḍāwī, they are not found in the other classical commentaries.

[F] The word «and» (*wa*) in the expression «I am going to receive you *and* raise you to Myself» merely serves to structure the sentence. The āya indicates that God performs the actions which are mentioned but does not indicate how or when. However it is indicated that Jesus is alive and it is established from ḥadīth that he will return to kill the Antichrist. God will 'receive' him after that. This interpretation is listed fourth by Rāzī. No authority is mentioned. The argument is not quite as specious as it sounds. In Arabic there are two words for 'and' – *fa* and *wa*. Whereas the former invariably implies that the actions which it links are consecutive, the latter does not.

[G] What is intended is 'I am going to receive you away from your desires and the pleasures of your carnal soul.' Then God said «and raise you to Myself». That was because a person who has not realised the annihilation of all that exists apart from God cannot attain the station of knowledge of God. Also when Jesus was raised to heaven his state became like the state of the angels in the extinction of lust and anger and blameworthy traits of character. This interpretation is listed fifth by Rāzī who attributes it to Abū Bakr al-Wāsiṭī (d. after 932). It is also alluded to by Bayḍāwī although he puts it slightly differently: '[I am going] to destroy in you the desires which prevent ascent to the world of the spirits.' This is a Ṣūfī interpretation and will be dealt with in Chapter 17.

[H] The verb *tawaffā* means to take something in full. As God knew that some people would imagine what He raised was Jesus' spirit not his body He used this word to indicate that He raised him completely, body and spirit, into heaven. Advocates of this interpretation allege that its correctness is indicated by another āya which says «They will not hurt you at all» [4:113]. This interpretation is listed sixth by Rāzī. No authority is mentioned.

[I] The expression «going to receive you» means going to make you like someone who is received [in death] because when Jesus was raised up to heaven all report and trace of him ceased on earth. He was like one who had been received [in death] and the application of the name to what shares most of its characteristics and qualities is admissible and good. This interpretation is listed seventh by Rāzī. No authority is mentioned.

[J] The statement is elliptical and the word 'work' has to be understood. What is meant is 'I am going to receive your *work*' in the sense of receive your work in full, 'and raise your *work* to Myself'. This is in line with what is said elsewhere in the Qur'ān, «Unto Him good works ascend» [35:10]. Thus God's intention in this āya is to announce to Jesus His acceptance of his obedience and his deeds and to make known to him that he would receive his reward for the troubles and hardships which he met with in establishing God's religion. This interpretation is listed ninth by Rāzī. No authority is mentioned.

DISCUSSION

We saw in the last chapter that, since at least the time of the Catholicos Timothy, Christian polemicists and apologists have generally assumed that in 3:55 and 5:117 the verb *tawaffā* means 'cause to die'. There are three things which can be said in their favour:

1. The other 24 instances of the verb are in some way associated with death.
2. In three instances the verb is used in connection with Muḥammad's death.
3. Although the classical commentators were unanimous that Jesus did not die *on the cross*, some of the interpretations which they mentioned – [A], [C], [D], [F] and [I] – presuppose that the verb normally means 'cause to die' or 'receive in death'.

In view of this it is hardly surprising that in recent years several cautious Christian scholars have also assumed that the normal meaning of the verb is 'cause to die'. Cragg, whose apologetic stance is overt but subtle, suggests something remarkably similar to interpretation [I] when he says that 3:55

> can well be read as the Qur'ān's clue to the inner experience of Jesus within that gathering sense of threat and rejection accompanying his ministry amid the vested interests and passions which he challenged. In his consciousness it must have seemed like an anticipation of death – death casting its shadow over his faithful course in God's Name.[5]

Räisänen, who eschews apologetics, is in effect opting for interpretation [C] when he concludes that although 4:157 states that the Jews did not kill Jesus or crucify him, 3:55 none the less implies that God somehow caused him to die and raised him into His presence.[6]

Detailed examination of the Qur'anic usage and of the exegetical tradition does, however, suggest that the issue is more complex. The verbal root *wfy* conveys the idea of 'fulfilment' or 'completion'. This idea is clearly present in forms II, IV and X. It is therefore reasonable to suppose that it is also present in form VI and that *tawaffā* means 'to receive completely' or 'to bring to completion'. Although death is normally a concomitant there is no reason why there should not be exceptions. We should also note that the agent is invariably God or His angels and that the verb is often used when a seemingly premature demise is described or envisaged. In such cases the verb may in addition be intended to convey the idea that, despite appearances to the contrary, the human life or the prophetic mission was brought to completion by God. That this is so in 3:55 seems to be implied by the use of the first person pronoun followed by the definite article instead of the finite verb. When viewed in this light, interpretations [B] and [E] gain in plausibility. Nor need much weight be given to the fact that several of the other interpretations presuppose that the verb normally means 'cause to die' or 'receive in death' for in all probability those interpretations were evolved in dialogue with Christians. For instance interpretation [D] employs an exegetical device used by Jews and Christians to interpret their own Scriptures[7] and interpretation [C] explicitly mentions Christian beliefs.

13 Muslim Interpretation Of «*shubbiha la-hum*»

In Chapter 11 I discussed the principal non-Muslim interpretations of 4:157. I will now examine how the classical commentaries deal with the key expression which I provisionally translated «a semblance was made to them».

TABARĪ

In commenting on 4:157, Ṭabarī[1] groups the early interpretations of *shubbiha la-hum* under two headings:

[A] Some said that all the disciples were made to look like Jesus and that the Jews killed one of them thinking that he was Jesus.

Under this heading he mentions two reports. The first he traces back to Wahb b. Munabbih by a single isnād:

> Ibn Ḥumayd told us. He said Ya'qūb al-Qummī told us on the authority of Harūn b. 'Antara on the authority of Wahb b. Munabbih. Wahb said:
>
> 'Jesus went into a house together with seventeen of his companions. The Jews surrounded them but when they burst in God made all the disciples look like Jesus. The pursuers, supposing that they had bewitched them, threatened to kill them all if they did not expose him. Then Jesus asked his companions which of them would purchase paradise for himself that day. One man volunteered and went out saying that he was Jesus and as God had made him look like Jesus they took him, killed him and crucified him. Thereupon «a semblance was made to them» and they thought that they had killed Jesus. The Christians likewise thought that it was Jesus who had been killed. And God raised Jesus right away.'

The second report he also traces back to Wahb b. Munabbih by a single isnād but by a different route. This version begins with an account of Jesus' last meal with his disciples in the course of which he spoke about his death. Contrary to what Ṭabarī leads us to expect, it is not said that all the disciples were made to look like Jesus. Instead we are told that after the meal they went out and were scattered:

Al-Muthannā told me concerning it. He said 'Isḥāq told us. He said Isma'īl b. 'Abd al-Karīm told us. He said 'Abd al-Ṣammad b. Ma'qil told me that he heard Wahb say:

'When God notified Jesus Son of Mary that he was to leave this world he became anxious about death and it troubled him. So he called the disciples and made a meal for them and told them, "Come to me tonight for I am in need of you." When they were gathered around him that night he made them dine and waited on them in person. When the meal was over he began to wash their hands and to help them perform the ablutions and to wipe their hands on his clothing. They were indignant about that and disliked it so he said, "If anyone refuses anything which I do tonight, he is not of me and I am not of him." So they consented to it. Then when he had finished he said, "As for what I have done to you tonight, in that I served you the meal and washed your hands in person, let it be an example for you. Since you indeed consider that I am better than you, do not be haughty in relation to each other but rather expend yourselves for each other as I have expended myself for you. As for my need for which I turn to you for help, implore God on my behalf and spare no efforts in petitioning Him in order that my term may be postponed."

'Now when they prepared themselves to petition God and intended to spare no efforts sleep took hold of them with the result that they were unable to pray. So Jesus began to awake them and to say, "Glory be to God! Will you not persevere in helping me for just one night?" They said, "By God we do not know what is wrong with us. We used to be in the habit of keeping vigil and continuing far into the night but tonight we were incapable of doing so for whenever we wanted to petition God something prevented us." Jesus said, "He will remove the shepherd and the sheep will be scattered." And he began to make similar statements to this, lamenting his fate. Then he said, "The truth is one of you will certainly disbelieve in me before the cock crows three times and one of you will certainly sell me for a paltry price and will indeed eat my price." So they went out and were scattered.

'The Jews were looking for Jesus. They took hold of Simon, one of the disciples, and they said, "This is one of his companions." And he denied it and said, "I am not one of his disciples." So they left him. Others took hold of him and he likewise denied it. Then he heard the sound of the cock and he wept and it grieved him.

'On the morning of the next day one of the disciples went to the Jews and said, "What will you give me if I lead you to the Messiah?"

He accepted their offer of thirty dirhams and led them to him. And a semblance had been made for them (*wa-kāna shubbiha 'alay-hum*) before that, and they took him and made certain of him and bound him with a cord and began to lead him and to say to him "You used to bring the dead to life and to drive away Satan and heal the jinn-possessed so why not deliver yourself from this cord?" And they spat on him and cast thorns on him until they brought him to the wood upon which they wanted to crucify him. And God raised Jesus to Himself. And they crucified the semblance which was made to them (*mā shubbiha la-hum*). And [Jesus] tarried seven [hours].

'Then his mother, and the woman whom God had freed from jinn-possession when Jesus treated her, came weeping to where the crucified [semblance] was. And Jesus came to them both and said, "Why are you weeping?" They said, "Because of You." He said, "God raised me to Himself and I came to no harm. This [corpse] is something which was «made a semblance to them». Order the disciples to meet me at such and such a place." Eleven met him at the place. Jesus missed the one who had sold him and led the Jews to him so he asked his companions about him. They said, "Because he regretted what he had done he committed suicide by strangling himself." Jesus replied, "If he had turned toward God, God would have turned toward him". Then he asked them about a young man called John (*Yuḥanna*) who followed them and he said, 'He is with you. Depart. Everyone of you will have to converse in the language of a [different] people. Let him warn them and let him summon them."'

[B] Others said that Jesus asked his companions for a volunteer. One of them accepted to have Jesus' semblance projected on him and to be killed in his place. Ṭabarī gives nine reports under this heading which can, I suggest, be subdivided into four sub-groups according to their relative complexity:

1. The eighth and ninth reports are traced back to Mujāhid and actually say no more than that the Jews crucified someone else whom they thought looked like Jesus. Is this the original core of the story? Or are these abbreviated versions of more detailed comments?
2. The first and second reports are traced back to Qatāda. They are very brief but fit Ṭabarī's summary. The fourth report which is traced back to al-Qāsim b. a. Bazza and the seventh which is traced back to Ibn Jurayj are similar.

3. The third report is traced back to al-Suddī. In addition to mentioning the projection of Jesus' image onto a volunteer and Jesus' ascension to heaven, it explains why the Jews disagreed and were in doubt. They knew that Jesus and 19 disciples had gone into the house and realised that there was one missing when they came out.
4. The fifth and sixth reports are traced back to Ibn Isḥāq. He too stresses that the Jews realised that they were a man short. He does, however, have a more accurate knowledge of the Christian tradition and he attempts to take issue with it. In one version he says that there were twelve disciples and he correctly names ten of them. The initial anachronistic reference to King David may be based on a misunderstanding of *Luke* 2:11 which speaks of Jesus' birth in the 'City of David':

Ibn Ḥumayd told us. He said Salma told us on the authority of Ibn Isḥāq. He said:

'The name of the King of the Israelites who gave orders for Jesus, himself an Israelite, to be killed, is said to have been David. When they resolved on doing that to him who was a servant of the servants of God he did not find death detestable – [although] in accordance with what was mentioned to me he did detest it – nor did he truly fear it, nor did he call upon God to remove it from him, as they allege, saying, "O God, if You avert this cup from any of Your creatures then avert it from me." And [they allege that] even his skin dripped with blood because of the torment.

So he entered the anteroom into which [the Jews] had resolved to burst in on him to kill him. Jesus was with his companions, they were thirteen in all counting him. When he was sure that they were going to burst in on him he told those of his disciples who were his companions [at the time]. They were twelve men Peter, James son of Zebedee, John the brother of James, Andrew, Philip, Bartholomew, Matthew, James son of Halqiya, Thaddeus, two youths and Judas Iscariot. Ibn Ḥumayd said that Salma said that Ibn Isḥāq said, "According to what was mentioned to me there was a man among them whose name was Sergius so there were thirteen men besides Jesus. The Christians denied it." (That is to say they denied that he was the one by whom the semblance was made (*huwa 'l-ladhī shubbiha*) to the Jews in the place of Jesus.) He said "I do not know whether he was the twelfth of these or the thirteenth." So they denied it when they avowed that the Jews crucified Jesus and [when] they disbelieved in what Muḥammad (the peace and blessing of God be upon him!) brought by way of report about it. If they were thirteen then on entering the anteroom there were fourteen of them counting Jesus. If they were twelve then on entering the anteroom there were thirteen of them counting Jesus.'

In the other version, which is introduced with an identical isnād, Ibn Isḥāq says that he was told by a Muslim convert from Christianity that after Sergius had had Jesus' semblance projected onto him, Judas saw him and did not doubt that it was Jesus:

> A man who was a Christian and became a Muslim told me that when God's message «I am going to raise you to Myself» came to Jesus he said, "O company of disciples, which of you would like to be my companion in paradise on the condition that he is made to resemble me to the people so that they kill him in place of me?" Sergius said, "I would, O Spirit of God." He said, "Sit in my seat." So he sat in it and Jesus (the blessings of God be upon him) was raised. They burst in on [Sergius] and took him and crucified him. So he was the one whom they crucified and «a semblance was made to them» through him (*bi-hi*). The number of them when they entered was known. They had seen them and counted them. So when they burst in on him they found Jesus, as they thought, and his companions, and noticed that one of them was missing. Hence he was the one «they differed» over. And they did not know Jesus until they gave Judas Iscariot (*Yūdas Rakrīyāyūtā*) thirty dirhams to point him out to them and acquaint them with him. He said to them, "When you burst in on him I shall kiss him. He will be the one whom I kiss, so seize him." Now when they burst in on him, after Jesus had been raised, Judas saw Sergius in the form of Jesus and did not doubt that it was Jesus himself. So he bent over him and kissed him. Then they seized him and crucified him. Then Judas Iscariot regretted what he had done and committed suicide by strangling himself with a rope. He is cursed amongst Christians although he had been numbered amongst Jesus' companions. Some of the Christians allege that it was Judas Iscariot who was made his semblance to them and that they crucified him despite his saying, "I am not one of his companions. I am the one who pointed him out to you!" God knows best.

After listing all the reports together with their asānīd, Ṭabarī states his preference for the two which he mentioned under the first heading on the authority of Wahb b. Munabbih. We should note that he favours them not because of their pedigree but because they are less problematic than the others. According to Wahb's first report Jesus' semblance was projected on all the disciples. According to his second report the disciples dispersed before the appearance of Jesus' semblance. Either way it is understandable why even the Christians were confused about the crucifixion. If on the other hand Jesus' semblance had been projected on a single volunteer the other disciples would have continued to see Jesus and the man with his semblance together in their midst. Therefore the semblance would only have misled the Jews who came in from the outside; Jesus' disciples would have known the truth all along.

Unfortunately, this is not the end of the matter because Ṭabarī cites traditions about the crucifixion of Jesus' semblance in the course of his comments on two other passages, one which occurs earlier than 4:157 and one which occurs later. First, there is his comment on 3:54 «And they schemed and God schemed and God is the best of schemers».[2] In dealing with this āya Ṭabarī does not mention Wahb b. Munabbih. He simply cites al-Suddī's account of how Jesus' semblance was projected onto a single volunteer. Are we to assume then, that Ṭabarī commented on the whole Qur'ān in sequence and that between commenting on 3:54 and 4:157 he changed his mind because he came to hear of many more traditional comments including those of Wahb? That is possible but unlikely. It is much more probable that he cited only al-Suddī in his comments on 3:54 because as far as he knew only al-Suddī was on record as mentioning the substitute specifically in connection with that āya. In other words the theory that a substitute was crucified first became an established element in the exegesis of 4:157 and was subsequently invoked by al-Suddī to explain 3:54.

The other āya is 61:14: «O you who believe, be God's helpers as when Jesus the Son of Mary said to the disciples, 'Who will be my helpers towards God?' And the disciples said, 'We are God's helpers.' Some of the Children of Israel believed and others disbelieved. Then we aided those who had believed against their enemy and they became pre-eminent.»[3] Once again Ṭabarī makes no mention of Wahb b. Munabbih. Here too he simply cites one tradition of how Jesus' semblance was projected onto a single volunteer. This time, however, it is a tradition which is not reported in his comments on 4:157. I shall give it in full including the isnād:

'Abū al-Sā'ib told me. He said Abū Mu'āwiya told us on the

authority of al-A'mash on the authority of al-Minhāl on the authority of Sa'īd b. Jubayr on the authority of Ibn 'Abbās. He said:

'When God desired to raise Jesus to heaven twelve men who were Jesus' companions were in a house. Jesus came out to them from a spring in the house and his head was dripping with water. And he said, "One of you will disbelieve in me twelve times after having believed in me". Then he said "Which of you will have my semblance projected upon him and be killed in my place and share my exalted rank?" A youth who was the youngest of them in years stood up and said, "I will". Jesus told him to sit down. Then he repeated his request and the youth again stood up and said, "I will". Jesus said, "Yes you are the man". The semblance of Jesus was projected onto him and Jesus was raised to heaven from a skylight in the house.

A search party came from the Jews and they took his semblance (*shabah*) and killed him and crucified him. One of them disbelieved twelve times after he had believed in him. They split into three groups. One group said, "God was amongst us (what God wished) then He was raised up to heaven" – they were the Jacobites [i.e. the Monophysites]. One group said "The Son of God was amongst us (what God wished) then He raised him to Himself" – they were the Nestorians. One group said "God's servant and messenger was amongst us (what God wished) then He raised him to himself" – they were the Muslims. And the disbelieving parties triumphed over the Muslims and killed them. Islam did not cease being blotted out until God sent Muḥammad, the peace and blessings of God be upon him.'

ZAMAKHSHARĪ

The two traditions reported by Zamakhsharī in his comments on 4:157 are not identical with any of those which we have encountered.[4] Unfortunately he does not mention on whose authority they were transmitted. The first tradition is of the same type as those in Ṭabarī's group [B] and describes how Jesus' semblance was projected onto a volunteer:

> It is related that a band of Jews reviled him and his mother so he prayed against them saying, 'Our God you are my Lord, by your word you created me. Our God curse those Jews [cf. 5:78] who

have reviled me and my mother.' So God transformed those who had reviled them into monkeys and pigs. So the Jews agreed to kill him. [However] God informed him that he would raise him to heaven and purify him [cf. 3:55] from the company of the Jews. So he said to his companions, 'Which of you will consent to have my semblance cast upon him so that he is killed and crucified and enters paradise?' A man of them said 'I [will]'. God projected his semblance upon him and he was killed and crucified.

In the second tradition the semblance is projected onto the *face* of the betrayer:

And it is said that there was a man who feigned belief in Jesus so when they wanted to kill Jesus he said, 'I will point him out to you.' When this hypocrite entered Jesus' house God raised Jesus and projected his semblance onto him. So they burst in on him and killed him supposing that he was Jesus. Then they disagreed and some of them said, 'He is a god, it is not true that he has been killed'. Some of them said, 'He has been killed and crucified'. Some of them said, 'If this was Jesus then where is our companion? And if this is our companion then where is Jesus?' Some of them said, 'He has been raised to heaven.' And some of them said, 'The face is Jesus' face but the body is that of our companion.'

Zamakhsharī then attempts to determine the grammatical subject of *shubbiha*. [The verb is the third person singular masculine perfect passive of *shabbaha* 'to make similar', 'to make resemble'.] He considers three possibilities:

1. The subject is the Messiah. The objection to this is that the Messiah is the one who was resembled not the one who resembled.
2. The subject is the person whom they killed. The objection to this that the person whom they killed has not been mentioned.
3. The verb is impersonal. It is like the common expression *khuyyila la-hu* ('It seemed to him'). It is as though what was said were (*waqaʿa la-hum al-tashbīhu*) ('the resemblance occurred to them').

Zamakhsharī seems to favour the first because he does not put forward any objection to it. Nevertheless he reconsiders the second and deems it admissible on the grounds that the person whom they killed is implied in the statement «We killed . . .» [4:156]. It is as though what was said were 'The person whom they killed (*man qatalū-hu*) was made to resemble [the Messiah] for them.'

Despite apparently being open to the possibility that the verb *shubbiha* is impersonal, Zamakhsharī seems not to have doubted that Jesus' semblance was projected onto someone.[5] For in commenting on 3:54 he writes:

> «And God schemed» in that He raised Jesus into heaven and projected his semblance onto the one who wanted him to be taken by force so that he was killed.[6]

RĀZĪ

Rāzī first mentions the projection of Jesus' semblance when commenting on «Who will be helpers in God's cause?» [3:52].[7] He explains that some think that Jesus spoke these words when he called his disciples from being fishermen but that others think that the context was the end of his ministry when the Jews were set on killing him. According to him, those who take the latter view have two options:

1. They can link Jesus' summons with his offer of paradise to whichever of the 12 disciples volunteered to have his semblance projected on him.
2. They can interpret it as a summons to fight because of what is said in 61:14.

In connection with the first option he mentions that, according to the Christian Gospel, after the Jews arrested Jesus, Simon drew his sword and cut off the high priest's servant's ear but Jesus healed it.

The projection of Jesus' semblance is next mentioned in the comments on «And God schemed» [3:54].[8] Rāzī gives five possible explanations. The first is similar to the tradition which Ṭabarī attributes to Ibn al-'Abbās but it has some novel features. The second is reminiscent of one of the traditions mentioned by Zamakhsharī. The others are in a different vein. I will give only the salient features:

1. The King of the Jews wanted to kill Jesus but Gabriel never left him for an hour which is the meaning of «And We strengthened him with the Holy Spirit» [2:87]. The angel made Jesus enter a room and made him escape by the skylight. His semblance had previously been projected onto someone else and that person was crucified. Those present split into three groups who revered Jesus as God, the Son of God and the servant and messenger of God respectively.
2. The twelve disciples were gathered in a house. One of them

indicated to the Jews where Jesus was. Jesus was raised and they crucified the hypocrite thinking him to be Jesus because his semblance had been projected on him.
3. According to Ibn Isḥāq, after Jesus was raised into heaven the Jews persecuted the disciples. However, the Roman Emperor became a Christian, hid the crucified body, venerated the wood of the cross and punished the Jews.
4. God gave the King of Persia authority over them and he killed them.
5. God caused His religion to triumph.

When commenting on 3:55, Rāzī states that the wording of 4:157 indicates that God projected Jesus' semblance onto someone else. He then mentions a number of rational objections to this and attempts to refute them.[9]

(1) If one man's semblance can be projected onto another, then so-called eyewitness evidence must be treated with scepticism. Perhaps even the Companions of Muḥammad were deluded when they thought that they were transmitting instructions which he had given them, for there can be no certainty that it really was Muḥammad whom they saw. But if such scepticism is in order the whole edifice of Muslim sacred law will be undermined.

Rāzī's reply is that God does have the power to give one person the appearance of another. Nevertheless God has an habitual practice which he normally sticks to. His intervention to save Jesus is, like all miracles, an exception. It should not therefore lead to generalised doubt.

(2) God ordered Gabriel to look after Jesus in all circumstances. The tip of one of his wings would have been sufficient to defend the entire world against the collective opposition of all humanity. So why did the angel not kill Jesus' enemies or inflict them with illness or paralysis so that they were prevented from laying hands on him?

Rāzī's reply is that if Gabriel had repulsed the enemies of Jesus, or if God had given to Jesus himself the power to repel them, the miracle would have been reduced to an irresistible constraint (*iljā'*), and that was not possible. (The point here is that, from an orthodox Muslim point of view, miracles require a specific divine intervention. They do not stem from a capability bestowed by God on a creature.)[10]

(3) God could simply have snatched Jesus from his pursuers and raised him to heaven. What was the interest in projecting his sem-

blance on someone else thereby sending an unfortunate individual to his death for no purpose.

Rāzī's reply is that a miracle was called for and a miracle required this sort of ruse. (To us this sounds rather lame but we must remember that as an Ash'arite he would have strongly disapproved of the question in the first place. Who are we to argue whether or not God's acts are just!)[11]

(4) In projecting the semblance of Jesus onto another person God threw men into ignorance and doubt.

Rāzī's reply is that Jesus' disciples were present. They knew what happened and could have dispelled the doubt. (We should note that this reply does not take Wahb's versions of the story into account. We saw earlier that Ṭabarī favoured those versions precisely because they explained why even the disciples were deluded.)

(5) Why did the disciples not illuminate subsequent generations about what happened? The Christians, who have spread throughout the earth, are animated by an intense love for Jesus and are given to exaggeration in everything to do with him. Yet they declare that the disciples saw him dead and were witnesses of his crucifixion. For Muslims to deny this is to attack the solidity of a universal tradition transmitted from generation to generation (*tawātur*). Now to attack such a tradition leads necessarily to attacking the prophetic mission of Muḥammad and Jesus, even their existence and that of all other prophets.

This is a very serious criticism but Rāzī's knows how to deal with it. Those present at the time of the crucifixion were few in number. It is possible for a small group of people to prevaricate. Consequently if a universal tradition transmitted from generation to generation is based ultimately on the testimony of a very small group it cannot be the basis of reliable knowledge.

(6) The universal tradition among Christians is that the individual who was crucified remained alive for quite a long time after the crucifixion. If that individual had been someone other than Jesus he would surely have declared it. The news would have spread and would have been transmitted. Yet we find nothing of that.

This objection reinterprets the Christian reports about Jesus' resurrection in terms of his substitute's having survived crucifixion. Rāzī seems not to take the objection very seriously. He says that even if we admit that the crucified person was preserved from death in answer to Jesus' prayer, it could still be the case that he kept quiet and did not say anything about what had happened.

Having replied to the six objections Rāzī concludes:

> In sum, these questions are things to which one can give significations that are admissible from certain points of view. But as it has been solidly established by a decisive miracle that Muḥammad is reliable in everything which he teaches us about Jesus, it is impossible that these questions, although they are entirely admissible, should become objections to the decisive text of the Qur'ān. God is the Master who guides in the good direction.

This seems to imply that the text of the Qur'ān necessitates belief in the projection of Jesus' semblance onto someone. Yet when Rāzī deals explicitly with 4:157 he takes a more liberal view. He repeats Zamakhsharī's grammatical discussion of *shubbiha la-hum* almost verbatim but without attributing it to him. Then he repeats the first and fifth of the rational objections wording them slightly differently. His answer to these objections is that the schools of ulama differ. There are two approaches as follows.

[A] Many of the speculative theologians say that when God caused Jesus to ascend into His presence the Jewish authorities feared a revolt. They therefore took someone else and crucified him making him out to be Jesus. The people were easily duped because they did not know Jesus except by name. The Christian tradition that it was Jesus who was crucified originated with the testimony of very few people who probably agreed to propagate what they knew to be untrue.

[B] According to others God projected Jesus' semblance onto someone else. In which case there are four possibilities:

1. Jesus was in a house with his disciples. The leader of the Jews sent Ṭīṭāyūs to bring him out to be killed. When he entered the house God caused Jesus to ascend through the roof and projected his semblance onto him so that he was the one who was killed and crucified.
2. They appointed someone to watch Jesus. When Jesus went to a mountain and ascended to heaven his semblance was projected onto that person and it was he who was crucified.
3. The semblance was projected onto one of the twelve who volunteered.
4. The semblance was projected onto a hypocrite who feigned discipleship.

BAYḌĀWĪ

In commenting on 3:54 Bayḍāwī assumes that God's plotting refers to His causing Jesus to ascend and projecting his likeness onto someone else.[12]

In commenting on 4:157 he repeats the two traditions mentioned by Zamakhsharī in that context. Then he mentions the tradition about the Jew Ṭīṭānūs which he probably derived from Rāzī despite the different spelling of the name. He also repeats Zamakhsharī's grammatical discussion in summary form and then adds: 'or it may be that [in actual fact] nobody was killed although it was falsely claimed and spread about that [Jesus] had been.'[13]

IBN KATHĪR

In the course of his comments on 4:157 (and more briefly in his comments on 3:52–4) Ibn Kathīr gives what is perhaps his own paraphrase based on several traditional reports and indirect knowledge of the gospels.[14] He narrates that the King of Damascus, who was a worshipper of the stars, was informed that Jesus was leading people astray. He instructed his deputy in Jerusalem to crucify him and put thorns on his head. On the eve of the Sabbath the deputy went to the house where Jesus and 12, 13 or 17 of his companions had gathered. Then follows the familiar account of how Jesus' semblance was projected onto a young volunteer who was subsequently arrested after Jesus himself had been taken up. A novel feature is that the arrest and crucifixion are said to have taken place at night-time which explains why the Jews were so easily mistaken. The Jews boasted that they had crucified Jesus. Only those Christians who had been in the house knew that this was incorrect. The others, who were ignorant and not very intelligent, believed the Jews. Ibn Kathīr adds that it is said that Mary sat beneath the one who had been crucified and wept and that he addressed her. God knows best.

Ibn Kathīr's principal treatment of the traditions concerning the crucifixion of a substitute occurs in the course of his comments on 4:158.[15] Here his primary source seems to be Ṭabarī. Because he attaches great importance to the pedigree of traditional interpretations, he gives precedence to the report which Ṭabarī mentioned in his comments on 61:14 and which he traced to Ibn al-'Abbās. He furnishes it with two more isnāds. One begins with Ibn abī Ḥātim and Aḥmad b. Sinān but is identical with Ṭabarī's from al-A'mash onwards. He comments that it is sound to Ibn 'Abbās. The other begins with Al-Nasā'i (d.303/915 compiler of one of the six canonical collections of aḥādīth) and Abū Kurayb but is identical with Ṭabarī's from Abū Mu'āwiya onwards. Having made out the best possible case for the report from Ibn 'Abbās, he cites the two reports from Wahb and explicitly mentions that he has derived these from Ṭabarī. In both instances he comments that the sequence of names is very rare. Then, again drawing on Ṭabarī, he gives the two reports from Ibn Isḥaq but without comment. He does not mention that Ṭabarī gives seven other reports.

DISCUSSION

Despite differences of opinion about the details the commentators were agreed that 4:157 denies that Jesus was crucified. The most widespread view was that it implies that the Jews erroneously crucified Jesus' 'semblance' and not Jesus himself. Speculative thinkers offered more mundane explanations but this was probably a later development, an attempt to overcome rational objections to the projection of Jesus' semblance onto a substitute.

Ayoub has suggested that the substitute theory itself passed through several stages of development.[16] Initially it was envisaged that the substitute was a volunteer. In the next stage 'there was a growing interest in historical accounts' and the use of 'gospel materials and hagiography'. In time there developed a preference for 'punishment substitutionism' which envisaged the crucifixion of the betrayer or of the person sent to arrest Jesus. Finally by the sixth/twelfth century there was an attempt 'to interpret the entire passage in one complete story'. Ayoub seems to be right about the final stage. He is also correct when he points to the development of a preference for punishment substitution. This development probably occurred in response to the objections which were voiced to the crucifixion of an innocent party. We should note, however, that the actual theory of punishment substitution – as distinct from the Muslim preference for the theory – is much more ancient and is traced back by Ṭabarī to the time of Ibn Isḥāq. Slightly more questionable is Ayoub's suggestion that the reports which envisage the substitution of a volunteer are earlier than those which make use of gospel materials. This must be discussed in greater detail.

If we take the material in Ṭabarī at face value, the most ancient tradition is the one which describes how the semblance was projected onto a single volunteer and how Jesus was raised through the skylight of the house. This is the only tradition which is traced back to a Companion, namely Ibn al-'Abbās. The traditions which make use of gospel materials are traced back to Wahb and Ibn Isḥāq, that is to say they ostensibly originated in the first half of the second/eighth century. On this reckoning, Ayoub is correct. However, if we examine the three asānīd supporting the tradition attributed to Ibn al-'Abbās – the one isnād in Ṭabarī and the two in Ibn Kathīr – we find that they all include the name of the Kūfan traditionist al-A'mash [d.148/764]. It is therefore possible that in actual fact this tradition also originated in the first half of the second/eighth century but in Kūfa where speculation about the Shī'ite Imams was already rife. In Chapter 16 we shall encounter an additional piece of evidence which seems to point in this direction. I presume that it was considerations of this kind, together with the brief reports which Ṭabarī attributes to the Iraqis Qatāda and al-Suddī, which led Massignon to conclude that the substitute theory itself originated in Shī'ite circles.[17] However, we should note that the asānīd supporting the traditions which make use of gospel materials do not include the names of any Kūfan traditionists. Moreover these traditions furnish evidence that there were Christians alive in that period who denied that Jesus had been crucified. For this reason I am inclined to regard these traditions as primary and those which mention a volunteer as a secondary development catalysed by Shī'ite speculation.

The relationship between the Christians known to Wahb and Ibn Isḥāq and the Christians who lived in Medina a century earlier is more problematic. I am, however, impressed by the similarity of the Muslim traditions which make use of gospel materials to the Gnostic speculations which I mentioned in Chapter 11. If these Gnostic speculations, which originated long before the rise of Islam, survived into the first half of the second/eighth century, the probability that they were in circulation during Muḥammad's life-time is substantially increased.

14 Creating Birds from Clay and Raising the Dead to Life

There are two passages in the Qur'ān which give a summary list of Jesus' miracles. The first occurs in the course of the angelic annunciation to Mary:

> «And [He shall appoint him] a messenger to the Children of Israel [saying] 'Lo! I have come to you with a sign from your Lord. Lo! I create for you from clay something resembling the form of birds and I blow into it and it becomes birds by God's leave. And I heal the blind fom birth and the leper and I bring the dead to life by God's leave. And I declare to you what you eat and what you store up in your houses. Surely in that there is a sign for you if you are believers. (3:49)»

The second passage is very similar but this time it is retrospective. It is part of what God said to Jesus after raising him into His presence:

> «When God said, 'O Jesus Son of Mary remember my favour to you and your mother, how I strengthened you with the Holy Spirit so that you spoke to mankind when you were in the cradle and when you were of mature age. [Remember] when I taught you the Scripture, Wisdom, the Torah and the Gospel and when you created from clay something resembling the form of birds by My leave and when you blew into it and it became birds by My leave and you healed the blind fom birth and the leper by My leave and brought forth the dead by My leave . . .'» (5:110)

It is the miracle of the birds and the raising of the dead which have attracted the most attention. I shall therefore concentrate on them.

SOME NON-MUSLIM RESPONSES TO THE QUR'ANIC MIRACLES OF JESUS

Christian polemicists and apologists have frequently suggested that by attributing these miracles to Jesus the Qur'ān implies that he was allowed to exercise divine prerogatives.[1] Several things can be said in favour of this claim. First, the verb used to denote Jesus' 'creating' is *khalaqa*, a verb which the Qur'ān reserves almost exclusively for God's activity.[2] Second, the substance which Jesus employed was 'clay' (*ṭīn*), the very substance from which, according to the Qur'ān, God created Man.[3] Third, the verb *nafakha* used to indicate Jesus' 'blowing' into the birds is used elsewhere of God's blowing his Spirit into Man at the creation[4] and into Mary when she conceived.[5] Finally there are a number of passages in the Qur'ān which stress that it is God who gives life and causes death. On the other hand, one should of course notice that the Qur'ān stresses that Jesus performed the miracles «by God's leave». Nevertheless, Kenneth Cragg has suggested that even this proviso is potentially a mediating feature between the Qur'ān and the New Testament because the latter asserts that everything which Jesus said and did was by divine authority and permission.[6]

Christian historians have been more concerned to discover the source from which Muḥammad derived his information. The canonical gospels mention three people whom Jesus raised from the dead: Jairus' daughter, the widow of Nain's son and Lazarus.[7] They do not mention the miracle of the birds. The closest pre-Islamic parallel to this is found in an apocryphal writing known as *The Infancy Story of Thomas*:

> When this boy Jesus was five years old he was playing at the ford of a brook, and he gathered together into pools the water that flowed by, and made it at once clean, and commanded it by his word alone. He made soft clay and fashioned from it twelve sparrows. And it was the Sabbath when he did this, and there were also many other children playing with him. Now when a certain Jew saw what Jesus was doing in his play on the Sabbath he at once went and told his father Joseph: 'See, your child is at the brook, and has taken clay and fashioned twelve birds and has profaned the Sabbath.' And when Joseph came to the place and saw [it], he cried out to him, saying: 'Why do you do on the Sabbath what ought not to be done?' But Jesus clapped his hands and cried to the sparrows: 'Off with you!' And the sparrows took flight and went away chirping.[8]

The parallel is not exact. In the Qur'ān Jesus creates birds; here he creates twelve sparrows. In the Qur'ān he blows into them; here he claps his hands and issues an oral command. Nevertheless, it is striking that, in the Qur'ān as in the *The Infancy Story of Thomas*, two distinct stages are envisaged: Jesus' fashioning the birds from clay and his bringing them to life. Moreover the second Qur'anic version somewhat puzzlingly mentions God's permission in connection with both stages. This makes admirable sense if on the basis of the *The Infancy Story of Thomas* we assume that the fashioning of the birds involved an infringement of the Sabbath. In other words the Qur'ān seems to expect prior knowledge of the story on the part of the hearers. Independent confirmation of this is given by Ibn Isḥāq, the biographer of the Prophet. He refers to the miracle of the birds and the raising of the dead in his account of the beliefs of the Christians of Najrān who sent an embassy to Muḥammad at Medina:

> They argue that he is God because he used to raise the dead, and heal the sick, and declare the unseen; and make clay birds and then breathe into them that they flew away; and all this was by the command of God Almighty, «We will make him a sign to men.» (19:21)[9]

In view of this it seems likely that the Qur'anic revelations about Jesus' miracles were intended as a corrective to Christian teaching. The Qur'ān does not deny that Jesus performed the miracles which the Christians attributed to him but it puts them in perspective by stressing that they were performed «by God's leave», that is to say they are not proofs of his divinity.

Further light is thrown on this phrase when the miracles are considered in the context of Muḥammad's own prophetic ministry. According to the Qur'ān the revelations which Muḥammad received were likewise brought down to him by God's leave (2:97). Moreover, like Jesus' miracles, these revelations are described as signs (2:110).

THE CLASSICAL SUNNĪ COMMENTATORS AND THE MIRACLE OF THE BIRDS[10]

The commentators deal at length with a number of technical matters connected with syntax, minor variant readings and the morphology of Arabic nouns. They also report a tradition traced back to Ibn Isḥāq which describes how Jesus created a bird from clay when he was still a school-boy and others attributed to Ibn Jurayj and Wahb which allege that what Jesus created was a bat. For further details reference should be made to my article in *Muslim World*.[11] Here I will simply summarise what Zamakhsharī and Rāzī say about the verb *khalaqa* ('create') and the latter's discussion of the significance of Jesus' blowing into the birds.

Whereas Ṭabarī leaves the verb *khalaqa* without comment, Zamakhsharī glosses it with *qaddara* which generally means 'determine' or 'make in proportion'. Elsewhere he defines 'creating' (*khalq*) as 'the bringing of a thing into being by proportioning it and making it regular' (*ījādu 'l-shay'a 'ala taqdīrin wa-istiwā'in*). In support of this he cites the expression 'to fashion a sandal' (*khalaqa 'l-na'ala*).[12]

Rāzī's treatment of the verb *khalaqa* is much more extensive. He argues that it has the meaning of *taqdīr* (determining, measuring), *taswīya* (arranging, making regular) and *taṣwīr* (fashioning, representing). In support of this he mentions several non-Quranic expressions including the one cited by Zamakhsharī. He also adduces evidence from pre-Islamic poetry such as the words of Zuhayr b. Abī Sulmā in his eulogy of Harim Ibn Sinān:

> You indeed cut what you have measured (*khalaqta*).
> Some of the people measure (*yakhluqu*) then do not cut.[13]

The most important evidence is, however, that of the Qur'ān itself. First, in one instance God is spoken of as «the best of creators (*aḥsanu 'l-khālaqīna*)» (23:14). Since human beings cannot be creators in the sense of 'causing to be' (*takwīn*) and 'originating' (*ibdā'*) the word 'creator' (*khāliq*) should here be interpreted in terms of 'determining' and 'arranging'. Second, there are three āyas where *khalaqa* and its derivatives are applied to lying (29:17, 26:137 and 38:7). Rāzī suggests that this is because the liar determines and fashions a falsehood in his imagination. Third, there is the evidence of the two āyas in which Jesus is the subject of the verb. Finally there is the Qur'anic assertion that God «determined (*khalaqa*) for you all that is in the earth» (2:29). Rāzī argues that the perfect tense of *khalaqa* indicates God's activity in the past. Yet it is nonsense to suppose that everything that is on the earth at present had already been 'created' by God if what is meant by this is that He had already brought it into being and originated it. The meaning must be rather that He 'determined' or 'predetermined' (*qaddara*) everything.

None of the five commentaries consulted links Jesus' blowing into the birds with God's blowing His Spirit into Man. Rāzī does, however, mention the possibility that Jesus' breath was in some way special. What he says in the context of commenting on 3:49 is tantalisingly brief and ambiguous. He remarks that some theologians claim that this āya indicates that the spirit is a fine substance like the wind and is thus presented as breath. He indicates that there is debate about whether it is permissible to say that God endowed Jesus' breath with particular efficacy so that when he blew into things it caused them to come to life.[14] He espouses the alternative view, namely that God created life by His own power at the moment when Jesus blew. In support of this he adduces two āyas from the Qur'ān. First, God is described as «[He] who created (*khalaqa*) death and life» (67:2). Second, when Abraham was involved in a dispute he said, «My Lord is He who gives life and causes death» (2:258). Abraham's argument would have been worthless if this were true of anyone else. So far Rāzī's position is I think perfectly clear but he does not stop at this point. He adds that according to the Qur'ān Jesus was begotten solely by Gabriel's blowing into Mary and that therefore, since Gabriel is a pure spirit and a pure spiritual being, it of course follows that Jesus' breath was life and spirit.

TRADITIONS ABOUT RAISING THE DEAD WHICH ARE CITED IN THIS CONTEXT

Ṭabarī's comments on the references to Jesus' raising the dead are very brief. In the course of dealing with 3:49 he records that Wahb alleged that sometimes Jesus would heal as many as 5,000 sick people and that these healings were invariably brought about by petitioning God.

Zamakhsharī states that it is narrated that Jesus raised to life Sām b. Nūḥ while people were watching and that they said it was sorcery and asked him for a sign.[15] Sām b. Nūḥ is evidently Shem the son of Noah. Muslims were well aware that he had died long before Jesus' time.[16] I am unable to trace the source of the story that Jesus raised him from the dead.

Rāzī refers to the tradition from Wahb and then mentions that according to al-Kalbī Jesus used to raise the dead [by invoking God] with [the words] 'O Living One, O Everlasting One'. He also refers explicitly to three people whom Jesus raised:

> He raised to life 'Ādhar who was a friend of his. He called Sām b. Nūḥ from his grave and he came out alive. He passed by the dead son of an old woman so he petitioned God and the [man] came down from the bier, returned to his family and continued to live and a child was subsequently begotten by him.

'Ādhar is the Arabic form of Lazarus. Sām b. Nūḥ we have already dealt with. The dead son of the old woman sounds like the widow of Nain's son but this is the only place in which I have come across the delightful ending to the story.[17]

Ibn Kathīr gives by far the most developed tradition of how Jesus used to raise the dead. It seems to imply that Jesus already knew parts of the Qur'ān or that parts of the Qur'ān were identical with the Gospel which was revealed to him:

> Ibn Abī Ḥātim has said, My father told us, Mālik b. Isma'īl told us, Muḥammad b. Ṭalḥa – he means Ibn Maṣrif – told us on the authority of Abū Bishr on the authority of Abū 'l-Hudhayl. He said:
>
> 'When Jesus Son of Mary (on him be peace!) wanted to bring the dead to life, he used to pray two prostrations. In the first he would recite [the ṣūra which begins] «Blessed is He in whose hand is the sovreignty» [67:1] and in the second [he would recite the ṣūra which begins] «*Alif lām mīm*» [32:1f] [and is called] *the Prostration*.[18] When he had finished them both he would extol God and laud Him. Then he would invoke the seven names: O Eternal One, O Hidden One, O Enduring One, O Peerless One, O Separate One, O Unique, O Self-Subsistent One. If distress afflicted him he invoked another seven: O Living One, O Everlasting One, O God, O Beneficent, O Endowed with Majesty and Nobility, O Light of the Heavens and the Earth and what is between them and Lord of the Mighty Throne, O Lord. This used to have an astounding effect.'

The expression 'Ibn Abū Ḥātim has said'[19] indicates that this is taken from a written work, presumably one which was compiled by the traditionist Ibn Abī Ḥātim of Raiy (d.327/939). The authority to whom the tradition is traced back should probably be identified as Ghālib b. al-Hudhayl al-Ūdī Abū al-Hudhayl of Kūfa who ranks as a Successor.[20] The content of the tradition is best understood in the light of popular beliefs about the power of the divine names and about the merits of reciting certain ṣūras of the Qur'ān. For the former we may compare the story which al-Qushayrī narrates concerning the merchant who was attacked by brigands; after the threefold repetition of a similar invocation he was delivered by a green-clad cavalier on a brilliant white horse who descended from the third heaven.[21] Beliefs about the merits of reciting certain ṣūras are enshrined in the ḥadīth literature. According to two traditions preserved by Ibn Ḥanbal, the Prophet never went to sleep without first reciting ṣūras 67 and 32[22] and he declared that reciting the former would procure forgiveness.[23] I know of no instance where Muslims have recited it in order actually to raise the dead but there is a ḥadīth of very weak authority which mentions how it preserved someone from being taken to hell. The man knew only this ṣūra and when he was buried it rose up against the angel of death and interceded with God on the man's behalf pleading that if the man were burned in hell it would perish with him in the flames.[24]

FURTHER TRADITIONS ABOUT JESUS' RAISING THE DEAD

In the course of commenting on the words attributed to Jesus in 3:52 «'Who are my helpers towards God?'» Ṭabarī cites a long tradition which mentions among other things how Jesus brought to life a king's son, a sheep, a calf and a king:

> What Mūsa b. Harūn told me. He said 'Amr told us. He said Asbāṭ told us on the authority of al-Suddī:
>
> 'When God sent Jesus with the order to summon the Children of Israel they rejected him and drove him out. So he departed with his mother and roamed the earth with her. Now they alighted in a certain locality where a [Jewish] man offered them hospitality and treated them very well. This city was ruled by a king who was a brutal tyrant. One day the man returned home in a sorrowful and distressed state. Mary was with his wife at the time and said to her: "What is the matter with your husband? I see that he is sorrowful."'

The wife confided in her that it would soon be her husband's turn to feed the king and his soldiers and that he did not have sufficient means to do it. Mary told her not to worry and begged Jesus to intercede on the man's behalf. Jesus was reluctant to help because he foresaw that it would have evil consequences. Nevertheless he complied with his mother's request and gave instructions that when the time drew near the man should fill his cooking pots and casks with water and then inform him. This the man did and in answer to Jesus' prayer the contents of the cooking pots turned into meat, rich gravy and bread whereas the contents of the casks turned into wine beyond compare. The king was most impressed and forced his host to reveal the origin of the wine,

Now the king had a son whom he had loved more than anyone and whom he had hoped would succeed him but he had died a few days earlier. He reflected that a man who changed water into wine by petitioning God would undoubtedly have his request granted if he petitioned God on behalf of his son in order to bring him back to life. So he called for Jesus, spoke with him and asked him to petition God so that his son would come back to life. Jesus replied that that should not be done because if his son came back to life evil would occur. Since the king affirmed that he was not worried about what might happen Jesus said to him: "If I make him come to life again will you let me and my mother leave and go wherever we like?" The king replied that he would. Jesus petitioned God and the young man came back to life. The king's subjects, perceiving that the son was alive, plotted together and took arms saying, "Look how the king who devoured us right up until his old age now wants to see his son succeed him so that he can devour us in the same way!" And they fought one another.

Jesus and his mother departed accompanied by their Jewish companion. The Jew had two loaves with him, Jesus had one. Jesus suggested that they should share their food. The Jew accepted but when he saw that Jesus had only one loaf he regretted doing so. While Jesus was asleep he began to eat one of his loaves. Hardly had he swallowed a mouthful when Jesus asked him what he was doing. "Nothing at all", replied the Jew, who carried on until he had finished eating the bread. In the morning when Jesus asked him to bring his food he came with only a single loaf. "Where is the other loaf?" asked Jesus. "I never had more than one," he replied. Jesus kept silent and they departed.

On the way they passed by a shepherd. Jesus called him and said: "O shepherd slaughter one of your sheep for us." The shepherd agreed and told him to send his companion to fetch it. Jesus sent the Jew who came back with the sheep. They slit its throat and roasted it. Jesus said to the Jew: "Eat but be sure not to break a single bone." They both ate and when they were satisfied Jesus threw the bones into the skin and struck it with his staff saying: "Get up by God's leave." The sheep stood up bleating and Jesus said: "Shepherd! Take your sheep!" "Who are you?" the shepherd asked him. He said: "I am Jesus son of Mary." "You are a magician!" he said to him and fled. Then Jesus said to the Jew: "By Him who brought to life this sheep after we had eaten it, how many loaves did you have?" The Jew swore that he had had only one.'

After a similar incident in which Jesus brought a calf to life, the Jew still maintained that he had had only one loaf.

'They continued until they alighted in a certain locality. The Jew lodged at one end and Jesus lodged at the other. The Jew took a staff like Jesus' staff and said, "Now it is I who will bring the dead to life." Now the king of that city was gravely ill. The Jew began summoning anyone who desired a physician and the news was brought to the king. So the Jew was informed about the king's ailment. He said: "Bring me in to him and I will heal him. If you think that he has already died I will bring him back to life. He was told, "The king's ailment has thwarted all the efforts of the physicians before you. There is no physician who is able to cure him. The only effect that their remedies have is that he gives orders for them to be crucified." The Jew said: "Bring me in to him and I will heal him." So they brought him in and he struck the king's foot with his staff so that he died. Then, the king being dead, he set about striking him with his staff and saying: "Get up by God's leave." So he was taken to be crucified. Then Jesus arrived and approached him. He had already been raised aloft on the wood. Jesus said: "If I bring your companion back to life for you will you leave my companion alone?" They said: "Yes". And God brought the king back to life for Jesus and he got up and caused the Jew to be brought down from the cross. The Jew said: "O Jesus you are the man who has done me the greatest kindness. I will never be separated from you."

Jesus said – according to what Muḥammad b. al Ḥusayn b. Mūsa told us. He said Aḥmad b. al-Mufaḍḍal told us. He said Asbāṭ told us on the authority of al-Suddī – to the Jew, "I implore you by Him who brought the sheep and the calf to life after we had eaten them and who brought this man back to life and who made you come down from the cross after you had been raised aloft to be crucified, how many loaves did you have?" The Jew swore by all that that he had only had a single loaf. "All right", said Jesus.

They continued on their way. When they passed by a treasure which the lions and wolves had dug up the Jew asked whose it was. Jesus told him to leave it alone because it would fall to people who would perish because of it. His companion who coveted these riches but feared to disobey him continued with him. At that moment four men passed by the treasure. When they saw it they agreed to take it. Two of them told the other two to go into town and buy some food, drink and riding animals to carry all these goods. So the two men went off and bought riding animals, food and drink. One of them said to his fellow, "What if we were to put poison in our two companions' food so that when they ate it they died and we had all the wealth between us. Shall we do that?" He said: "Yes". The other two said to one another, "When they bring us the food let us both rise against our companions and kill them. Then we will have the food and the riding animals between us." When they brought them their food they rose up and killed them. They sat down to the food, ate some of it and died. Jesus knew about it and he said to the Jew, "Bring the treasure out so that we can share it." Seeing that Jesus was dividing it into three parts, he said to him: "O Jesus fear God and do not treat me unfairly. Here we are just you and I so for whom is the third part?" Jesus said, "One part is for you, one part is for me and that part there is for the person who had the loaf." He said, "If I tell you who it was will you give me that part of the treasure?" Jesus said that he would. The Jew said: "It was me." Then Jesus said to him: "Take your share and mine as well as the share of the person who took the loaf. That is your share in this world and the next." Hardly had he loaded his treasure and taken several steps when the ground swallowed him up'

The initial isnād occurs 530 times in Ṭabarī's commentary. The isnād given in support of the final two episodes occurs 860 times. According to Horst,[25] from whom these figures are derived, both of them are cited much more frequently in some parts of the *Tafsīr* than in others. Sezgin[26] assumes that all the traditions supported by them are extracts from a commentary written by al-Suddī who originated in the Hejaz but died in Kūfa in 128/725. However Asbāṭ, wrote a commentary based on that work and it is possible that some of the traditions go back no further than him. This particular tradition is not retained by Ibn Kathīr. One reason why he may have omitted it is that after the time of Asbāt it seems to have been transmitted in Shī'ite circles.[27]

The tradition itself is an extraordinary mixture of biblical and folk-tale motifs. Note that the raising of the king's son is said to have taken place after Jesus had gained a reputation by turning water into wine. The original source of that episode is perhaps the healing of the son of the royal official (Greek *basilikos*) mentioned in *John* 4. John tells us that the man's son was on the point of death and that Jesus received the request for a miraculous cure when he was in Cana of Galilee, the city where he had performed the miracle of the wine. Jesus' use of a staff makes him like Moses. With the novelistic rescue of the Jew from the cross we may compare the similar rescue of Chaereas in the Hellenistic romance *Chaereas and Callirhoe*.[28]

THE MEANING OF THE QUR'ANIC PROVISO

We must now deal with the expressions *bi-idhni 'llāhi* «by God's leave» and *bi-idhnī* «by My leave».

In paraphrasing the miracle of the birds in 3:49 Ṭabarī does not give a synonym for «by God's leave» nor does he subsequently discuss the matter. When dealing with the reference to raising the dead, where the proviso is repeated, he links it with Jesus' habit of petitioning God before performing healings.

Zamakhsharī likewise only discusses the expression in 3:49 when it is repeated after the reference to raising the dead. But his explanation is different; he says that it was spoken as a rebuttal of any who would attribute divinity to him because of what he did. At 5:110 where God says «by My leave» he glosses it as *bi-tashīlī*, 'by my facilitation' or 'by my supplying'.

Rāzī goes into greater detail. In commenting on 3:49 he says that the expression means *bi-takwīni 'llāhi wa-takhlīqi-hi* 'by God's causing to be and determining'. In support of this interpretation he cites «No soul can ever die except by God's leave» (3:145), that is except God bring about his death. Rāzī adds that Jesus mentioned this proviso to abolish all doubt by making it clear that although he made the representation of the birds from clay it was God who created the life. In commenting on 5:110, however, he notes that in this version of the miracle of the birds the proviso is mentioned twice – that is to say in connection with the initial fashioning from clay as well as in connection with the coming to life. Rāzī simply says that this is to emphasise that what occurred originated in God's determining power rather than in Jesus' creative power.

Bayḍāwī only comments on the expression at 3:49. He says that Jesus indicates thereby that it is God and not he himself who makes the birds come alive.

In his comments on 3:49 Ibn Kathīr says that the birds flew visibly by leave of God who granted this miracle for Jesus thereby indicating that He had sent him. In his comments on 5:110 he says that they became birds 'by God's leave and creation' and in the same āya when the expression occurs in connection with the raising of the dead he says that they rose from their tombs 'by God's leave and His power and His decree and His volition'.

OTHER RELEVANT CONSIDERATIONS

Although Jesus' creation of birds and his raising the dead to life are only mentioned in the Qur'ān at 3:49 and 5:110, Rāzī sees fit to refer to these miracles in several other contexts.[29] In the course of commenting on 3:61, he tells us about his own experience of Muslim-Christian dialogue with a Christian of Khwārāzm, a region situated to the east of the Caspian Sea:

> I said to the Christian, 'What proves to you that Jesus is God?' He answered, 'What proves it to me is the miracles manifested by him: the raising of the dead, the healing of the leper and the healing of the man born blind. That could only happen by the power of God Most High.'[30]

The fact that this type of Christian apologetics was still alive in Rāzī's day and age may explain why he was at pains to put the miracles in perspective. He insists that the miracles accomplished by Jesus were not on a par with God's creation of life in the womb from a drop of sperm.[31] Moreover other prophets accomplished miracles as great as those of Jesus: God gave life to Moses' rod and transformed it into a serpent, He also divided the Red Sea using Moses as His intermediary.[32] According to Qur'ān 3:33 God preferred Adam and Noah and the family of Abraham and the family of 'Imrān above all creatures. Therefore instead of arguing that the miracles prove Jesus' divinity Christians should recognise that God caused them to happen in order to honour Jesus. God chose him in preference to other men and appointed him to perform great miracles.[33]

In a similar vein Ibn Kathīr explains that the prophets were enabled to perform those miracles which were the most appropriate for convincing their contemporaries:

> Many of the ulama say that God sent each one of the prophets with what suited the people of his period. What predominated in the

period of Moses (on whom be peace) was magic and the aggrandizement of magicians. So God sent him with a miracle which dazzled and bewildered every magician and when they were confident that it was from the Almighty the Omnipotent they were led to submission and became God's devoted servants [cf. 7:120ff., etc.]. As for Jesus (on whom be peace), he was sent in the period of physicians and natural scientists. So he brought them signs which nobody could have had access to except he were supported by Him who prescribed the way. For from whence would a physician obtain the power to give life to an inanimate object or for the cure of the blind from birth and the leper and for the raising of one who was in his tomb pledged for the Day of Judgement? Likewise Muḥammad (the blessings and peace of God be upon him) was sent in the period of those who were skilled in Arabic and of the eloquent and the troops of poets. So he brought them a Scripture from God (Mighty and Majestic is He). And if «man and jinn were to unite to produce the like» of it [17:88] or «ten ṣūras the like of it» [11:13] or «a ṣūra the like of it» [2:27, 10:38] they would never be able «though they were helpers one of another». [17:88] That is nought save the speech of the Lord (Mighty and Majestic is He). The speech of creatures will never bear a resemblance to it.[34]

DISCUSSION

From the material reviewed in this chapter it is clear that the Qur'an's attribution of unprecedented miracles to Jesus is not a cause of embarrassment to the Muslim commentators. On the contrary, from their point of view, since Jesus is a prophet the miracles which God vouchsafes him must be sufficiently great to convince those to whom he is sent. Hence in common with popular Muslim piety the commentators tend to exaggerate the miraculous rather than play it down.

There is little evidence that any of the classical commentators or their precursors had accurate knowledge of the Christian beliefs about Jesus' miracles. The traditions which they quote have little in common with either the canonical or the apocryphal gospels. Even the discussion of *khalaqa* is presented as something which is pertinent solely to Muslim theology without reference to Christian belief in the Logos as God's agent in creation. Nevertheless there is evidence that the commentators were trying to respond to ongoing Christian polemic and apologetics.

There is a surprising absence of traditional material relating to the proviso «by God's leave» and the commentators have to fall back on theological considerations. When the *Infancy Story Of Thomas* and the *Sīra* of Ibn Isḥāq are taken into account it does, however, seem likely that the proviso is intended as a corrective to Christian teaching.

The commentators have on the whole made a thorough job of putting Jesus' miracles into perspective. Nevertheless they have not really grappled with the similarity between the miracle of the birds, God's creation of Man and His breathing into Mary. There is in particular a need for a more detailed study of the verb *khalaqa*, for Rāzī's discussion is intriguing but not exhaustive. For instance it is surely noteworthy that in the Qur'ān, where the finite verb occurs 173 times in the active voice, God is the subject in no less than 162 instances. Moreover eight of the remaining 11 instances are scarcely exceptions for in them it is used mockingly; the subject is the pagan deities or Man whose creative power is implicitly denied. Might it not be the case that in the one instance where the finite verb is used of human beings creating a falsehood it is also used mockingly – implying that they cannot create anything substantial? Certainly the two instances in which Jesus is the subject stand out as exceptional and should not be used as primary data for establishing the meaning of the verb.

15 The Virginal Conception

The Qur'ān refers to Mary's chastity (66:12) and reproves the Jews for speaking a calumny against her (4:156). It seems to endorse the virginal conception but on the understanding that it was analogous to the creation of Adam by divine fiat (3:47 and 59). However, in one of the accounts of the annunciation we are told that, after Mary had taken to herself a curtain, the Spirit

> «presented himself to her as a perfectly proportioned human being» (19:17b)

and reassured her with the words,

> «'I am only a messenger of your Lord [and have come] so that I may bestow upon you (*li-'ahaba la-ki*) a pure boy.'» (19:19)

Who is meant by the Spirit in this instance? How did he 'bestow' the child on Mary? What is the relationship between this passage and the two oblique references to God's breathing His Spirit into her (21:91 and 66:12)? And how is all this to be reconciled with the assertion that Jesus was strengthened by the Spirit (2:254) and that the Messiah was a Word and Spirit from God (4:171)? With these problems in mind I will first adduce some partial parallels from ancient Christian writings. Then I will discuss the similarity of Mary and 'Ā'isha. Finally, I will review the salient features of the classical exegesis of 19:17–22.

THE SECTARIAN CHRISTIAN BACKGROUND

In Chapter 3 I gave some illustrations of how the *Diatesseron*, the apocryphal infancy gospels and Nestorian anti-Orthodox polemic all help to shed light on the Qur'anic representation of Mary. Here I will make some further suggestions.

Orthodox Syrian Christians sometimes likened the virginal conception to the creation of Adam. For instance Ephraim of Nisibis wrote:

> The virgin's conceiving teaches us that He who brought Adam into the world by causing him to come out of the virgin earth without carnal intercourse, also formed the second Adam in the virgin's womb without carnal intercourse.[1]

The Qur'anic statement (3:59) seems, however, to be closer to the teaching of Nestorius who is said to have asserted:

> the Lord Jesus to have been like in all and equal to Adam: Adam indeed [was created] without seed and Jesus too without seed; the first only a man and the second, too, a man and nothing more.[2]

The background to the Qur'anic description of the Spirit's presenting himself to Mary in the form of a perfect human being is less easy to determine. If we assume (on the basis of 16:102, 26:193 cp. 2:97) that the Spirit is Gabriel, then the closest parallel is furnished by Ephraim of Nisibis. Although Ephraim believed in the virginal conception, he linked the name Gabriel with the Syriac word *gabro* which means a man or a husband. Commenting on the annunciation he wrote:

> Since Elizabeth had a husband Gabriel did not go to her. He went to Mary so that by reason of his name he might symbolically take the place of a husband.[3]

Alternatively it might be thought (on the basis of 4:171) that the Spirit who presented himself to Mary was none other than the Messiah to whom she subsequently gave birth. At first this seems improbable because of the way in which the Spirit refers to himself as a messenger. There is, however, an apocryphal writing which furnishes a precedent for identifying the agent of the annunciation with the Word who became flesh. This is the so-called *Epistula Apostolorum* which purports to be a letter addressed to the worldwide Church by the 11 disciples recording a conversation which they had with Christ after his resurrection. In the course of the conversation he told them:

> At that time I appeared in the form of the archangel Gabriel to [the virgin] Mary and spoke with her, and her heart received [me]; she believed and laughed and I, the Word, went into her and became flesh; and I myself was servant for myself, and in the form of the image of an angel.[4]

There is also evidence that in Jewish-Christian milieus the Messiah was thought of as Word, Spirit and Angel[5] but not as divine. For instance the Ebionites identified the Messiah with the Spirit whom God created like the archangels. They held that the same Spirit had previously assisted Adam and other prophets.[6] They rejected the virginal conception holding that Jesus was begotten in the normal way and that he was assisted by the Messiah/Spirit from the moment of his baptism. Another sect, the Elkesaites, seem to have acknowledged the virginal conception but to have held that the Messiah had been born of a virgin on previous occasions.[7]

Before we leave the question of the Christian background something should be said about Mary's taking to herself a curtain (19:17). Christian historians usually draw attention to a partial parallel in the *Protoevangelium of James*. This writing mentions that seven virgins including Mary were chosen to make a curtain for the temple and that Mary's specific task was to weave the pure purple and scarlet which she took and worked in her house.[8] Another apocryphal work which might be relevant in this connection is the so-called *Gospel of Bartholomew*. This records that Mary told the apostles that, when 'one in the form of an angel' appeared to her, the curtain of the temple was rent and there was a violent earthquake.[9]

'Ā'ISHA AND MARY[10]

There is one passage in the Qur'ān in which Mary is cited for an explicitly hortatory purpose. This occurs at the end of the 66th ṣūra. The passage states that God has proposed the wife of Pharaoh together with «Mary daughter of Imrān who guarded her chastity» as examples for the believers (66:13–14). This is directly related to the first part of the ṣūra which is concerned with a domestic problem occasioned by Muḥammad's wives. The details of that problem need not detain us and in any case they cannot be deduced directly from the text. Suffice it to note that the trouble was caused by two wives (66:3f) and that it was suggested that unless they had a change of heart they might be divorced and replaced with women who were better Muslims, either women who had already been married (like Pharaoh's wife?) or virgins (like Mary?) (66:4f). According to the most plausible tradition the two wives who caused the trouble were Ḥafṣa and 'Ā'isha. They would certainly fit the bill admirably for Muḥammad married Ḥafṣa after she was widowed whereas Ā'isha was his only virgin bride.[11]

Taking our lead from this passage we may enquire whether any of the other things which the Qur'ān says about Mary were relevant to Muḥammad's *ménage*. If the Qur'anic information about the Prophet's wives is supplemented with details derived from early Muslim tradition, and if attention is focused on Ā'isha some quite remarkable parallels emerge.

When the Prophet moved to Medina he was about 50 years old and had only one wife, Sawda, who was at least 30. The residence which was built for him also served as the first mosque.[12] It consisted principally of an enclosed courtyard in which he conducted business, addressed his followers and led communal prayers. In the pre-Islamic period marriage was uxorilocal, that is to say wives used to remain in their family homes where they were visited by their husbands. Muḥammad departed from this custom and established virilocal marriage as the norm. Thus Sawda lived with him in the mosque or rather in her own apartment which opened onto the courtyard. Muḥammad soon contracted a further marriage with 'Ā'isha. His relationship with her must, to begin with, have been more that of a guardian than a husband for she was only nine and was allowed to keep her toys. Nevertheless 'Ā'isha had to leave her family and live at the Prophet's residence.[13] Quarters were built for her resembling those of Sawda and opening onto the *eastern* side of the courtyard. In addition to being separated from her folk, 'Ā'isha was screened off from them because of a revelation instructing Muslims to speak to the Prophet's wives from behind a 'curtain' (*ḥijāb* 33:53). There are various traditions as to why the *ḥijāb* was introduced but the underlying reason was that the mosque was frequented by large numbers of people and it was undignified for the women to be exposed to all and sundry. God wished to 'purify' them (33:33) and give them unique status as mothers of the believers (33:12).

Many of these details tally with what the Qur'ān says about Mary. The two principal versions of her story associate her with Zechariah. He was a prophet, advanced in years and married to a woman who was barren. He is mentioned in connection with an important place of worship. While Mary was still only a girl she was put in the care of Zechariah because her mother had dedicated her to God. In one version of the story it is implied that Mary lived in the *miḥrāb* (3:37) which was either the place of worship itself or a chamber adjoining it. In the other version she is said to have withdrawn from her folk to an 'easterly' place and screened herself from them with a 'curtain' (*ḥijāb*) (19:16).[14] Moreover she was told by the angels that God had 'purified' her and preferred her above all the women of creation (3:42).

There is a further important resemblance between 'Ā'isha and Mary: both were accused of sexual immorality.[15] When the Muslims were returning from a campaign 'Ā'isha was accidentally left behind at the camp site. Apparently her howda had been loaded onto the camel while she was in the privy and because she was so light no one had realised that the howda was empty. Tongues began to wag when she returned to Medina accompanied by a handsome young man who had also fallen behind for some reason and had not spent the night with the troops. The accusations provoked a serious crisis which was only resolved when Muḥammad received a revelation declaring her innocence. Tradition identifies this revelation as 24:11ff. The passage does not name 'Ā'isha but it clearly refers to a false accusation of unchastity made against an eminent Muslim woman. The accusers are lambasted for speaking lies and not bringing four witnesses. The believers are reprimanded for listening to scandal-mongering and not dismissing it as slander; they should have realised that it was «a tremendous calumny» (*buhtān 'aẓīm* 24:16). The case of Mary is of course different in as far as she was visited by God's Spirit and returned to her people with a child. There are, however, a number of similarities. In the first place the encounter with the Spirit took place when she was alone and he presented himself to her as a handsome young man (19:17). Second, her people suspected her of unchastity and her virtue had to be defended by revelation (19:27–33). Finally, the Qur'ān criticises the People of the Scripture for having spoken «a tremendous calumny»[16] against her (4:156).

CLASSICAL EXEGESIS OF 19:17–22[17]

The classical commentaries incorporate traditional material concerning the circumstances of Mary's seclusion, the identity of the Spirit who was sent to her, the form in which he appeared and the manner of the insufflation. I will first attempt to summarise the traditions. Then I shall mention some of the more speculative interpretations discussed by Rāzī. For further details reference may be made to my annotated translation in *Islamochristiana*.[18]

The commentators invariably suppose that the *ḥijāb* taken by Mary was something which concealed her. The word is usually translated 'curtain' or 'veil' but it could denote any kind of screen. According to a tradition, which Ṭabarī traces back to Ibn al-'Abbās, Mary went to the east where she was screened from sight by the brilliance of the sun. According to a second tradition which he traces back to al-Suddī, she was screened by a wall during her monthly periods and the Spirit presented himself to her after she had cleansed herself. Rāzī refers to several rival accounts including the following which I have not found elsewhere:

> At the side of the house of Zechariah her sister's husband she had a private chamber where she dwelt. Whenever Zechariah went out he used to lock her in. So she desired to find solitude in the mountain to delouse her head. Then the roof fell in for her and she went out to the desert and sat in an elevated place behind the mountain. Then the angel came to her.

None of these traditions is mentioned by Ibn Kathīr. Instead he informs us that according to Ibn Isḥāq the encounter took place when Mary had gone out to draw water but that according to Nawf al-Bikālī she was concealed by the dwelling place in which she had devoted herself to worship.

Ṭabarī assumes that the Spirit who was sent to Mary was Gabriel. He reports that this was the view of Qatāda, Ibn Jurayj and Wahb. The other commentators agree that this is the correct interpretation but none the less mention the alternative view, namely that the Spirit was the Messiah. Ibn Kathīr gives the following report traced back by a single isnād to the Companion Ubaiy:

> The spirit of Jesus is one of the group of spirits with whom [God] took a pact in the time of Adam [cf. 33:7 and 7:172]. It is he, that is to say the spirit of Jesus, who presented himself to her in the form of a perfect human being. So she conceived the one who addressed her and he became incarnate in her [entering her through her] mouth.

Despite its pedigree, Ibn Kathīr dismisses this interpretation as reprehensible and supposes it to have been derived from the People of the Scripture.

As regards Gabriel's appearance, Rāzī knows of a tradition that he took the form of a beardless youth and another that he appeared to her in the form of a companion of hers called Joseph who was one of the servants of the temple. He also mentions a novel interpretation of 19:18 which hinges on the fact that the word which is usually translated 'God-fearing' is sometimes used as the name of a person:

> There was at that time a debauched man named Taqī who used to chase the women. Mary (peace be upon her!) thought that he was the person whom she saw.

Bayḍāwī says that Gabriel may have presented himself to Mary in the form of a perfect human being in order to arouse her desire and thereby facilitate the descent of the maternal fluid into the womb.[19]

Although the insufflation is not mentioned in 19:22 the commentators infer that it must have taken place at this time. Rāzī gives a summary of the various traditions:

> Then they differed, on the basis of [reported] sayings, concerning the particulars of that breathing:
> (1) Wahb's saying that Gabriel breathed into her bosom until it reached the womb.
> (2) Into her hem and it reached the vulva.
> (3) The saying of al-Suddī. He seized her sleeve and breathed into the side of her chemise and the breath entered her breast.
> (4) That the breathing was into her mouth and it reached her womb so she conceived instantly.
> If you concede this it is evident that in this sentence there is an ellipsis. It is «It is a thing ordained – and he breathed into her – and she conceived him.»

As well as relaying the traditional exegetical material, Rāzī summarises the opinions of the Mu'tazilites and engages in debate with them on a number of issues. These include whether it is possible for an angel to take the form of a human being, whether the angelic annunciation constituted a miracle and whether an angel could literally bestow a child.

Some of the Mu'tazilites including Abū Muslim[20] favoured the view that the Spirit who presented himself to Mary was not Gabriel but the Messiah. Others followed Abū Ḥaywa[21] in reading *rawḥa-nā* (Our refreshment) instead of the canonical *ruḥa-nā* (Our Spirit). Judging by Rāzī's analysis, they probably adopted these stratagems because of their objection to the notion of an angel appearing in human form, a notion which was as abhorrent to them as that of the projection of Jesus' semblance onto a substitute. They held that such occurrences were not permissible because they would lead to mistaken identity and undermine the value of eye-witness testimony. As atomists they also had difficulty in envisaging how Gabriel's enormous body could have shrunk to the size of a human being. They further argued that if Gabriel could appear in human form he could equally well appear in the form of something smaller such as a fly, a bed bug or a gnat. Rāzī does his best to counter these arguments and lends his support to the canonical reading and to the traditional view that the Spirit was Gabriel.

There was a further problem connected with Gabriel's appearing to Mary in human form: clearly he must have done something to prove to her that he was indeed an angel and not a man in which case the annunciation must have been miraculous. This was difficult to reconcile with the orthodox position that a miracle (*mu'jiz*) was proof of prophethood and that only a man could be a prophet.[22] 'Abd al-Jabbār attempted to get round the problem by suggesting that because the annunciation took place in the time of Zechariah it was a miracle performed on his behalf. Rāzī retorts that this is a weak argument because if a miracle is done for a prophet the least to be expected is that he knows about it. He therefore suggests that what took place should be regarded either as a divine favour (*karāma*)[23] granted to Mary or portents (*arhāṣ*) preceding the birth of Jesus.

According to the standard text of 19:19 the Spirit spoke of himself as the one who would bestow the child on Mary. There is, however, an interesting variant. Instead of *li-'ahaba la-ki* – «'that I may bestow upon you'» – Abū 'Amr[24] read *li-yahaba la-ki* «'that He may bestow upon you'»'. Despite the fact that Abū 'Amr's system was one of the seven which subsequently came to be considered canonical, Ṭabarī rejects his reading on the grounds that it departs from the consonantal text. Ibn Kathīr on the other hand accepts both readings and states somewhat cryptically that each requires the other. This was probably Rāzī's position as well because he writes:

> Gabriel's saying «'so that I may bestow upon you'» can be understood figuratively in one of two ways:
>
> (1) The gift occurred through Gabriel's good offices because it was he who blew into her bosom by the order of God Most High. Therefore he represented himself as the one who bestowed [the boy] on her. The attribution of the deed to the secondary cause which occasioned it [rather than to God who willed it] is also employed in the āya where God Most High said concerning the idols, «Behold! They have led many mankind astray» [14:36].
>
> (2) When Gabriel (peace be upon him!) brought her tidings concerning that, the accurate bringing of the tidings produced the bestowal [of the son].

Rāzī then goes on to consider the possibility that Gabriel was endowed with special creative powers:

> If someone says, 'What is there to indicate that Gabriel (peace be upon him!) is not able to assemble atoms (*ajzā'*) and create life, intellect and rational speech in them?', what is [usually] said in reply is that Gabriel is a body (*jism*) and that a body is incapable of

such things. As for his being a body this entails his being temporal (*muḥdath*) and everything which is temporal is either spatial (*mutaḥayyiz*) or persists in what is spatial. As for no body being able to do such things that is because if one body were able to do them every body would be able to do them since bodies are alike (*mutamāthila*). This is a weak argument because [all that is necessary to refute it] is for the opponent to say, 'We are not agreed that everything which is temporal is either spatial or persists in what is spatial. On the contrary there are existent things (*mawjūdāt*) which persist in themselves and which are neither spatial nor persisting in what is spatial. Their being like that does not necessitate their being likenesses (*amthāl*) of God Most High's essence (*dhāt*), because sharing positive attributes (*al-ṣifāt al-thubūtiyya* does not require resemblance. How much less [does this require resemblance in the case of Gabriel when] we submit that as regards the negative attributes (*al-ṣifāt al-salbiyya*) Gabriel is a body.[25] Why then do you say that a body is not able to do such things? We maintain that the statement that bodies are alike may mean either that they are alike in so far as they occupy spaces and move in directions or it may mean that they are alike in the entirety of their quiddity (*māhiyya*). Now we agree to the former [but not to the latter since] we hold that their occupying spaces are attributes belonging to these essences and participation in qualities does not necessitate participation in the quiddities that have those attributes. Since we submit that bodies are alike [in this sense] why is it not admissible to say that God Most High endowed some of them with this ability (*qudra*) but not others so that that was true of them and not of mankind?

Rāzī concludes that the sole basis for rejecting this possibility is the consensus of the Muslim community.

DISCUSSION

The patristic texts about Jewish Christianity are as brief and opaque as the Qur'anic references to the annunciation and conception which they have been invoked to explain. Nevertheless, when considered together with the apocryphal writings cited in the first section of this chapter, they further our knowledge of the soil from which Islam sprang. The Qur'anic Christology seems to reflect the teaching of a Jewish Christian sect but one which was slightly different from those known to the church fathers. Alternatively, the Qur'anic Christology may have been forged through contact with Nestorian Christians who had moved in the direction of a gnosticised Jewish Christianity. We may also note in passing that the traces of the Ebionite distinction between the human Jesus and the angel/spirit Messiah could account for the tension between the Qur'ān's insistence on the humanity of Jesus and the Gnostic-sounding denial of the crucifixion in 4:157.

The similarity of 'Ā'isha and Mary is intriguing. We must reckon with the possibility that Muḥammad's domestic arrangements in the 'mosque' at Medina were made with the story of Mary in mind. His primary motive was probably the desire to emphasise the fact that he was a prophet like Jesus. In the process, however, he also blazed the trail for the establishment of virilocal marriage. This was not the only social reform of his which was reinforced by the story of Mary. His campaign to eradicate the pre-Islamic practice of burying girl children alive because of the shortage of food (cp. 16:58) must surely have been furthered by the account of how, when Mary's mother was distressed at giving birth to a daughter, God accepted the child and miraculously fed her (3:36f.). The Qur'anic āya exonerating 'Ā'isha from the charge of unchastity is a different matter and came later. It would have made sense to the Muslims who were by then long familiar with the story of how Mary's innocence had likewise been defended by revelation.

The classical commentaries contain a wealth of traditional exegetical material about the annunciation and conception. Some of it appears to have come from Christian sources. For instance the story of Mary's going out to draw water and the story of the miraculous falling in of the roof and her subsequent solitude in the mountain are perhaps both derived ultimately from midrashic elaboration of the Syriac version of *Daniel* 2:34 ('a stone was cut out by no human hand') and *Isaiah* 51:1 ('Look to the mountain and the well . . .'), texts which were treasured as prophecies of the virginal conception.[26] Mary's going out to draw water also figures in the *The Protoevangelium of James* and the scene is very effectively depicted in a mosaic in the little Byzantine church of St Saviour in Chora (now Kariye Camii, Istanbul).[27]

The Mu'tazilite debates which were fuelled by the account of how the Spirit presented himself to Mary seem not to owe anything to Muslim-Christian dialogue. Most intriguing is the suggestion that if Gabriel could appear in human form he could equally well appear as a fly, a bed bug or a gnat. Was this suggestion based on *Qur'ān* 2:26?

Or was it an allusion to Waraqa's description of the Spirit as the Nāmūs, a word which can also denote a mosquito?

We saw in Chapter 8 that although the classical commentators rejected any suggestion that the virginal conception was a proof of Jesus' divinity they none the less accepted it as literally true. This is borne out by a detailed examination of their comments on 19:17-22. Even Rāzī, who considered that Gabriel might have been able to *create* Jesus in Mary's womb, seems not to have entertained the thought that he could have been given power to *procreate* him. Nevertheless there are occasional hints that, although no sexual act was involved, Mary's carnal desire was aroused. We shall see later that this theme looms large in the theosophical commentary of Qāshānī.

16 The Representation of Jesus in the Shī'ite Commentaries

When dealing with the Qur'anic references to Jesus the classical Shī'ite commentators raise similar issues to those raised by their Sunnite counterparts and generally propose more or less the same solutions. In order to avoid needless repetition I shall concentrate on the additions, omissions and subtle differences evinced by their work.

THE SHĪ'ITE COMMENTARIES[1]

Like the Sunnites, the Shī'ite commentators make considerable use of traditional material. However, since they believe that the 12 Imams were infallible and that they inherited Muḥammad's knowledge, they treat traditions derived from them as on a par with those from the Prophet himself. They also take into account the interpretations attributed to the Companions and Successors but tend to play down their importance.[2]

The oldest extant Shī'ite commentary on the whole Qur'ān is the *Tafsīr* of Abū al-Ḥasan 'Alī b. Ibrāhīm al-Qummī (d.307/919)[3] which dates from the period of the Lesser Occultation and exhibits a strong anti-Sunnite tendency. It consists primarily of traditions which Qummī's father had learned from the disciples of the sixth Imam. Scant attention is paid to linguistic problems and many difficult passages of the Qur'ān are passed over without comment.

Shortly after the death of Qummī, the Būyids took control of Iran and part of Iraq where they held sway for over a century. At around the same time the Ḥamdānids came to power in Mosul and Allepo. These were Shī'ite dynasties and under their patronage Shī'ite scholarship flourished. Shī'ite theologians were now free to engage in open debate and they developed their own rationalistic theology which was strongly influenced by that of the Mu'tazilites of Baghdad. One of the most distinguished scholars of this period was Abū Ja'far al-Ṭūsī better known as Sheikh al-Ṭā'ifa (d.460/1067). He produced a major Qur'anic commentary called the *Tibyān* or 'Exposition'.[4] This work is less hostile towards the Sunnites and frequently refers to the interpretations ascribed to the Companions and Successors as well as to the traditions of the Imams. It also contains detailed discussions of variant readings, valuable information about Mu'tazilite exegesis and numerous references to the theories of the grammarians. Ṭūsī lived to see the demise of the Shī'ite dynasties and was forced to leave Baghdad when it was captured by the staunchly Sunnite Seljuq Turks in 454/1055.

Under the Seljuqs Shī'ite theology stagnated although there were a handful of notable scholars in northern Iran. One of these, Abū 'Alī al-Faḍl b. al-Ḥasan al-Ṭabarsī (d.548/1153) who lived in Khurasān, was the author of a commentary entitled *Majma' al-Bayān fī Tafsīr al-Qur'ān*,[5] ('Combination of the explanations concerning the exegesis of the Qur'ān'). This draws extensively on both Ṭabarī and Ṭūsī and represents the common ground between Sunnite and Shī'ite scholarship. I shall only refer to it when it helps clarify the earlier works or provides additional information.

JESUS' RETURN[6]

In commenting on 4:159 Qummī cites the following tradition without further explanation:

> My father told me on the authority of al-Qāsim b.Muḥammad on the authority of Sulaymān b. Dā'ūd al-Munqarī on the authority of Abū Hamza on the authority of Shahr b. Ḥawshab. He said:
> 'Al-Ḥajjāj told me, "There is an āya in the Book of God which has thwarted my efforts to understand it."
> I said, "O Emir which āya is it?"
> He said, "It is His statement «And [there is] not one of the people of the Scripture except [he] will most certainly believe in him before his death». By God if I give orders for a Jew or Christian to be decapitated and I watch him with my own eyes I do not see him move his lips before he is extinguished."
> I said, "May God cause you to thrive O Emir! It is not in accordance with how you have interpreted it."
> He said, "How is it then?"
> I said, "Jesus will descend to the world before the Day of Resurrection and there will remain neither Jew nor Christian who does not believe in him. And he will pray behind the Māhdī."

He said, "Woe to you! How do you know that? Where did you derive it from?"
I said, "Muḥammad b. 'Alī b. al-Ḥusayn b. 'Alī b. a. A. Ṭālib told me."
He said, "By God you have derived it from a sound source!"

The story of Shahr b. Ḥawshab's encounter with al-Ḥajjāj is familiar to us already. We came across it in Zamakhsharī and Rāzī who probably derived it from the commentary of al-Kalbī. The āya which puzzled al-Ḥajjāj is the same. So too is al-Ḥajjāj's assumption that the death referred to is that of the Jew or the Christian and his unsuccessful attempt to observe this experimentally. The explanation attributed to Shahr b. Ḥawshab is, however, entirely different. According to Zamakhsharī and Rāzī he held that the āya did indeed refer to the death of the Jew or Christian and he explained that the dying man's confession was inaudible to al-Ḥajjāj because it was addressed to the interrogating angels. Moreover, the commentators differ over Shahr b. Ḥawshab's teacher in these matters. According to Zamakhsharī and Rāzī it was Muḥammad b. 'Alī b. al-Ḥanafiyya; according to Qummī it was Muḥammad b. 'Alī b. al-Ḥusayn b. 'Alī b. a. Ṭālib better known as al-Bāqir (d.117/735?) the fifth Imam.

Ṭūsī's comments on this āya are more extensive, He refers to the three traditional interpretations found in Ṭabarī:

[A] «believe in him» means believe in Jesus and «before his death» means before Jesus' death when he returns to kill the Antichrist. (Ṭūsī adds that this will be when the Mahdī has come forth.)

[B] «believe in him» means believe in Jesus and «before his death» means before the Scripturist's death.

[C] «believe in him» means believe in Muḥammad and «before his death» means before the Scripturist's death.

Moreover he deals with them in the same order as Ṭabarī and attributes them to the same authorities as him but without citing either the asānīd or the traditions.

His treatment of the first interpretation is intriguing. He correctly states that Ṭabarī chose this interpretation and that he said that it only concerned those of the People of the Scripture who would still be alive when Jesus returned. He further adds that this is the interpretation mentioned by 'Alī b. Ibrāhīm [al-Qummī]. Then he mentions Shahr b. Ḥawshab's encounter with al-Ḥajjāj but words Shahr's explanation of the āya rather differently:

> 'Muḥammad b. 'Alī [b. al-Ḥanafiyya] told me that God will send an angel to him [i.e. to each Jew] who will shake him violently [*or* shake the dust off him, *yanfuḍu-hu*] and strike him on the head and on the back and say to him 'You called Jesus a liar'. So he will believe in him then.

Here the interrogating angel is not sent at the moment of death but in the last days, probably – although this is not absolutely clear – in order to rouse the deceased from his tomb. Thus although the wording of Ṭūsī's version is closer to Kalbī's than to Qummī's, he follows Qummī in supposing that Shahr b. Ḥawshab understood «before his death» to mean before Jesus' death when he returns to kill the Antichrist. Ṭūsī adds that [the Mu'tazilite] al-Balakhī (d.319/931)[7] interpreted it along these lines but that [the Sunnī grammarian] al-Zajjāj (d.310/922)[8] considered this interpretation weak. Al-Zajjāj thought that the āya required the belief of all the People of the Scripture. He allowed that it might mean that all those who were still alive when Jesus returned would declare their belief in him. However, since only a few of them would still be alive he favoured the second interpretation.

Ṭūsī refers to Ṭabarī's objection to the second interpretation and counters it in much the same way as Ibn Kathīr does. He also refers to Ṭabarī's objection to the third interpretation but does not consider it conclusive because he is able to point to another āya in which there is an allusion to something which has not previously been mentioned: «. . . until it disappeared behind a curtain» [38:32]. Where 'it' is the sun. He also suggests that «his death» may refer to both the death of the Scripturist and the death of Jesus. Thus he seems to admit all three interpretations.

Qummī does not comment on 43:61. Ṭūsī refers briefly to the two traditional interpretations which we encountered in Ṭabarī and he mentions the reading of Ibn al-'Abbās but not that of Ubaiy. He states that, of those who hold that the āya alludes to Jesus' return, some say that 'prescription' (*taklīf*, i.e. the imposition of [further] religious and legal duties by God) will have been abolished so that Jesus will not be a messenger (*rasūl*) to the people of that time, whereas others say that 'prescription' will still exist but that Jesus will be without a prescriptive rōle (*ghair mukallaf*) in the government of the Mahdī.

THE CRUCIFIXION[9]

Qummī does not discuss the meaning of *inn-ī mutawaffī-ka*. Ṭūsī, on the other hand, mentions three of the four principal interpretations which we have encountered in the Sunnī commentaries:

1. God grasped Jesus from the earth without causing him to die. He ascribes this to al-Ḥasan, Ibn Jurayj and Ibn Zayd. (These are three of the six authorities mentioned by Ṭabarī.)
2. God caused Jesus to ascend while he was asleep. He ascribes this to Ibn al-'Abbās and Wahb. (Ṭabarī traces it back to Rābi'.)
3. It is an example of *al-taqdīm wa 'l-takhīr*. He says that this interpretation was mentioned by [the Kūfan grammarian] al-Farrā' [d.207/822].[10] (Ṭabarī does not name an authority for this interpretation but Ibn Kathīr attributes it to Qatāda.)

The reason why Ṭūsī does not mention the other traditional interpretation, namely that God caused Jesus to die, is probably that he did not distinguish between death and sleep. This is certainly the case with Ṭabarsī. A further interesting feature of Ṭabarsī's comments on this āya is that he illustrates *al-taqdīm wa 'l-takhīr* by reference to another āya: «How [dreadful] were My punishment and My warnings» [54:18]. This clearly means 'How [dreadful] were My warnings and My punishment', because elsewhere God says: «We do not punish until we have sent a messenger» [17:15].

Qummī does not discuss the meaning of *shubbiha la-hum* in 4:157 but in connection with 3:55 he cites a tradition about the projection of Jesus' semblance onto a disciple who volunteered to be crucified in his place. It is supported by the following isnād:

> My father told me on the authority of Ibn abī 'Umayr on the authority of Jamīl b. Ṣāliḥ on the authority of Ḥumrān b. A'yān on the authority of Abū Ja'far.

Here Abū Ja 'far is probably the fifth Imam, Muḥammad b. 'Alī al-Bāqir. He lived in Medina although most of his supporters were in Kūfa. I will not quote the tradition in full because it is almost identical to the one which the Sunnī commentators Ṭabarī and Ibn Kathīr trace back to Ibn al-'Abbās.[11] The main differences are that Jesus ascends from the corner of the house (rather than through the skylight) and that he himself predicts that the disciples will split into three groups: two groups who will invent lies about God in the Fire whereas the other group will follow Simon and speak the truth about God in Paradise. The Simon in question can hardly be Simon Peter. In view of the belief of some of the Gnostics that Simon of Cyrene was crucified the reference is perhaps to him in which case we should probably identify him with the volunteer.

In commenting on *shubbiha la-hum*, Ṭūsī says that they (the early interpreters) differed concerning the manner in which this occurred:

(1) Wahb said Jesus' semblance was projected on all seventeen of his disciples who were with him in a house.

(2) Qatāda, al-Suddī, Ibn Isḥāq, Mujāhid and Ibn Jurayj differed concerning the number of the disciples but agreed that the semblance was projected onto only one person: Sergius or Judas.

Ṭūsī probably derived this information from Ṭabarī whose preference for Wahb's interpretation he mentions. He then goes on to mention an interpretation which we have not encountered in any of the Sunnī commentaries. He says that according to al-Jubbā'ī the Jewish leaders took a man, killed him and crucified him on a high place. No one was able to get close to him. Moreover his appearance altered and his form changed beyond recognition. They did this in order that the general public would think that it was Jesus, for when they had tried to arrest Jesus he had ascended into heaven and they feared that this might inspire the Jews to believe in him. The person who propounded this rational explanation, Abū 'Alī al-Jubbā'ī (d.303/915), was a distinguished member of the Baṣran branch of the Mu'tazilites. He had perhaps learned from some Christian informant that according to one of the gospels Jesus' acquaintances stood at a distance (*Luke* 23:49). He may also have heard the Christian interpretation of Isaiah's prophecy of the suffering servant of God whose 'appearance was so marred beyond human semblance and his form beyond that of the sons of men' (*Isaiah* 52:14).

Ṭūsī also discusses whether it is possible for God to project the likeness of one person onto another so that they cannot be distinguished. He maintains that God is indisputably capable of doing this although it is not his normal practice. He states that according to the Shī'ites it may occur as a miracle (performed by a prophet) or as a divine favour performed for one of the righteous saints or infallible Imams but that according to the Mu'tazilites it can only take place in the time of the prophets.

THE MIRACLES[12]

Qummī has very little to say about Jesus' creating birds from clay and raising the dead. Commenting on 3:49 he glosses «I create» (*akhlaqu*) as 'I fashion' (*aqaddaru*). He passes over the whole of 5:110–11 with the comment that it is *muḥkam*, that is to say clear and unambiguous.

Ṭūsī says that 'creating' (*khalq*) here has the meaning of fashioning (*taqdīr*) without bringing into existence (*iḥdāth*) and he mentions the tradition that Jesus fashioned a bat. He says that «I blow into it» means:

> I blow into it the spirit (*rūḥ*) which is a subtle body like wind (*rīḥ*) and which is not the life. For the spirit lives only in so far as God Most High puts the life into it. All bodies are alike; God makes live those of them that He wills.'[13]

In the course of his comments on 5:110 Ṭūsī mentions al-Jubbā'ī's interpretation:

> Abū 'Alī [al-Jubbā'ī] said, 'He may have blown it into the body in the way that God reports [in the Qur'ān] that Gabriel did [in the case of Jesus in Mary's womb] and in the way that it has been transmitted on the authority of the Prophet (on him be peace) that [God] sends an angel to [the foetus in the womb] at the completion of a hundred and twenty days to blow the spirit into it and to write down the time when [the person] will die and whether he is destined to be happy or wretched.'

Ṭūsī's explanation of the proviso «by God's leave» is that it indicates what

> God did without Jesus. As for the forming and blowing on the other hand, Jesus did it because it was part of what he was destined to do (*mimmā yadkhulu taḥta maqdūri 'l-qadari*). The changing of an inanimate body into an animal is not like that; no one is able to do that except the Most High. And in saying «and I bring the dead to life by God's leave» Jesus figuratively ascribes the action to himself but its true meaning is 'I call upon God to bring the dead to life and God brings them to life and they live by God's leave.'

Of the three Shī'ite commentators whom I have selected, only Ṭabarsī mentions the people whom Jesus raised from the dead. He states that it is said that Jesus brought four persons to life:

> 'Āzar who was a friend of his. He had been dead for three days. Jesus said to his sister, 'Come with us to his tomb.' Then he said, 'Our God, Lord of the seven heavens and Lord of the seven earths, you sent me to the Children of Israel to summon them to your religion and to announce to them that I would raise the dead to life.' So he brought 'Āzar to life and he came out from his tomb and he continued [to live] and a child was begotten by him. [Then there was] the son of the old woman whom he passed by when he was dead and on his bier. Jesus invoked God and he sat up on his bier and came down from the necks of the men [who were carrying him], put his clothes on and returned to his folk. He continued to live and a child was begotten by him. [There was also] a twelve year old girl. Jesus was asked whether he could bring her to life. She had died the previous day. He invoked God and she lived and remained [alive] and produced a child. [Finally there was] Sām b. Nūḥ. He invoked God for him by the greatest name. So he came out from his tomb. Half of [the hair on] his head had turned grey. He said 'Is this the Resurrection?'. Jesus replied 'No, but I invoked the greatest of God's names for you.' – It is said [literally 'he said'] that they used not to turn grey in that time because Sām b. Nūḥ lived for five hundred years and he was [still] a youth – Then Jesus told him to die. He said, 'On the condition that God protects me from the agonies of death.' So Jesus invoked God and He did.

Like Rāzī, who as we have seen also mentions three of the four incidents but not in such detail, Ṭabarsī says that according to al-Kalbī Jesus used to raise the dead by praying 'O Living One, O Everlasting One.' Like Ibn Kathīr he further explains that this type of miracle was granted to Jesus because of the predominance of medicine at the time of his mission, whereas it was magic which predominated in the time of Moses and eloquence in the time of Muḥammad.

THE VIRGINAL CONCEPTION[14]

Like their Sunnī counterparts, the Shī'ite commentators relativise God's choice of Mary by citing *aḥādīth* which describe her as above the women *of her time*. In chapter eight I mentioned one such ḥadīth which put Mary on the same level as Muḥammad's first wife Khadīja. There are others which put them both in the same class as Pharaoh's wife Āsiya and Muḥammad's daughter Fāṭima. The latter has a special place in Shī'ite devotion because she was the wife of 'Alī, the mother of Ḥasan and Ḥusayn and the ancestress of the nine subsequent Imams. There is therefore a tendency for Shī'ites to regard her position as supreme. This tendency is reflected in Ṭūsī and Ṭabarsī who state that according to Abū Ja'far (the fifth Imam) Fāṭima is the mistress of the women of the worlds. Nevertheless both of these commentators were aware that this was not the only point of view and that according to al-Zajjāj and al-Jubbā'ī, God chose Mary above the women of the worlds in the absolute sense in that he chose her to give birth to the Messiah Jesus.

Not withstanding the tendency to exalt Fāṭima above Mary, the Shī'ite commentators assume without question that Mary conceived while still a virgin. Like the Sunnites they suppose that the Spirit who presented himself to her was Gabriel. To the question of how it was that an angel appeared to a woman despite the fact that only men could be prophets, Ṭūsī gives the same three answers as Rāzī but in greater detail. First, he states that according to al-Jubbā'ī this was a miracle performed for Zechariah (Rāzī ascribes this view to 'Abd al-Jabbār). Second, he says that according to Ibn al-Akhshād it was proof of Jesus' prophethood like the appearance of shooting stars and other portents before the sending of Muḥammad. Third, Ṭūsī declares that 'according to us' (*'inda-nā*) it could have been a miracle and a divine favour performed for Mary herself because such things are possible in the case of Imams and saints as well as prophets. Ṭabarsī mentions only the first two answers, attributing the one to al-Jubbā'ī and his son and the other to al-Balakhī. Moreover, he views the virginal conception in the same light as the appearing of the angel – that is to say it was a miracle performed for Zechariah or Jesus rather than for Mary!

Ṭūsī's discussion of the reading of 19:19 is more detailed than any that I have encountered in the Sunnī commentaries. It will be remembered that the majority read this āya *li-ahaba la-ki* ('so that I may bestow on you') but that Abū 'Amr and Nāfi' read it *li-yahaba la-ki* ('so that [your Lord] may bestow on you'). The two readings differ in respect of a single consonant: *hamza* in the one case, *yā'* in the other. Ṭūsī states al-Ḥasan [al-Baṣrī] said that 'so that I may bestow on you' means 'so that I may bestow on you by God's leave'. Then he mentions the opinions of various grammarians:

(1) Abū 'Ubayda [Baṣran grammarian d.210/825] considered Abū 'Amr's reading weak because it departed from the consonantal text (*muṣḥaf*).

(2) Ibn Khālawayh [grammarian and specialist in readings d.370/981] said that Abū ʻAmr's defence was that the letters of extension and softness [*alif*, *wāw* and *yā*'] and those with a *hamza* are transformed into each other. For instance *li-allā* (in order not to) is pronounced *li-yallā*.

(3) Abū ʻAlī [al-Qālī] the grammarian [of Baghdad, d.355/967] said that it is possible that whoever read it with *yā*' intended *hamza*' and only changed it to *yā* in accordance with the school of Abū 'l-Ḥasan [al-Fārisī, Baṣran grammarian who was also active in Baghdad, Aleppo and Shirāz, d.376/987] or made it a cross between the two in accordance with the teaching of al-Khalīl [Baṣran grammarian d.170/786].

Finally, Ṭūsī mentions that the reading with *yā*' had the support of Ubaiy and Ibn Masʻūd and that he himself considers it the better reading.

DISCUSSION

In the classical period, Shīʻite and Sunnite exegesis of the Qur'anic passages which refer to Jesus were remarkably similar. There are two obvious reasons for this: on the one hand both Ṭūsī and Ṭabarsī made extensive use of the great Sunnī commentary by Abū Jaʻfar al-Ṭabarī and on the other hand Rāzī drew on the commentary by al-Kalbī and took an interest in the Muʻtazilites. This is not, however, the whole story and a comparison of Qummī and Ṭabarī suggests that, in the pre-classical period, proto-Shīʻites and proto-Sunnites drew upon very similar traditions which the former traced to the Imams and the latter traced to the Companions and Successors.

In comparison with the Sunnite commentators the Shīʻites tend to further reduce Jesus' uniqueness. There is no doubt that he was born of a virgin and that his mother was chosen above all women but the virginal conception is in the same category as the portents which preceded the mission of Muḥammad and Mary is no greater than Muḥammad's daughter Fāṭima. His return to kill the Antichrist is not in question but when he does return his role will be subordinate to that of the Mahdī who is identified with the Twelfth Imam. In general it is assumed that his likeness was projected onto a substitute who died in his place but similar things could happen in the case of the Imams or saints. According to Qummī Jesus ascended from the corner of the house, presumably the same corner as the one containing the spring from which he had previously emerged to greet his disciples. This curious detail is perhaps linked in some way with the belief that the twelfth Imam went into occultation by disappearing down a well in the corner of a room in Sāmarrā.[15]

The Shī'ite commentaries throw further light on the development of the exegetical traditions although there is still much which remains obscure. In Chapter 13 we saw that there were grounds for thinking that the report concerning the projection of Jesus' likeness onto a volunteer might have originated in Kūfa in the first half of the second/eighth century despite its being ostensibly traced back to Ibn al-'Abbās. The similarity of this report to the one which Qummī attributes to the fifth Imam strengthens our suspicions but falls short of actually proving them. In Chapter 9 we examined Zamakhsharī's version of Ibn Ḥawshab's encounter with al-Ḥajjāj and it was suggested that this furnished evidence that the interpretation of 4:159 was a divisive issue in Kūfa at the beginning of the second/eighth century. Unfortunately the presence in Qummī and Ṭūsī of different versions of this encounter leaves us in some doubt concerning which of the two interpretations was originally considered sectarian. I am inclined to think that these Shī'ite versions have more historical plausibility than Zamakhsharī's version and that, to the consternation of the authorities, the early Shī'ites understood «before his death» to mean before Jesus' death.

17 The Representation of Jesus in the Ṣūfī Commentaries

Ṣūfism was discussed briefly in Chapter 7 and we have occasionally encountered allusions to Ṣūfī interpretations in the commentaries of Rāzī and Bayḍāwī. In this chapter I will examine the representation of Jesus in two Ṣūfī commentaries: those compiled by Qushayrī and Qāshānī.

THE ṢŪFĪ COMMENTARIES

Qushayrī

Abū al-Qāsim 'Abd al-Karīm al-Qushayrī (d.465/1072) was born in Ustuwā in 376/986 when Khurāsān and Transoxania were ruled by the Sāmānids. His parents were well-to-do Arabs and he received a thorough education in Islamic sciences becoming one of the leading Ash'arite teachers of his time and earning the nickname 'the Professor' (*al-ustādh*) of Khurāsān. His best known work is the *Risāla*. It was written in 448/1046 with the express purpose of rescuing Ṣūfism from the bad reputation which had become attached to it because of the *Malāmatīya* and it is still regarded as the standard handbook on moderate Ṣūfism.[1] Qushayrī's mystical or esoteric commentary *Laṭā'if al-Ishārāt* ('The Subtleties of the Allusions')[2] was begun the previous year but not completed until considerably later. This mature work was written for the edification of those who were following the Ṣūfī path. It deals only with the inner meanings of the text, meanings which cannot be determined by recourse to tradition or by the rigorous application of a set method. However, from the Ṣūfī standpoint, these meanings are not arbitrary. They are alluded to in the text and are grasped intuitively by those who meditate on the spiritual significance of the Qur'ān. It is also important to realise that this type of interpretation was not intended to rival or supplant traditional exegesis but to supplement it. In Qushayrī's case this should be obvious from the fact that long before he began the *Laṭā'if al-Ishārāt* he completed a large Qur'anic commentary *al-Tafsīr al-Kabīr* written on traditional lines and expounding the external meaning of the Qur'ān. Unfortunately, of this earlier work, only the section dealing with ṣūras 57:21 to 66:12 has survived.[3]

Qāshānī

Our second Ṣūfī commentator, 'Abd al-Razzāq Kamāl al-Dīn al-Qāshānī (d.730/1329), lived in Kāshān in Persia in the period when it was dominated by the Il-Khānid Mongols. Little is known about him other than that he wrote several books on Ṣūfism and that he was a champion of the theosophical system of Ibn al-'Arabī to whom his own *Ta'wīlāt al-Qur'ān* ('Esoteric Explanations of the Qur'ān') is sometimes wrongly attributed.[4] In the preface to this work he cites and explains an ḥadīth which enjoyed considerable vogue in Ṣūfī circles:

> 'Not an āya of the Qur'ān has come down but it has a back (*ẓahr*) and a belly (*baṭn*); every letter has a limit and every limit has a point of ascension.'
>
> I understood by it that the 'back' is the external meaning (*tafsīr*) and the 'belly' is the esoteric meaning (*ta'wīl*). The 'limit' is the extreme point which understanding of the verbal meaning can reach. The 'point of ascension' is the contemplative level to which one ascends to contemplate the All-Knowing King.[5]

He subsequently declares that he is concerned exclusively with esoteric explanation. This, he says, varies in accordance with 'states' of the hearer, the 'moments' in the stages of his spiritual journey and the spiritual levels that he has reached. Every time the hearer progresses to a higher 'station' a new door of understanding is opened and he becomes aware of the subtlety of a further meaning prepared for him.

The presence within Qāshānī's commentary of interpretations corresponding to different spiritual levels makes for very difficult reading. The problem is exacerbated by the fact that he does not deal systematically with the spiritual cosmology or with the stages of spiritual realisation and that he uses slightly different terminology from Ibn al-'Arabī. I cannot deal with these matters in detail although I will refer to them briefly in the concluding discussion.[6] It is nevertheless desirable to be aware from the outset of the two broad types of esoteric interpretation which we shall encounter: *taṭbīq* and *ta'wīl*. The former is the 'application' of the Qur'anic symbolism to the spiritual psychology of the Ṣūfī or to the various stages of his spiritual journey. The latter is esoteric interpretation in the strict sense and elicits allusions to the divine essence or the spiritual cosmology.

JESUS' RETURN

Qushayrī[7]

Qushayrī passes over 4:159 without comment but in dealing with 43:61 he states that it refers to Jesus whom God will send down from heaven as a sign of the hour. He also mentions in connection with 3:46 that Jesus' speaking to mankind in his maturity may apply to the period after his return. In other words he simply refers in summary fashion to the traditional exegesis of these āyas and sees no inner significance in Jesus' return beyond its literal meaning.

Qāshānī[8]

Qāshānī's treatment of this issue is much more extensive. In the course of his comments on 3:56–8 he explains why it is that Jesus must return:

> Since Jesus did not reach the seventh heaven, which Muḥammad attained during his heavenly ascent and which is designated symbolically by the «Lotus of the limit» [53:14] – which I take to mean the Station of Ultimacy in Perfection – and since Jesus has not attained the degree of divine love, he must descend a second time in a bodily form and follow the Muḥammadan religion in order to attain Muḥammad's spiritual degree. God best knows the reality of the things.

This receives further clarification in his comments on 4:159 where he states that Jesus was raised to the fourth heaven and that since he did not attain to true perfection (*ilā 'l-kamāli 'l-ḥaqīqī*) he must descend at the end of time and in a different body. Every one of the People of the Scripture will believe in him then, on the Day of Resurrection, before his death by extinction in God (*qabla mawti 'Īsā bi-'l-fanā'i fī Allāh*).

Qāshānī assumes without question that the external meaning of

43:61 is that the return of Jesus is one of the signs of the hour. He gives an esoteric interpretation not of the Qur'anic text but of one of the aḥādīth associated with it:

> [Jesus] will descend in a narrow pass of the Holy Land called Afīq. In his hand he will have a lance with which he will kill the Antichrist. He will smash the Cross, destroy synagogues and churches and enter the temple when folk are at the morning prayer. The imam will step back but Jesus will send him out in front again and he will pray behind him in accordance with the religion of Muḥammad (may God bless him and grant him peace!).
>
> The narrow pass named Afīq is an allusion to the external appearance in which [Jesus] will be embodied. The Holy Land [is an illusion to] the pure matter of which his body will be composed. The lance is an allusion to the powerful and incisive form in which he will appear. Killing the Antichrist with it is an allusion to his overcoming the misleading tyrant who will come forth in his time. Breaking the Cross and destroying synagogues and churches is an allusion to his abolition of the different religions. His entering the temple is an allusion to his attaining the Station of Essential Sainthood in the Divine Presence, which is the Station of the Pole. The people's being at the morning prayer is an allusion to the agreement of the Muḥammadans to the probity of belief in the Divine Unity at the rising of the dawn of the Day of the Great Resurrection with the appearing of the light of the Sun of Oneness.
>
> The imam's stepping back is an allusion to his awareness of Jesus' precedence, at any rate in the standing pertaining to the Station of Polarity. Jesus' sending him back forward and his following his example in accordance with the Muḥammadan religious law is an allusion to his following the chosen religious confession and to his not changing to the systems of religious law [of the Jews and Christians?] although [God] used to teach them the evident Divine Unity and inform them about the states of the Great Resurrection and the rising of the face of the One who Remains. That is [the correct esoteric interpretation] if Jesus is the Mahdī in accordance with what has been transmitted in the ḥadīth, 'No Mahdī except Jesus Son of Mary.'
>
> If on the other hand the Mahdī is not Jesus but someone else, then Jesus' entering the temple is his attaining to the Position of Contemplation (*ilā maḥalli mushāhadatī*) without [attaining to] the Station of the Pole. [In that case] it is the imam who will step back

who is the Mahdī. He will step back, despite his being the Temporal Pole, out of deference to the etiquette governing the relationship between a person endowed with sainthood towards one endowed with prophethood. Jesus' sending him back forward is because of his knowing that in fact he has precedence because of his Position of Polarity. His praying behind him in accordance with the Muḥammadan revealed law and his emulating him in it serves as a confirmation of his detailed observance of that law both outwardly and inwardly.

God knows best [which of these two interpretations is correct.]

THE CRUCIFIXION

Qushayrī[9]

Qushayrī says nothing about the traditional interpretations of 3:55 which link it with God's rescue of Jesus from the machinations of the Jews. Instead he concentrates exclusively on the esoteric meaning:

> When God said, «'O Jesus, I am going to receive you'» – what is alluded to in this (*al-ishāra fī-hi*) is 'I am going to receive you from yourself, grasp (*qābiḍ*) you from you and cause you to ascend from the attributes of mankind and purify you entirely from your own volition so that you become disposed by Us for Us. Nothing will depend on your free will. The pouring upon you of sainthood (*tawallin*) will be continuous.'

We saw in Chapter 12 that both Rāzī and Bayḍāwī referred briefly to this interpretation and that Rāzī attributed it to Abū Bakr al-Wāsitī. What is implied is that Jesus was brought into a special relationship with God, characterised as being grasped by Him. The Arabic verb *qabaḍa* conveys the idea of grasping in the hand. In Ṣūfī parlance *qabḍ* is a quasi technical term denoting 'compression' in which the individual is left completely to God. Qushayrī evidently does not think of this as the inner significance of what happened when Jesus was raised bodily into heaven. On the contrary, he has in mind a mystical state into which Jesus was drawn in the course of his earthly life for he adds that it was because of this quality that the bringing to life of the dead was manifested through his good offices. He also gives a second and slightly different explanation of what was involved in this mystical state:

> And it is said that the Lord purified his heart from the perusal of things that change and the spectacle of images and impressions in all states and stages.

In commenting on 4:157f, Qushayrī summarises two of the traditional reports of how God projected Jesus' semblance onto a substitute who was then crucified in his place. According to the first version of what happened the semblance was projected onto Jesus' betrayer. According to the second version it was projected onto a volunteer. He makes no attempt to choose between the two on the grounds of strength of attestation or implicit rationality. Instead he draws out the inner significance of both stories.

The moral of the story of Jesus' betrayer is summed up by the proverb: 'He who digs a pit for his brother will fall into it.' As for the story of the volunteer: 'If a person patiently endures the full measure of destruction he will not lack a recompense from God.' Moreover the Qur'ān contains the following promise: «We do not allow the reward of those who have done good deeds to be lost». (18:30)

In view of this Qushayrī mentions speculation about the fate of the volunteer:

> When Jesus was made to ascend to the place of proximity the spirit of the man who saved him was made to ascend to the place of nearness.

This is somewhat cryptic but there are two points which we should note. First, in Qur'anic usage 'proximity' to God (*zulfa* cf. 67:27) has less positive connotations than 'nearness' to Him. We are probably intended to infer that the volunteer immediately took Jesus' place in paradise becoming 'one of those brought near' (cf. 3:45) whereas Jesus himself was temporarily given a lower position. Second, Qushayrī avoids specifying whether or not Jesus was made to ascend bodily. However, since he explicitly states that in the case of the volunteer it was the man's spirit which ascended, we are encouraged to draw our own conclusions.

Qāshānī[10]

When commenting on 3:54f, Qāshānī begins by giving the 'application' on the level of the individual's spiritual psychology. Jesus' sensing unbelief corresponds to the heart's sensing the contrariety of the spiritual forces of the carnal soul. His request for helpers corresponds to the heart's need for spiritual strength to assist it in turning to God. The disciples who rallied to his help correspond to the best part and the most sincere of the spiritual forces of the carnal soul:

> «they schemed» that is the forebodings and imaginings [schemed] to murder the heart and destroy it by varieties of seductions «and God schemed» by making the intellectual arguments and decisive proofs triumph over their imaginings and sceptical remarks, and by his raising Jesus, [that is] the heart, into the heaven of the Spirit and by projecting its likeness onto the carnal soul so that their murdering should befall it. «And God is the best of schemers» hence His scheme triumphed.

Qāshānī is probably still thinking of the 'application' when he continues:

> And He said to Jesus [the heart] «'I am going to receive you'» that is, going to grasp you to Me from among them «'and raise you to Myself'» that is, into the heaven of the Spirit in proximity to Me'.

A little further on he adds:

> As for the esoteric interpretation (*ta'wīl*), apart from the application (*bi-ghayr 'l-ṭatbīqi*), it is that they schemed by sending one who would murder Jesus (on him be peace), so «a semblance was made to them» a corporeal form which was the external appearance of Jesus [who in accordance with his true nature is] the Spirit of God as being the form of the essential truth of Jesus. They took it to be Jesus himself whereas God caused Jesus (on him be peace) to ascend to the fourth heaven because of his spirit's overflowing with the spirituality of the Sun. And they did not know in their ignorance that God's spirit could not be killed.
>
> When Jesus knew for certain his state, before the ascending, he said to his companions: 'I am going to rejoin my father, your heavenly father,' [cp. *John* 16:16 etc.], that is I am going to cleanse myself of the world of filth and rejoin the Holy Spirit which gives the forms which provoke the cosmic deployment of the spirits and perfections, the Master who educates men by inbreathing the Spirit so that he spreads his effusion on you.

Having commented on 3:55f in such detail, Qāshānī is left with nothing to say about 4:157, but concerning 4:158 he remarks:

> The raising of Jesus (on him be peace), the transporting of his spirit at the departure from the lower world to the higher world, and his

being in the fourth heaven, is an allusion to the overflowing (*fayḍān*) of the source of his spirit, the spirituality of the celestial body, the Sun which is tantamount to the heart of the world and what it reverts to. That spirituality is a light which moves that celestial body by its loveliness (*bi-ma'shūqīyati-hi*) and the beaming of its rays on its active soul (*'alā nafsi-hi 'l-mubāsharat-*) to move it.

THE MIRACLES

Qushayrī[11]

Qushayrī has little to say about Jesus' miraculous signs. He accepts them literally as overwhelming and dazzling demonstrations and he knows that there were others attributed to him besides those which are detailed in the Qur'ān. He seems particularly impressed by Jesus' raising the dead. Yet did Jesus work this miracle or did God perform it for him? Qushayrī does not actually pose the question. From his standpoint the distinction verges on the academic. It was because Jesus had been purified from his own volition and was entirely at God's disposal that the raising of the dead was manifested through his offices (literally 'at his hand') but such occurrences would have been impossible were it not for sublime power.

Qāshānī[12]

That Qāshānī also believed the miracles to be literally true is evident from his comments on the Qur'anic account of how Moses confounded the magicians in Egypt (7:104–41). There he mentions that the prophets were sent with signs appropriate to the epochs in which they lived: Moses' period was dominated by magic just as Muḥammad's was dominated by eloquence and Jesus' was dominated by medicine. Elsewhere, however, he concentrates on the inner significance of the miracles. He paraphrases 3:49 as follows:

> «Lo! I create for you» by instruction, purification and practical wisdom, from the «clay» of your carnal souls, which are ready but deficient, «something resembling the form of birds» flying to the side of holiness from intense desire; «and I blow into it» of the exhalation of divine knowledge and the breath of true life by the influence of companionship and instruction «and it becomes a

> bird», that is a living soul flying on the wing of desire and ardour to the side of the Truth. «And I heal the blind from birth» who is veiled from the light of the Truth, whose eye of discernment has never been opened and who has perceived neither the Sun of the countenance of the Truth nor the light, and whose family have never acknowledged the antimony of guidance; «and the leper» whose soul is blemished by the disease of vices and corrupt doctrines and the love of this world and the dirt of carnal appetites, [I heal] by the medicine of souls. «And I bring to life» the dead of ignorance with the life of knowledge.

His paraphrase of 5:110 is very similar but there are some interesting additions. For instance he interprets «by My leave» to mean:

> by My knowledge and My power, and My facilitating through My manifesting the attributes of My life, knowledge and power for you

And he states that Jesus brought forth the dead 'of ignorance from the tombs of the body and the earth of the carnal soul'.

THE VIRGINAL CONCEPTION

Qushayrī[13]

Qushayrī's comments on the story of Mary are for the most part confined to the external meaning. He remarks for instance that God preferred Mary above the women of the worlds in the sense that she was the only woman to bear a child without a father and that in this she was unique because no woman resembled her or ever will.

Qāshānī[14]

Qāshānī discusses the virginal conception at great length sparing no efforts in his endeavour to explain how such an occurrence could be possible. In normal circumstances pregnancy cannot take place without the male and female generative fluids combining in the womb. The man's fluid, he tells us, is much hotter than the woman's fluid and its power to make coagulate is proportionally stronger as is that of rennet in comparison with cheese. Correspondingly, the woman's fluid has a greater propensity to be coagulated. Thus when the two come together they complement each other perfectly and the foetus is formed. Now if the constitution of the female were strong and the constitution of her liver were hot, the generative fluid discharged from her right kidney would be much hotter than that discharged from her left kidney. If they came together in the womb and the constitution of the womb were also strong because of abstinence and barrenness, the discharge from the right kidney might perform the role of the male fluid with the result that the woman would conceive. None of that would happen, however, unless something first provoked the discharge of the generative fluid. This, according to Qāshānī, was why God's Spirit presented himself to Mary as a perfectly proportioned human being. The apparition aroused her passion as if in an erotic dream although the effect was much more powerful and her generative fluid was consequently propelled into the womb and the child was formed.

Taken out of context Qāshānī's digression into physiology might give the impression that he was a *savant grivois* not unduly overawed by Mary's sanctity. That this is far from true is evident from the comments on 19:16–17a which precede the digression:

> The «easterly place» is the place of the holy world [to which she withdrew] at the time of her contact with the Holy Spirit in her isolation. «She withdrew» from the stronghold of the natural disposition and the refuge of the carnal soul. Her «family» were the natural and psychic forces. The «curtain» which «she took to herself» «from them» was the enclosure of holiness which is forbidden to the «family» of the world of the carnal soul by the «curtain» of the breast which is the utmost amount of knowledge of the material powers and the range of their operation. If she had not been devoted to the holy world in her isolation, the sending of the Holy Spirit to her would have been impossible.

Moreover, in his comments on 3:34 and 47 Qāshānī shows that the virginal conception is applicable to the spiritual life. In normal circumstances,

> Just as the body in its material birth is conceived in the womb of the mother by the action of the father's sperm, likewise the heart in the true birth is conceived in the womb of the predisposition of the soul by the breath of the sheikh or instructor. It is to this birth which Jesus alluded when he said, 'He who has not been born twice will not enter the Kingdom of heaven' [cp. *John* 3:3].

Mary's case was different:

> «She said 'My Lord how can I have a child...?'» The soul is astonished at its conceiving and giving birth without a mortal touching it, that is without instruction from a sheikh and without training from a mortal teacher. This is the meaning of her virginity. «He said, 'It shall be so. God creates what he wills.'» He chooses whom he wills by attraction and unveiling and he offers him the station of the heart without him having to follow formation or spiritual instruction.

DISCUSSION

In general the Ṣūfī commentators assume that traditional exegesis provides the correct understanding of the external meaning of the Qur'ān. Indeed, we have seen that on occasions they give a mystical exposition of certain aspects of traditional exegesis rather than of the Qur'anic text itself. For instance Qushayrī discusses the inner meaning of the reports about the projection of Jesus' likeness onto a substitute and Qāshānī gives an esoteric interpretation of the ḥadīth about Jesus' return. Sometimes, however, they seem, on the contrary, to be out of step with traditional exegesis. Qushayrī ignores the ḥadīth relativizing Mary's position and states that she was unique in an absolute sense, a view which we have elsewhere seen attributed to the Mu'tazilite scholar al-Jubbā'i. Moreover he gives an esoteric interpretation of 3:55 in terms of 'compression' that cannot be reconciled with the standard explanation which links it with God's rescuing Jesus from his Jewish assailants. Qāshānī sidesteps this issue by relegating Qushayrī's interpretation to the position of *taṭbīq*. Nevertheless, although he preserves the link between 3:55 and God's rescuing Jesus, he appears to abandon the substitute theory in favour of the view that it was Jesus' outward form and not his spirit which was crucified.

Much more research would be needed to ascertain the extent to which the Ṣūfī commentators were heirs to a tradition of esoteric interpretation. It is, however, possible to make a few provisional observations. The general tenor of Qāshānī's commentary is markedly different from Qushayrī's and there is little continuity between the two. Nevertheless there are signs that both writers were indebted to their predecessors. If Rāzī's attribution is correct, Qushayrī's interpretation of 3:55 originated over a century earlier with Abū Bakr al-Wāsiṭī. Qāshānī's discussion of Jesus' miracles is similar to that of the Brethren of Purity and he follows Ibn al-'Arabī in supposing that Mary's desire had to be aroused in order for conception to occur. As is to be expected, Qāshānī also adopts Ibn al'Arabī's theosophical system in broad outline.

Qāshānī seems to envisage three principal stages on the path to spiritual realisation. The first stage is that of unification at the level of acts and consists of self-abandonment to God in the realisation that all acts come from Him. This is 'the station of the soul' and is in principle attainable by all believers through observance of the revealed law. The second stage is that of unification at the level of attributes and is characterised by true contemplation and the stripping off of one's own qualities in order to assume the divine attributes. This is 'the station of the heart.' It is, as we have seen, the station which was bestowed on Mary in her seclusion. It is also the station which Jesus attained at his ascension when he rejoined 'the heart of the world', which is another name for 'the Universal Rational Soul'.[15] In Qāshānī's spiritual cosmology the World of the Universal Rational Soul is called the World of Royalty; it is inhabited by 'the Holy Spirit' (Gabriel) and the other angels by whom God governs the affairs of heaven and earth. The third and final stage is that of unification at the level of Essence. This is 'the station of the spirit' also known as 'the station of ultimacy in perfection' and 'the position of contemplation', 'true perfection' and 'extinction in God'. It is the station which Muḥammad attained during the *mi'rāj* but to which Jesus will not accede until the Day of Resurrection.

If the above analysis is correct, Qāshānī's understanding of Jesus' words about being born again and about returning to the Father is radically different from the standard Christian interpretation of them. He takes them to refer to an intermediate stage in spiritual realisation – a stage beyond which neither Jesus nor his followers can progress without Islam. The 'Kingdom of Heaven' is equated with the World of Royalty and the 'Father' to whom Jesus returns is taken to be a designation for Gabriel. Nevertheless it is interesting that Qāshānī should have appropriated these Christian texts. His interpretation of the miracles may also be derived ultimately from Christianity for once again one is reminded of St John's Gospel in which the healing of the man who was born blind and the raising of

Lazarus from the dead have symbolic overtones to do with illumination and new life. The interpretation is, however, attuned to the symbolic universe of the Qur'ān where unbelievers are said to be blind (2:18, etc.) and where birds which are held in flight solely by the Beneficent epitomise total dependence on God (67:19).

Postscript

Abū Ḥayyān (d.745/1343), a post-classical author and near contemporary of Ibn Kathīr, compiled a comprehensive commentary on the Qur'ān based on earlier works. Its title, *al-Baḥr al-Muḥīṭ* – 'the Ocean' or more literally, 'the Enveloping Sea' – puts my own attempts at plumbing the depths of Qur'anic exegesis into perspective. I have done no more than take provisional soundings at points which, with good reason, I deemed appropriate. Had I followed a different course and sunk my line elsewhere I would doubtless have gained a different impression of the underlying ocean bed. Nevertheless, although a 'conclusion' would be premature, my investigations qualify me to make some observations.

Christians who are concerned with contemporary Islam and with Muslim-Christian dialogue often pay scant attention to the classical commentaries and concentrate instead on more recent popularist writings. Yet although ordinary Muslims may have little or no first-hand knowledge of traditional exegesis, this does not detract from its importance as one of the massive institutions which contribute to the maintenance of their religious worldview. This is particularly true of the *Tafsīr* of Ibn Kathīr. It owes its prestige to its author's association with Ibn Taymīya whose theology inspired the Wahhābī movement in eighteenth-century Arabia, which in turn had a marked influence on Islamic fundamentalism in the Indian sub-continent. These considerations alone should be sufficient to show that the classical commentaries cannot simply be dismissed as a relic of the past.

The classical commentaries represent Jesus in a manner which is fairly constant and it makes little difference whether their authors are Sunnites or Shī'ites. The Qur'anic picture is fused with that of the 'authentic' aḥādīth which refer to Jesus' future descent to kill the Antichrist and which relativise the Qur'anic statement about God's choice of Mary. The commentators are unanimous in accepting the literal truth of the virginal conception and of the miracles which the Qur'ān ascribes to Jesus but they interpret them as proofs of his prophethood, not of his divinity. They are also unanimous in maintaining that *Qur'ān* 4:157 denies that Jesus was crucified. They generally assume that this āya is best understood in the light of traditions which describe how Jesus' semblance was projected onto someone else while he himself was raised bodily into heaven – or to be more precise into the third heaven where Muḥammad encountered him on his night journey.

Nevertheless despite the essential unity which I have just outlined, their works are far more rich and varied than I was given to expect. Ibn Kathīr is only one classical commentator among many. In comparison with him, Ṭabarī is more tolerant of diversity while Rāzī and Ṭūsī are more open to speculation. In addition a whole new dimension is opened up by the esoteric commentaries of Qushayrī and Qāshānī.

Classical exegesis of course has its limitations. For the most part the commentators are lawyers with a concern to fix the meaning of the sacred text. Although they quote freely from the early poets, never once have I caught them remarking on the rhyme, rhythm or alliteration which are so characteristic of the Qur'ān. Nor is their interest in history sufficiently critical to lead them to question the traditional vision of Islam. Consequently they frequently seem incapable of distinguishing between the Qur'anic representation of Jesus and subsequent layers of interpretation. Although I myself have occasionally attempted to do this by referring to Christian polemic, *ghulāt* beliefs and other factors whose influence I have detected, I am under no illusions about the enormity of the task which still lies ahead. Moreover, judging by the experience of Christian scholars who have made considerable progress in extricating the New Testament from the interpretative matrix of patristic and reformation theology but who have had little impact on ordinary Christians, I doubt whether a thorough-going critical understanding of classical exegesis would radically alter the status of Jesus in the Muslim imagination.

Although the critical study of the Qur'anic commentaries is still in its infancy, the critical study of the Qur'anic representation of Jesus is well established. For the most part it has been the privileged domain of non-Muslim scholars particularly of Christians. With some justification Muslims have frequently suspected them of covert polemical or apologetic intentions. At their worst, Christian apologists who force their interpretation on the Qur'ān remind me of the agents of the *Reconquista* who built their cathedral in the heart of the mosque at Cordoba. At their best, Christian historians who detect elements of Christian provenance embedded in the Qur'ān are more like skilled archaeologists who have unearthed vestiges of Constantinople beneath the surface of Istanbul. They know that Aya Sofya Camii was once a Christian church but that it could not be 'restored' merely by removing the minarets with which it is now adorned. Its 'meaning' is now inextricably bound up with the many splendid Ottoman buildings which surround it on every side.

Notes

INTRODUCTION

1. Muslim scholars.
2. Ṭaha Hussayn, *Al-Ayyām*, vol. 2, (Cairo: Dār al-Ma'ārif, 1939), English Translation: Taha Hussein, *The Stream of Days: A Student at the Azhar* (London: Longmans, Green, 1948).

1 JESUS IN THE QUR'ĀN

1. Whenever dates are given the first figure refers to the Muslim Era (H), the second to the Common Era (G). The Muslim year comprises 12 lunar months and is 11 days shorter than the solar year. In some instances the Common Era dates are only approximate and have been calculated on the assumption that: $G = H + 622 - H/33$.
2. See R. Bell and W.M. Watt, *Introduction to the Qur'ān* (Edinburgh University Press, 1970) pp. 40–8. In broad outline the Muslim tradition has met with widespread acceptance from non-Muslim scholars. It is, however, rejected by J. Wansbrough, *Quranic Studies* (Oxford: OUP, 1977) esp. pp. 43–6.
3. Ṣūras and āyas are numbered in accordance with the standard Egyptian Edition of the Qur'ān which is the basis of most modern translations. Some older translations including those of Bell and Arberry follow Flügel's numbering of the āyas which differs only slightly from this. A conversion table is given in Bell and Watt op. cit. pp. 202f.
4. Taking the word as an elative *aḥmad* rather than a name Aḥmad. There is no distinction between upper and lower case letters in Arabic.
5. This point is made forcefully by Mohammad Arkoun, 'Ceux qui prétendent réduire à un exposé systématique, conceptuel, linéaire, un texte libre, «désordonné», éclaté en milliers d'unités textuelles, commettent un contresens linguistique grossier. On ne peut transposer un langage de structure mythique dans un simple langage dénotatif sans appauvrir à l'extrême un système complexe de connotations.' *La pensée arabe*, 2nd edn (Paris: Presses Universitaires de France, 1979) p. 18.

2 'ĪSĀ THROUGH CHRISTIAN EYES

1. See Section A of the Bibliography.
2. Cited by G.C. Anawati, 'Polémique, apologie et dialogue Islamo-Chrétiens. Positions classiques et positions contemporaines', *Euntes docete* (Rome, Urbaniana) XXII (1969), p. 385.
3. I.S. Allouche 'Un traité de polémique Christiano-Musulmane au IX 'siècle', *Hespéris* XLVI (1959), pp. 129ff.

4. Muḥammad presumably understood himself to be the one referred to in *Qur'ān* 61:6. At an early date Muslims linked this passage with Jesus' promise of the Paraclete. Already in the eighth century the Nestorian Catholicos Timothy I marshalled arguments against this. See H. Putman *L'Eglise et l'Islam sous Timothée I (780–823)* (Beirut: Dar el-Machreq, 1986), pp. 238ff.
5. Allouche, ibid.
6. A-Th.Khoury, *Les théologians Byzantins et l'Islam* (Louvain and Paris: Nauwelaerts, 1969), p. 146.
7. Cited by G.C. Anawati ''Īsā', *Encyclopaedia of Islam*, 2nd edn (Leiden: Brill, 1960–), vol. II, p. 85.
8. Muḥammad's encounter with Baḥīrā is mentioned in Islamic tradition. The notion that he was an Arian is probably derived from the Byzantine theologian John of Damascus (died before 753?). John regarded Islam as a Christian heresy. He did not mention Baḥīrā by name but he said that Muḥammad, or Mamed as he called him, 'having casually been exposed to the Old and the New Testament and supposedly encountered an Arian monk, formed a heresy of his own' – J.D. Sahas, *John of Damascus on Islam* (Leiden: Brill, 1972) p. 132f. The Sergius legend, on the other hand, seems to be an entirely Christian invention although it was still taken seriously by at least one Christian polemicist as recently as the seventeenth century. See Daniel, *Islam amd the West* (Edinburgh University Press, 1960), pp. 5 and 288.
9. Muḥammad's contacts with these individuals will be discussed in Chapter 4.
10. Cited by Anawati, 'Polémique, apologie . . .' p. 385.
11. Cited by Anawati ''Īsā' p. 85.
12. Sahas, op. cit. p. 136f.
13. C-J. Ledit, *Mahomet, Israël et le Christ* (Paris: La Colombe, 1956), p. 152.
14. R.C. Zaehner, *At Sundry Times: An Essay in Comparative Religions* (London: Faber & Faber, 1958), p. 201.
15. Ledit, op. cit. pp. 155f.
16. Zaehner, op. cit., p. 206.
17. Ibid. p. 209.
18. See e.g. Ledit, op. cit. p. 154.
19. In view of the debt of the apologists to earlier polemicists it is understandable that Muslims frequently view their work in this uncharitable light.
20. See A. Race, *Christians and Religious Pluralism* (London: SCM, 1983), pp. 38–69.
21. This is purely conjecture but it corresponds to the author's own experience at one stage.
22. K. Cragg, *Jesus and the Muslim* (London: George Allen & Unwin, 1985), p. 30.
23. G. Parrinder, *Jesus in the Qur'ān* (London: Faber & Faber, 1965).

3 'ĪSĀ AND THE CHURCH HISTORIAN

1. For a succinct survey see A. Havenith, *Les arabes chrétiens nomades au temps de Mohammed* (Louvain-la-Neuve: Cerfaux-Lefort, 1988). More detailed information is to be found in J.S. Trimingham, *Christianity among the Arabs in Pre-Islamic Times* (London and Beirut: Longman and Librairie du Liban, 1979).
2. The persecution was sometimes on a large scale. A century after Chalcedon a Patriarch of Alexandria was responsible for the massacre of 200,000 Monophysites. See E. Rabbath, *L'Orient chrétien à la veille de l'Islam* (Beirut: Librairie Orientale, 1980), p. 25.
3. See H. Lammens, 'Les Chrétiens à la Mecque à la veille de l'hégire', *Bulletin de l'Institut Français d'Archéologie Orientale*, XIV (1917), pp. 191–230.
4. These are the so-called *Ḥanīfs*. See W.M. Watt *Muḥammad at Mecca* (Oxford: OUP, 1953), pp. 162–4. At least two of them subsequently became Christians.
5. In one of his poems Adī b. Zayd makes his oath in front of the black stone 'In the name of the Lord of Mecca and of the Crucifix' – Rabbath, op. cit. p. 174.
6. On the origin of the Arabic versions of the New Testament see B.M. Metzger, *The Early Versions of the New Testament* (Oxford: Clarendon, 1967), pp. 257–61.
7. See A. Jefferey, *The Foreign Vocabulary of the Qur'ān* (Baroda: Oriental Institute, 1938).
8. See the section on the eschatological piety of Muḥammad in Tor Andrae, *Les origines de l'Islam et le Christianisme* (Paris: Adrien-Maisonneuve, 1955), pp. 67–200. The author has overstated his case as regards the voluptuous rewards of paradise: the hymns of Ephraim Syrus mention vines and fruit trees but not houris – see E. Beck, 'Les houris du Coran et Ephrem le Syrien', *MIDEO* VI (1959–60), pp. 405–8.
9. According to E. Gräf, 'Zu den christlichen Einflüsen im Koran', J. Henniger Festschrift *al-bahit* (Bonn: St Augustin, 1976), p. 118, this identification of Mary with the burning bush occurs in a hymn by Rabbula.
10. In Syriac (as in Hebrew and Greek) the two names are identical. See J. Bowman, 'The Debt of Islam to Monophysite Syrian Christianity', *Nederlands Theologisch Tijdschrift*, XIX (1964–5), p. 200.
11. H. Michaud, *Jésus selon le Coran*, (Neuchâtel: Delachaux et Niestlé, 1960), pp. 56–8.
12. See J. Bowman op. cit. pp. 187–90.
13. K. Luke, 'The Koranic Recension of Luke 1:34', *Indian Theological Studies*, XXII (1985), pp. 381–99.
14. E. Hennecke, *New Testament Apocrypha* vol. 1 (London: SCM, 1973) pp. 378–80. Note however that the parallels are not exact. For example according to the *Protoevangelium of James* it was Joseph who was chosen as Mary's guardian and not Zechariah.
15. Ibid. pp. 411f.
16. 'Nous avons trouvé ⟨ceci⟩ dans le livre de Josèphe, le grand prêtre qui

existait au temps du Christ . . . il affirme donc que Jésus parla, étant au berceau, et qu'il dit à sa mère: «Je suis Jésus, le fils de Dieu, le Verbe que vous avez enfanté, comme vous l'avait annoncé l'ange Gabriel, et mon Père m'a envoyé pour sauver le monde.' P. Peeters, *Evangiles Apocryphes* vol. 1 (Paris: Librarie Alphonse Picard et fils, 1914) p. 1. Peeters considers this to be a scholia added by a copyist. In a footnote he states 'Les anecdotes auxquelles cette scolie parait faire allusion, ont dû courir d'assez bonne heure parmi les chrétiens arabes, car elles ont passé dans le coran.' He does not, however, offer any evidence for considering the Christian version more ancient than the Qur'anic. Moreover it should be noted that the scholia is only found in the Bodleian manuscript and not in the more ancient Laurenziano manuscript now published with an Italian translation, M.E. Provera, *Il vangelo arabo dell'infanzia: secundo il ms. laurenziano orientale (n. 387)* (Jerusalem: Franciscan Printing Press, 1973).

17. E. Hennecke, op. cit. pp. 392f.
18. J.N.D. Kelly, *Early Christian Doctrines*, 3rd edn (Edinburgh: T. & T. Clark, 1965), p. 311.
19. The text which dates from around 550 CE. concludes a discussion of the Trinity with the words 'The Messiah is God but God is not the Messiah'. The Qur'ān endorses only the latter half of the statement. C. Schedl, *Muhammad und Jesus* (Vienna: Herder, 1978), p. 531.
20. In the last section it was mentioned that in 542 the Ghassanid phylarch Ḥārith succeeded in having two roving bishops consecrated to care for the Syro-Arab Monophysite communities. In 563, conscious of the Emperor's debt to him for assistance against the Persians, he visited him again bearing a document which he tried to have accepted. The document contained this statement. See A. Guillaume, *Islam*, 2nd edn (Harmondsworth: Penguin, 1956), pp. 16f.
21. See Trimingham, op. cit. pp. 167f.
22. This is an extremely complex issue and will be dealt with at length in Chapter 11.
23. They were also known as Collyridians because they offered Mary sacralised cakes (Gk. *kolluris* = a bread roll, cake). Ibid. p. 68.
24. This has been demonstrated by numerous scholars including Harnack and Schoeps. See most recently M.P. Roncaglia 'Éléments Ebionites et Elkésaïtes dans le Coran', *Proche-Orient Chrétien* XXI (1971), pp. 101–25.
25. It is possible that he is alluded to in the parable of 36:13–25.
26. On Manichaeism see F. Decret, *Mani et la tradition manichéenne* (Paris: Seuil, 1974).
27. Ibid. p. 98. The Christian heretic Montanus had done the same but by this time Montanism was extinct whereas Manichaeism was still flourishing. The identification of Muḥammad with the Paraclete would only have made sense if it was known that there were Christians who still expected the Paraclete to come. Jacob of Saroug's mystical treatises may provide evidence that there were Syriac-speaking Monophysites with expectations of this sort – see Bowman op. cit. p. 194. It should of course be borne in mind that the Qur'ān does not explicitly identify Muḥammad

with the Paraclete although this is how Muslims generally interpret 61:6.
28. See Hennecke op. cit. pp. 278f. It is unlikely that the *Gospel of Thomas* was written by Manichees and so the parallel does not necessarily point to Manichaean influence. See further W. Atallah, 'L'Évangile selon Thomas et le coran', *Arabica* XXIII (1976), pp. 309–11.
29. For a verse by verse study of Jewish parallels to material in ṣūras 2 and 3, which are both Medinan, see A.I. Katsh, *Judaism and the Koran* (New York: Perpetua, 1962).
30. For example: 'On the day when the first man was created, as it is said, "In the day when thou (Adam) wast created they were prepared," the Holy One, blessed be He, said to the ministering angels: Come let us descend and render loving service to the first man' – *Pirke de Rabbi Eliezer* (E.T. Friedlander), p. 89, cited by Katsh op. cit. p. 32f.
31. Chaim Rabbin, *Qumran Studies* (Oxford: OUP, 1957), pp. 112–30 makes out a case for thinking that the sectaries were related to the Qumran Community whose beliefs and practices are known to us from the Dead Sea Scrolls.

4 MUḤAMMAD AND THE CHRISTIANS

1. The most elaborate and best-known version is preserved by the Prophet's biographer Ibn Ishāq. See A. Guillaume, *The life of Muhammad: a translation of Ibn Ishaq's Sirat Rasul Allah* (Oxford: Clarendon, 1955), pp. 79–81. For a succinct discussion of this and of the versions transmitted by Ibn Sa'd and Tirmidhi see Ahmad von Denffer, *Christians in the Qur'ān and Sunna*, Islamic Foundation Seminar Papers 2, (Leicester: Islamic Foundation, 1979), pp. 7–9.
2. *Matthew* 2:4–14.
3. R. Blachère, *Histoire de la littérature arabe* (Paris: Adrien-Maisonneuve, 1966), pp. 727f.
4. Trimingham op. cit. pp. 177f.
5. Ṣaḥīḥ al-Bukhārī, ed. Aḥmad Muḥammad Shākir 9 parts bound in three volumes (Beirut: 'Ālam al-Kutub n.d.), part 1, pp. 3f.
6. W.M. Watt op. cit. 1953, p. 51.
7. These conflicting traditions are mentioned by the Muslim commentators on the Qur'ān. See e.g. the passage from Zamakhsharī translated in H. Gätje, *The Qur'ān and its Exegesis* (London: Routledge & Kegan Paul, 1976), p. 77.
8. For details about Salmān see Guillaume op. cit. 1955, pp. 95–98 and 452.
9. W.M. Watt, *Muhammad at Medina* (Oxford: OUP, 1956), p. 396.
10. Guillaume op. cit. 1955, pp. 146–50 and pp. 167–9.
11. According to tradition he invited them to embrace Islam. Only the Negus of Abyssinia accepted but the leader of the Copts sent presents including Muḥammad's future concubine Māriya. See Guillaume op. cit. 1955, pp. 652–9. The letters which he is purported to have addressed to the rulers are generally thought to be forgeries but their authenticity has been defended by M. Hamidullah, *Six originaux des lettres diplomatiques du prophète de l'Islam* (Paris: Tougui, 1986).

12. W.M. Watt op. cit. 1956, pp. 53–5.
13. Muslim traditions about this episode abound. According to Shī'ites, when the Christians saw Muḥammad, Fāṭima, Ḥasan and Ḥusayn standing under the shade of a cloak they were convinced that he was the brilliant light surrounded by four lesser lights mentioned in their scriptures. See L. Massignon, 'La mubāhala', *Annuaire de l'École Pratique des Hautes Études, Section des Sciences Religieuses* (1943–1944), pp. 5–26.
14. See Guillaume op. cit. 1955, pp. 648f. and the discussion in W.M. Watt op. cit. 1956, pp. 132–6.
15. R. Blachère, *Introduction au coran* (Paris: Maisonneuve et Larose, 1977) pp. 244f.
16. These traditions later became known as 'the causes of the revelation'. For a valuable survey of the literature see A. Rippin, 'The exegetical genre *asbāb al-nuzūl*: a bibliographical and terminological survey' *Bulletin of the School of Oriental and African Studies*, XLVIII/1 (1985) pp. 1–15.
17. See further D.S. Powers, 'The Exegetical Genre *nāsikh al-Qur'ān wa mansūkhuhu*' in A. Rippin (ed.), *Approaches to the History of the interpretation of the Qur'ān* (Oxford: Clarendon, 1988), pp. 117–38 and J. Burton (ed.), *Abū 'Ubaid al-Qāsim b. Sallām's K.al-nāsikh wa-l-mansūkh* (Cambridge: E.J.W. Gibb Memorial, 1987). The latter work contains an important introductory essay by Burton.
18. For the rationale see T. Nöldeke, *Geschichte des Qorans* part 1 (Leipzig: Dieterich'sche Verlags Buchhandlung, 1909), pp. 74–261. The table in Bell & Watt op. cit. (1970), pp. 205–13 gives the chronological order of the ṣūras according to Muir, Nöldeke, Grimme and the official Egyptian text. It occasionally omits details concerning the parts of ṣūras which these writers deemed to be later.
19. The Qur'anic version of the sleeper legend deals skilfully and magisterially with the issues on which Christians were divided – the number of sleepers and the length of time they spent in the cave. See F. Jourdan, *La tradition des sept dormants* (Paris: Maisonneuve et Larose, 1983).
20. See Guillaume op. cit. 1955, pp. 150–3.
21. Nöldeke op. cit. p. 130. He does not here refer to the length of the āyas which is one of the criteria which he normally relies on. In fact the āyas are no longer than one would expect in a ṣūra of the second Meccan period.
22. Because the Qur'ān purports to be in 'pure Arabic' Muslim commentators usually deny that it contains any 'foreign' vocabulary. When faced with loan words they either provide them with Arabic etymologies or insist that they had already been naturalised before the Qur'ān was revealed. The attempt to derive *hawāriyyūn* from the Arabic root *ḥwr* led to the fanciful notion that the disciples were 'fullers'.
23. Guillaume op. cit. 1955 pp. 270–7. Nöldeke op. cit. p. 190. From a Muslim stand-point the rival tradition is the more important because it is included in the ḥadīth collections of Bukhāri and Muslim. An attempt is sometimes made to reconcile the two traditions by suggesting that ṣūra three was recited when the embassy came from Najrān although it had been revealed several years before.

24. It should be noted, however, that a number of Non-Muslim scholars think that 85:4–7 refers to hell-fire and that, *pace* the majority of Muslim commentators, there is no allusion to the martyrs of Najrān. See R. Paret, *Der Koran: Kommentar und Konkordanz* (Stuttgart: Kohlhammer, 1980) pp. 505f.
25. J. Wansbrough op. cit. 1977.
26. G. Lüling, *Über den Ur-Qur'ān* (Erlangan: H. Lüling, 1974) and *Die Wiederentdeckung des Propheten Muhammad* (Erlangan: H. Lüling). I have not had access to these works but there is an extensive review in C. Gilliot, 'Deux études sur le coran', *Arabica*, 30, 1983, pp. 1–37, esp. 16–37.

5 MUḤAMMAD AND JESUS

1. The substance of the first section of this chapter is presented at greater length in my article 'Jesus and Mary in the Qur'ān: Some Neglected Affinities', *Religion*, XX (1990) pp. 161–75. The second section is reproduced from that article with the permission of the Editor.
2. Mohammed Arkoun, op. cit. 1979, pp. 10–13 and *Lectures du Coran*, (Paris: Maisonneuve et Larose, 1982) pp. 32–5.
3. For a discussion of the significance of this see Neal Robinson 'The Qur'ān as the Word of God' in A. Linzey and P. Wexler (ed.), *Heaven and Earth: Essex Essays in Theology and Ethics* (Worthing: Churchman, 1986), pp. 38–54.
4. Or at least of the first part, 'I bear witness that there is no God but God.'
5. Schedl op. cit. 1978.
6. For an explanation of the models see ibid. pp. 39–42.
7. Ibid. pp. 111–19.
8. Henri Michaud, *Jésus selon le Coran* (Neuchâtel: Delachaux et Niestlé, 1960), p. 42.
9. Ibid. p. 91.
10. There are explicit references to the tetraktys already in Philo of Alexandria (first century BC) – see C. Schedl *Baupläne des Wortes* (Vienna: Herder, 1974) p. 353. The alphabet symbolism is not found before the *Sepher Yeẓirah* which is of uncertain date but almost certainly pre-Islamic – see the article by G. Scholem in *Encyclopaedia Judaica* vol. 16, pp. 782–8. See further N. Sed, *La mystique cosmologique juive* (Paris, 1981), pp. 149–53, esp. note 37.

6 CURRENTS AND ENCOUNTERS

1. This is the impression which is given by the Muslim historians. Occasional references in Syriac works by Christians apparently suggest a less rosy picture. See P. Crone and M. Cook *Hagarism* (Cambridge: CUP, 1977), p. 6.
2. See H.A. Wolfson, 'The Muslim Attributes and the Christian Trinity', *Harvard Theological Review* XLIX/1 (Jan. 1956) pp. 1–18.

3. See D.B. Macdonald, *The Development of Muslim Theology, Jurisprudence and Constitutional Theory* (London: Darf, 1985 – New Impression of 1902 edition), p. 146.
4. On the Mu'tazilites see further A.N. Nader, *Le Système philosophique des Mu'tazila* (Beirut: Dar el-Machreq, 1984).
5. Aḥmad b.abī Ya'qūb b. Ja'far b. Wahb b. Wāḍiḥ al-Ya'qūbī, *Tarīkh* (Beirut: Dār al-Sādir n.d.) 2 volumes. The relevant section (vol. 1, pp. 68–80) is translated and discussed in A. Ferré, 'L'historien al-Ya'qūbī et les évangiles', *Islamochristiana*, 3, (1977), pp. 65–83.
6. Abū Ja'far Muḥammad b. Jarīr al-Ṭabarī, *Tarīkh al-Rusul wa-al-Mulūk*, 10 vols (Cairo 1960–69). An English translation of the whole is currently being undertaken by a team of scholars. The relevant section (vol. 1, pp. 585–605) is discussed in detail in A. Ferré 'La vie de Jésus d'après les *Annales de Ṭabarī*, *Islamochristiana* 5 (1979), pp. 7–29.
7. Arabic text and French translation, Maçoudi, *Les prairies d'or*, texte et traduction par C. Barbier de Meynard et Pavet de Courteille (Paris: Imprimerie Impériale, 1861), vol. 1, pp. 120–4.
8. French translation, Allouche, op. cit.
9. See R. Arnaldez, *Grammaire et théologie chez Ibn Hazm de Cordoue* (Paris, 1956), pp. 305–313.
10. *Matthew* 4:12–22, *Mark* 1:14–20, *Luke* 5:1–11, *John* 1:35–52.
11. See S.M. Stern, 'Quotations from Apocryphal Gospels in 'Abd al-Jabbār', *Journal of Theological Studies* N.S., vol. XVIII, part 1, April 1967, pp. 34–57 and ''Abd al-Jabbār's Account of how Christ's Religion was Falsified by the Adoption of Roman Customs', *Journal of Theological Studies* N.S., vol. XIX, part 1, April 1968, pp. 28–185.
12. English translation by A. Mingana (Manchester and London), 1922.
13. 'Alī al-Ṭabarī was not the first Muslim to point to the Paraclete passages in *John*. He was preceded by Ibn Isḥāq – see Guillaume op. cit. 1955, pp. 103f. Mingana op. cit. p. 141 gives the following note: 'In the *Shifā* of Yaḥsubi "Paraclet" is given as a name of Muḥammad (In the chapter of the Prophet's names).' For the numerical value of the Arabic letters see W. Wright op. cit. p. 28. The other NT proof texts cited by 'Alī al-Ṭabarī are *I John* 4:1–3, *I Peter* 4:17, *Luke* 22:36 and *Galatians*, 4:22–26.
14. The Arabic text was published along with a French translation by the Jesuit scholar Chidiac in 1939 under the title *Réfutation excellente de la divinité de Jésus-Christ d'après les évangiles*. I have only had access to the recent pirated edition in two volumes: Abū Ḥāmid Muḥammad b. Muḥammad al-Ghazālī, *al-Radd al-Jamīl li-Alhiyati 'Īsā bi-Ṣarīh al-Injīl* (Istambul: Waqf Ikhlas Publications, 1988). On the question of the attribution to Ghazāli see H. Lazarus-Yafeh, 'Étude sur la polémique islamo-chrétienne: Qui était l'auteur de al-Radd al-gamil li-Ilahiyat 'Isa bi-sarih al-Ingil attribué à al-Gazzali?' in *Revue des Études Islamiques* 1969/2, pp. 219–38.
15. See further J-M. Gaudeul and R. Caspar 'Textes de la tradition musulmane concernant le taḥrīf (falsification) des écritures', *Islamochristiana* 6 (1980), pp. 61–104. All the Qur'anic references to *taḥrīf* concern the Jews rather than the Christians. At 5:14 the Christians are accused of 'forgetting'. At 2:42, 2:140, 2:146, 2:159, 2:174, 3:71 and 3:187 there are

accusations of 'concealing' revelations which may apply to Christians as well as Jews.

7 SHĪ'ITES and ṢŪFĪS

1. See further S.H.M. Jafri, *The Origin and Development of Shi'a Islam* (London: Longman, 1979) and J.M. Hussaim, *The Occultation of the Twelfth Imam* (London: Muhammadi Trust, 1982).
2. For a succinct account of early Shī'ite schisms including the *ghulāt* see M. Momen, *An Introduction to Shi'i Islam*, (Yale: YUP, 1985), pp. 45–60.
3. See L. Massignon, 'Le Christ dans les Évangiles selon Ghazālī, *Revue des Études Islamiques* 1932, pp. 523–36, esp. p. 535.
4. A.J. Arberry (trans.), *The Doctrine of the Sūfīs* (Cambridge: CUP, 1935), pp. 158f.
5. A.J. Arberry, *Sufism* (London: George Allen & Unwin, 1950), pp. 33–5.
6. Many of the anecdotes collected in M. Hayek *Le Christ de l'Islam* (Paris: Seuil, 1959), pp. 133–214 come into this category.
7. Mentioned, e.g. by Hujwīrī Kashf al-Mahjūb translated by R. Nicholson (London, 1911), p. 40.
8. Ibid. p. 50. In some circles Jesus was later thought to have fallen short of the ascetic ideal because he owned a needle and thus disobeyed God's prohibition of earthly possessions – see e.g. Farid ud-Din Attar *The Conference of Birds* (Harmondsworth: Penguin, 1984), p. 207.
9. Hujwīrī op. cit. p. 375f.
10. Cited by M. Smith *The Way of the Mystics* (London: Sheldon Press, 1976), p. 224.
11. R. Nicholson *The Mystics of Islam* (London: George Bell, 1914), pp. 10f.
12. A. Schimmel, *Mystical Dimensions of Islam* (Chapel Hill: University of North Carolina Press, 1975), pp. 47ff.
13. 'The Truth' *(al-Ḥaqq)* is one of the names of God.
14. For an exhaustive treatment of this and related issues see L. Massignon, *La Passion de Hallāj*, 4 vols, 2nd edn (Paris: Gallimard, 1975), vol I, pp. 638–96.
15. Ibid. vol. II pp. 258f.
16. See I. Netton, *Muslim Neoplatonists: an Introduction to the thought of the Brethren of Purity* (London 1982) and Y. Marquet, 'Les Ikhwān al-Ṣafā et le christianisme', *Islamochristiana* 8 (1982), pp. 129–58.
17. There are two English translation: Muhyi-d-din Ibn 'Arabi, *The Wisdom of the Prophets* E.T. by Angela Culme-Seymour (Gloucestershire: Beshom Publications, 1975), pp. 68–82 and Ibn al-'Arabi *The Bezels of Wisdom* E.T. by R.W.J. Austin (London: SPCK, 1980), pp. 172–86 – the page numbers indicate the relevant chapter. There are important discussions by R. Arnaldez, *Jésus dans la pensée musulmane* (Paris: Desclée, 1988), pp. 149–84 and A.D 'Souza, 'Jesus in Ibn 'Arabī's "FUṢUṢ AL-ḤIKAM"', *Islamochristiana* 8 (1982), pp. 185–200.
18. J. Jomier 'Jésus tel que Ghazālī le présente dans «al-Ihyā'»' *MIDEO* (1987), pp. 45–81 has discussed most of the relevant texts. Cragg op. cit.,

1985, pp. 47–9 gives a selection and refers to articles by Margoliouth in *Expository Times*, vols 3 and 4, pp. 59ff., 107ff., 177ff., 503ff. and 561ff.

8 CLASSICAL EXEGESIS

1. There are 13,026 different asānīd in Ṭabarī's commentary of which this one is by far the most frequently cited. A mere 21 of them are cited more than one hundred times. 11,364 of them are cited only once. The figures are taken from H. Horst, 'Zur Uberlieferung im Korankommentar aṭ-Ṭabarīs', *Zeitschrift der Deutschen Morgenlandischen Gesellschaft*, Band 103, (Wiesbaden, 1953), pp. 290–307.
2. The technical terms to do with transmission may not have been so clearly defined in Ṭabarī's time. See further J. Robson, 'Ḥadīth', *Encyclopedia of Islam* (new edn), vol. III, (1977), pp. 23–8, esp. p. 26.
3. For further details concerning this isnād see Horst, op. cit. pp. 301f. and C. Gilliot *La sourate al-Baqara dans le commentaire de Tabarī*, unpublished doctoral thesis, (Université de Paris III, 1982), t.1, pp. 268–70.
4. See J. Robson, 'Al-Dj̲arḥ wa 'l-ta'dīl', *Encyclopedia of Islam* (new edn), vol, II, p. 462.
5. See C. Gilliot, 'Portrait «mythique» d'Ibn Abbās, *Arabica* 32 (1985), pp. 127–84.
6. Abū al-Fidā' Isma'īl Ibn Kathīr *Tafsīr al-Qur'ān al-'Aẓīm*, 7 volumes (Beirut: Dār al-Andalus 1385 H.), vol. 4, p. 452.
7. Ibid. vol. 2, pp. 37f.
8. Abū Ja'far Muḥammad b. Jarīr al-Ṭabarī, *Jāmi' al-Bayān fī Tafsīr al-Qur'ān*, 30 parts bound in 12 volumes (Būlāq 1324 H.), part 3, p. 207.
9. Ibid. p. 191.
10. Ibn Kathīr op. cit., vol. 4, pp. 440 and 474.
11. Ṭabarī op. cit. part 3, p. 192. He also quotes a line from Ru'ba.
12. An annotated edition of the *Masā'il Nāfi' b. al-Azraq* is given in pp. 234–91 of M.F. 'Abd al-Bāqī, *Mu'jam Gharīb al-Qur'ān* (Beirut: Dār al-Ma'rifa n.d.). See p. 246.
13. Ibn Hishām, *al-Sīrat al-Nabawiyya*, 4 volumes (Beirut: Dār al-Iḥyā al-Turāth al-'Arabī, n.d.), vol. 3, pp. 143f. I have taken the translation from Guillaume op. cit. (1955), pp. 408f. but substituting my own more literal rendering of the key verse.
14. Probably the foliage of the rose bay or some similar tree.
15. Ibn Manẓūr, *Lisān al-'Arab* (Beirut: Dār al-Ma'ārif, n.d.).
16. Ṭabarī op. cit. part 3, p. 122.
17. Ibid. part 3, p. 194.
18. Ibid. part 16, pp. 49f.
19. This is the interpretation which Ibn Kathīr prefers because the Qur'ān implies that God wished the angels to honour Adam. Alternatively when the angels prostrated themselves they may have been worshipping God, in which case Adam simply served to indicate the direction in which they were to pray. This would be analogous to God's commanding Muḥammad to «Establish the prayer from the declination of the sun . . .» (17:78). Ibn Kathīr op. cit., vol. 1, p. 135.

20. Ibid. vol. 2, p. 6.
21. Ibid. vol. 2, p. 459. This does not answer Ledit's point that pre-existence is implied in the reference to the Messiah as 'one of those brought near' (above, p. 11). At 56:11, 88 and 83:21, 28 the expression denotes those brought near to God in paradise. It is probably in this sense that it is applied to the Messiah in 3:45 where he is also described as «illustrious in the world and the hereafter». There may, however, be vestiges of an angel Christology at 4:172 where the Messiah is mentioned along with «the angels who are brought near».
22. On the history of the text and the systems of readings see Bell & Watt op. cit. (1970), pp. 40–56.
23. Nāṣir al-Dīn Abū Sa'īd 'Abd-Allāh b'Umar b. Muḥammad al-Shīrāzī al-Bayḍāwī, *Anwār al-Tanzīl wa-Asrār al-Ta'wīl* (Beirut: Dar al-Jīl 1329 H.), p. 166.
24. The surviving evidence has been published by A. Jeffery, *Materials for the History of the Text of the Qur'ān* (Leiden: Brill, 1937).
25. Parrinder op. cit. p. 96, R. Blachère, *Le Coran (al-Qor'ān)* (Paris: Maisonneuve and Larose, 1980) p. 593, Jeffery op. cit. (1937), p. 170.
26. The secondary literature on Ṭabarī's commentary is not extensive considering the size and importance of the work. For a good introduction see Loth (1888) and Goldziher (1920, pp. 86–98). There are two important studies of the asānīd (Horst op. cit. 1953; Gilliot, op. cit. 1982), a masterly survey of the material which refers to Christianity (Charfi, 1980), and an annotated analysis of the comments on 2:62 (Samir, 1980). One can only admire the stamina of those who are currently preparing abridged translations of the whole work in French (Godet, 1983–) and English (Cooper, 1987–) although it is regrettable that they are having to omit so much of the detail.
27. F. Sourdel, 'Une profession de foi de l'historien al-Ṭabarī', *Revue des Études Islamiques* (1968) part 2, pp. 178–99.
28. Abū Ḥāmid al-Asfarāyīnī d.406/1016 (quoted by Samir 1980, p. 559f.).
29. Zamakhsharī's biographical and bibliographical details have been researched by Ibrahim (1980) and Agius (1982). There are translated excerpts from the *Kashshāf* in Gätje (1976). For articles on his theology see note 35.
30. Abū al-Qāsim Jār Allah Mahmūd b. 'Umar al-Zamakhsharī, *al-Kashshāf 'an Ḥaqā'iq al-Tanzīl wa-'uyūn al-Aqāwil fī Wujuh al-Ta'wīl*, 4 vols (Beirut: Dār al-Fikr, n.d.). The general feel of this work is well conveyed by the extracts in Gätje op. cit. 1976.
31. There are general introductions by Arnaldez (1960) and Anawati (1965). On the author's theology see Goldziher (1912) and the recent French translation of his work on the divine names. Concerning his journeys and controversies see Kraus (1938) and Kholeif (1984).
32. The edition I have used is published under a different title (literally 'The Big Commentary') – Fakhr al-Dīn al-Rāzī, *al-Tafsīr al-Kabīr*, 8 volumes, (Beirut: Dār al-Fikr 1398 H./1978 CE). There are studies and translations of extracts by Arnaldez (1960, 1968), Fitzgerald (1978), Johns (1986) and Robinson (1988). On Rāzī's treatment of Christians in his commentary see Arnaldez (1974) and Jomier (1980).

33. The date of writing, the order of composition and the identity of the sections which were compiled by a subsequent hand are discussed by J. Jomier in 'Les mafātiḥ al-ghayb de l'Imam Fakhr al-Din al-Razi: quelques dates, lieux, manuscrits', *MIDEO* 13 (1977), pp. 253–90 and 'Qui a commenté l'ensemble des sourates al-'Ankabūt à Yāsīn (29–36) dans "Le tafsir al-kabīr" de l'Imām Fakhr al-Dīn al-Rāzī?', *Int. J. Middle East Studies* 11 (1980), pp. 467–85. The comments on a number of ṣūras conclude with a statement about the date of completion. The majority of the dates given fall between 595 and 603. However in one manuscript there is a statement at the end of the comment on ṣūra 114 which is dated 592. This could simply be a mistake or alternatively Rāzī may have begun his work by commenting on some of the shorter ṣūras near the end of the Qur'ān. In favour of this latter solution it is noteworthy that in his comment on 5:6 he refers to what he has already written about 98:5. Ibn Khallikān says that when Rāzī died in 606/1210 he left his commentary unfinished. Another possibility is that parts of it were subsequently lost, perhaps during the turmoil caused by the arrival of the Mongols less than 15 years later. Some manuscripts attribute the section of the commentary which covers ṣūras 29–36 to al-Khuwayyī. He was chief cadi of Damascus (d.637/1239) and may have studied briefly under Rāzī in Khurāsān. Jomier says that this section appears to have been written by someone who had heard Rāzī teach and who was familiar with the topography of Syria and Palestine. An addition to the margin of one manuscript further mentions that the section on ṣūras 46–57 was lost and that it was completed by al-Qumūli.
34. For further details concerning Rāzī's sources see J. Jomier, 'Fakhr al-Dīn al-Rāzī (m. 606H./1210) et les commentaires du coran plus anciens', *MIDEO* 15 (1982), pp. 145–72.
35. The details of Bayḍāwī's biography are assembled by Lutpi Ibrahim (1979). The same author has published a series of comparative studies of Zamakhsharī's and Bayḍāwī's theology covering such topics as reason and revelation, obedience and disobedience, divine justice, the position of the grave sinner (1980–82). See my *Bibliography*.
36. For details of the edition used see note 23. There are English translations of the sections dealing with ṣūras 3 (Margoliouth, 1894) and 12 (Beeston, 1963).
37. For the edition of Ibn Kathīr see note 6. I have not encountered any secondary literature in European languages apart from J.D. McAuliffe, 'Qur'anic Hermeneutics: the Views of al-Ṭabarī and Ibn Kathīr' in A. Rippin (ed.) *Approaches to the History of the Interpretation of the Qur'ān* (Oxford: Clarendon Press, 1988), pp. 46–62.
38. For an incisive description of 'la vision musulmane traditionelle' see Arkoun op. cit., 1979, pp. 20–4.
39. Ṭabarī op. cit., part 16, pp. 58f.
40. Ibid. pp. 38f.

9 JESUS' RETURN; QUR'ĀN 4:159

1. Guillaume op. cit., 1955, pp. 271f.
2. Ṭabarī, *Jāmi' al-Bayān*, part 6, pp. 14–17.
3. I am summarising the information. Ṭabarī invariably gives an isnād.
4. On the authority of Ḥumayd, Abū Rajā', Rabī' b. Anas, 'Awf and Manṣūr b. Zādhān. Ṭabarī was in some doubt about the last of these for he prefixes the report with the remark, 'I think he said'.
5. The examples given include falling from the top of a house, decapitation, and being eaten by lions.
6. By one route out of two.
7. The case of Ibn al-'Abbās is particularly glaring because the same pupil, Sa'īd b. Jubayr, is alleged to have reported him as advocating both interpretations. Ṭabarī op. cit., p. 15 lines 7ff., and p. 16 lines 4ff.
8. We saw in Chapter 8 that the short version of this isnād terminating in Qatāda is the most frequent of all the asānīd cited by Ṭabarī. It occurs 3060 times in suras 1–21 and 28–114. According to Horst there are 80 places where it extends back via Companions to the Prophet.
9. Zamakhsharī, *al-Kashshāf*, vol. 1, pp. 580f.
   Rāzī, *Tafsīr al-Kabīr*, vol. 3, pp. 342f.
   Bayḍāwī, *Anwār al-Tanzīl*, p. 135 lines 31ff.
10. Zamakhsharī does not cite any traditional authority in support of this statement. Remember that according to Ṭabarī, Ibn Zayd said that the belief of the Jews will be of no avail to them when Jesus returns.
11. 'Abd Allah Muḥammad b. Aḥmad b. 'Uthmān al-Dhahabī, *Mīzān al-I'tidāl fī Naqdi al-Rijāl*, 4 vols (Beirut: Dār al-Ma'rifa, 1382 H./1963) vol. 2, pp. 283–5.
12. For al-Hajjāj b. Yusuf's famous discourse see Maçoudi, *Les prairies d'or*, texte et traduction par C. Barbier de Meynard et Pavet de Courteille, 9 vols (Paris, 1861–67), vol. 5, pp. 294ff.
13. M. Momen, op. cit., pp. 34–7.
14. F. Sezgin, *Geschichte des Arabischen Schrifttums* vol. 1 (Leiden: Brill 1967), pp. 34f.
15. The comment is similar to those attributed to Ibn al-'Abbās by Ṭabarī but not identical.
16. It is unlikely that Rāzī is deliberately trying to conceal that this report is derived from al-Kalbī as elsewhere he does not hesitate to mention him by name.
17. This is an echo of a debate which began long before Rāzī's time. Ibn Qutayba (d.276/889?) was at pains to refute the *ahl al-kalām* by showing that there was no contradiction between ḥadīth which stated that there would be no prophet after Muḥammad and ḥadīth which referred to the return of Jesus. See A. Guillaume, *The Traditions of Islam* (Oxford: OUP, 1924), pp. 71f.
18. Ibn Kathīr al-Dimashqī, *Tafsīr al-Qur'ān al-'Aẓīm*, vol. 2, pp. 433–47.
19. The Christian ruler of Abyssinia.
20. *Qur'ān* 4:41, 16:84, 16:89, 28:75 and 50:21.
21. See Isaiah Goldfeld, 'The Tafsīr of Abdallah b. 'Abbās, *Der Islam* 58/1 (1981), pp. 125–35.

22. When Muslim hegemony was established Jews enjoyed the protected status which the Prophet had intended for them. It is therefore not surprising that interpreters failed to recognise that the āya in question was originally a threat. In its historical context, however, it was certainly no empty threat for in Medina Muhammad executed 600 members of the Jewish tribe of Qurayza because of their continuing hostility.
23. See Goldfeld, op. cit.

10 JESUS' RETURN – CONTINUED

1. Ṭabarī, *Jāmi' al-Bayān*, part 25, p. 54, line 8 to p. 55 line 11.
2. Commenting on this reading of Ubaiy, Schwally says, 'für ein schwieriges Wort ein anderes kaum leichteres eingesetz.', Nöldeke op. cit., part 2, p. 90.
3. See *Qur'ān* 7:63; 12:104; 38:87; 68:52; 81:27.
4. Zamakhsharī *al-Kashshāf*, vol. 3, p. 494 lines 20–7.
5. *mumaṣṣaratāni – see* Ibn Manẓūr, *Lisān al-'Arab* (Beirut: Dār al-Ma'ārif, n.d.), vol. 6, p. 4216, col. 1, lines 11f.
6. *Rāzī, al-Tafsīr al-Kabīr* vol. 7, p. 434, line 26 to p. 435 line 2.
7. Bayḍāwī, *Anwār al-Tanzīl*, p. 653, lines 1–4.
8. The reference is to Jesus' raising the dead and not to his own resurrection from the dead – *pace* Gātje op. cit., p. 129.
9. Ibn Kathīr, *Tafsīr*, vol. 6, pp. 235, lines 15–27.
10. *wa-fī-hi naẓrun* 'it requires consideration'. See E.W. Lane, *Arabic-English Lexicon* (London, 1863), p. 2812, col. 2.
11. See Guillaume op. cit. (1955), pp. 181–7.
12. Tabarī op. cit. part 15, pp. 2–14.
13. Ibid. p. 5 lines 21–4.
14. Ibid. p. 12 lines 22f–6.
15. Zamakhsharī op. cit., vol. 2, p. 437, line 16.
16. Rāzī op. cit. vol. 5 p. 370, lines 15–18, 24.
17. Bajḍāwī op. cit. p. 370, line 26.
18. Ibn Kathīr, vol. 4, pp. 238–280.
19. Ibid. p. 248, line 13.
20. Ibid. p. 262, line 20, p. 276, line 9.
21. Ibid. p. 251, line 13, p. 252, line 27.
22. The word he uses is *munkar*. Ibid. p. 245, line 8, p. 260, line 13, p. 261, line 13.
23. *wa-dhukira ma'a-hu qaṣabataini*. For this meaning of *qaṣaba* see Ibn Manẓūr, op. cit. vol. 5, p. 3641, col. 1.
24. Ṭabarī op. cit. part 16, p. 23 lines 3–15. The other four commentators do not mention Jesus or cite this ḥadīth at this point.
25. Byzantine name for Jerusalem.
26. A sort of worm which breeds in the noses of camels and sheep. Kasimirski, *Dictionnaire Arabe-Français* (Paris: Maisonneuve, 1860) vol. 2, p. 1302.
27. Ṭabarī op. cit. part 17, p. 69, line 17 to p. 70, line 1.
28. Ibn Kathīr op. cit. vol. 4, p. 594.

29. Ṭabarī op. cit. part 10, p. 82, lines 18–31.
30. In neither case are we given the name of the traditionist who transmitted the report from the Companion: 'on the authority of a sheikh on the authority of Abū Hurayra' and 'one who heard Abū Ja'far say.'
31. Zamakhsharī op. cit. vol. 2, p. 186 lines 16f. Nothing is added to the discussion by Bayḍāwī – op. cit. p. 253 line 3 – who merely refers back to his comment on the previous āya.
32. Rāzī op. cit. vol. 4, p. 426, lines 1–18.
33. Ibn Kathīr op. cit. vol. 3 p. 386 line 17 to p. 387 line 23.
34. According to Guillaume – op. cit. (1955) p. 639, note 1 – a rakūsī was defined as man midway between a Christian and a Ṣābi'. Since the latter is a man who changes his religion, Guillaume says that 'Ādī 'would seem to be, like so many of the Arabs at his time, a convert but not a practising Christian in the full sense.'
35. Ṭabarī, op. cit. part 3, p. 187, line 11 to p. 188, line 17.
36. *wa-lā a'ūdu ba'da-ha kariyya*
    umārisu 'l-kahlata wa'l-ṣabiyya
    The metre is as Ṭabarī says rajaz. The same verse is quoted by Ibn Manẓūr op. cit. vol. 5, p. 3947 col. 3, who adds:
    wa 'l-'azaba 'l-munaffaha 'l-ummiyya
    'and the rejected and illiterate spinster.'
37. Zamakhsharī op. cit. vol. 1, p. 430.
38. Razi op. cit. vol. 2, p. 449, line 26 to p. 450, line 1.
39. *yuḍāḥiku 'l-shamsa min-ha kawkabun shariqun*
    mu'azzarun bi-'ammīmi 'l-nabti muktahilu
    For the text of the whole poem see: al-A'shā, *Dīwān* (Beirut: al-Mu'assasa al-'Arabiya li-al-Tibā'ati wa-al-Nashri n.d.), pp. 144–9. The verse cited by Rāzī is on p. 145, line 9. In my translation *muktahil* is rendered 'in their perfection' and the word order is altered considerably.
40. Mu'tazilite exegete who lived in Isfahan. Rāzī cites him 32 times in his commentary on ṣūra 3. See Jomier, 'Fakhr al-Dīn al-Rāzī (m. 606H./1210) et les commentaires du coran plus anciens', *MIDEO*, 15, (1982), pp. 145–72, esp. p. 155.
41. Mu'tazilite exegete who lived in Baṣra but expelled from their circle for attacking the memory of 'Alī. Rāzī cites him 25 times in his commentary on sura 3. Ibid. p. 152.
42. I have been unable to identify this individual. According to Jomier – op. cit. (1982) p. 169 – this is the only reference to him in the whole of Rāzī's commentary on ṣūra three.
43. Bayḍāwī op. cit., p. 74, line 7.
44. Ibn Kathīr op. cit. vol. 2, p. 40.
45. Ibid. p. 678.
46. *Qur'ān* 46:15.
47. Guillaume op. cit., (1955), p. 104.
48. Al-Ya'qūbī knew that Luke's gospel gave Jesus' age as 30 when he began his ministry – see André Ferré op. cit. (1977) p. 73. Al-Mas'ūdī says that when God raised Jesus into His presence he was thirty three – see Maçoudi, op. cit., t.1, p. 124.
49. The poet was an almost exact contemporary of Muḥammad. Influenced

by Christianity, and at one time attracted to Islam, he died an unbeliever. This is from his most famous poem which is sometimes ranked as one of the *Mu'allaqāt*. For notes on the rare words and difficult expressions in these lines see al-Khātib al-Tibrīzī, *Sharḥ al-Qaṣā'id al-'Ashar* (Beirut: Dār al-Afāq al-Jadīda, 1980) p. 423. There is a splendid French translation of the whole poem in J. Berque *Les dix grandes odes arabes de l'Anté-Islam* (Paris: Sindbad, 1979), pp. 121–8.
50. See K.A.C. Cresswell, *A Short History of Early Muslim Architecture* (Harmondsworth: Penguin, 1958), p. 36.
51. Cited by P. Crone and M. Cook op. cit. p. 6.
52. See H. Putman, *L'Église et l'Islam sous Timothée I (780–823)*, (Beirut: Dar el-Machreq 1986), pp. 124–41.

11 THE CRUCIFIXION – NON-MUSLIM APPROACHES

1. Sahas op. cit. p. 133.
2. Putman op. cit. pp. 252–6.
3. See e.g. Parrinder op. cit. p. 121: 'The cumulative effect of the qur'anic verses is strongly in favour of a real death.'
4. T.F. Michel op. cit. p. 304.
5. E.E. Elder, 'The Crucifixion of Jesus in the Koran', *Muslim World* 1927, pp. 242–58, esp. 258.
6. Parrinder op. cit. p. 112 seems to favour this translation which on p. 109 he attributes to Massignon.
7. Zaehner op. cit. p. 213.
8. Ledit op. cit. pp. 149–52.
9. Cragg op. cit. 1985, pp. 167f. Almost thirty years earlier he expressed very similar views while writing under a pseudonym: see 'Abd al-Tafāhum, 'The Qur'an and Holy Communion' *Muslim World* 1959, pp. 239–48, esp. pp. 242f.
10. Bowman op. cit. p. 197.
11. Grégoire op. cit. pp. 113f.
12. Irenaeus Adv. Haer. 1.24.4. trans. *Anti-Nicene Christian Library* Vol. 5 (Edinburgh: T. and T. Clark, 1868), p. 91.
13. J.M. Robinson (ed.), *The Nag Hammadi Library in English* (Leiden: Brill, 1977), p. 332.
14. Ibid. p. 344.
15. 'Do not be concerned for me or for this people. I am he who was within me. Never have I suffered in any way', J.M. Robinson op. cit. p. 245.
16. Ibn Kathīr op. cit. vol. 3, pp. 306ff.
17. For example Parrinder op. cit. pp. 118f.

12 THE MEANING OF THE VERB *TAWAFFA*

1. My analysis is based on a concordance – Muḥammad Fu'ād 'Abd al-Bāqī, *al-Mu'jam al-Mufris li-'l-Alfāẓ al-Qur'ān al-Karīm* (Beirut: Dār al-Fikr, 1401 H./1981 CE.), pp. 756f. Unfortunately A.H. Mathias Zahniser's article – 'The Forms of Tawaffā in the Qur'ān: a contribution

to Christian-Muslim Dialogue', *Muslim World*, LXXIX/1, 1989, pp. 14–24 – reached me too late for me to take it into account. Zahniser refers to work by O'Shaugnessy, Welch, Crollius and Ritchie of which I was unaware. His own position is not far removed from mine.

2. Ṭabarī part 3, p. 202, line 20 to p. 205, line 2;
   Zamakhsharī vol. 1, p. 432, line 25 to p. 433, line 9;
   Rāzī vol. 2, p. 457, line 34 to p. 458, line 27;
   Bayḍāwī p. 75 lines 12–16;
   Ibn Kathīr vol. 2 p. 44 lines 2–22.
3. The final radical *y* is a semi-vowel.
4. Ṭabarī part 8, p. 89.
5. Cragg op. cit. 1985, p. 168.
6. Räisänen op. cit. p. 68.
7. It was employed by Rabbi Eliezer and Tychonicus.

13 MUSLIM INTERPRETATION OF *SHUBBIHA LA-HUM*

1. Ṭabarī part 6, p. 9, line 35 to p. 13, line 6.
2. Ibid. part 3, p. 202, lines 10–16.
3. Ibid. part 28, p. 60, lines 16–32.
4. Zamakhsharī vol. 1, pp. 579–80.
5. *Pace* M.M. Ayoub, 'Towards an Islamic Christology, II: The Death of Jesus, Reality or Delusion', *Muslim World*, LXX/2, (1980), pp. 91–121, esp. p. 100.
6. Zamakhsharī vol. 1, p. 432, lines 23f.
7. Rāzī vol. 2, p. 454, line 27 to p. 455, line 2.
8. Ibid. p. 458, lines 3–25.
9. Ibid. p. 459, line 14 to p. 460, line 12. Rāzī first states all six objections and then refutes them. In attempting to summarise his argument I have been greatly helped by R. Arnaldez, *Jésus fils de Marie prophète de l'Islam* (Paris: Desclée, 1980), pp. 198–202.
10. See further Chapters 14 and 15.
11. Rāzī vol. 3, p. 340, line 26 to p. 341, line 17.
12. Bayḍāwī p. 75, lines 8f.
13. Ibid. p. 135, lines 9–20.
14. Ibn Kathīr vol. 2, p. 428, lines 24 to 429, line 14 and p. 43, lines 8–16.
15. Ibid. vol. 2, p. 429, line 25 to p. 433, line 5.
16. Ayoub op. cit. pp. 97–9.
17. Massignon op. cit. (1932), p. 535.

14 CREATING BIRDS FROM CLAY AND RAISING THE DEAD TO LIFE

1. There is evidence that they did so already during the lifetime of the Prophet – see below. In the modern period this line of argument has rarely been pursued. It is, however, found in a recent work by Denise Masson:

Rien ne s'oppose en définitive d'après le Coran, à ce que Jésus soit considéré comme le Verbe éternel; il est comparé avec Adam qui à ce titre, mérite le respect des anges; il est doué du pouvoir de créer, de faire des miracles, de connaître ce qui est caché (D. Masson, *Le Coran et la révelation judéo-chrétienne: études comparées* (Paris: Maisonneuve, 1959), p. 213.)

2. See the *Discussion* at the end of the chapter.
3. *Qur'ān* 6:2; 7:12; 17:61; 23:12; 28:38; 32:7; 37:11; 38:71 and 38:76. The only other occurrence of the word *ṭīn* is at 51:33.
4. *Qur'ān* 15:29; 32:9 and 38:72.
5. *Qur'ān* 21:91 and 66:12.
6. K. Cragg, op. cit. (1985), pp. 33f.
7. *Matthew* 9:18–26/*Mark* 5:21–43/*Luke* 8:40–56; *Luke* 7:11–17; *John* 11:1–44.
8. E. Hennecke, op. cit. vol. 1, pp. 392f.
9. A. Guillaume op. cit. (1955) p. 271.
10. Ṭabarī part 3, pp. 190f. on 3:49; part 7, p. 83 on 5:110;
    Żamakhsharī vol. 1, p. 431. on 3:49; vol. 1, p. 653 on 5:110;
    Rāzī vol. 2, pp. 451f. on 3:49; vol. 3, p. 468f. on 5:110;
    Bayḍāwī p. 74 on 3:49; p. 166 on 5:110;
    Ibn Kathīr vol 2, p. 41 on 3:49; vol. 2, pp. 678f. on 5:110.
11. 'Creating Birds from Clay: a miracle of Jesus in the Qur'an and Classical Muslim Exegesis' *Muslim World*, LXXIX/1 (1989), pp. 1–13.
12. Zamakhsharī, op. cit. vol. 1, p. 228.
13. See Zuhayr b. Abī Sulmā, *Dīwān* (Beirut: Dār Ṣādir n.d.) p. 29. The meaning is that unlike others Harim executes the plans he determines on.
14. This is the view subsequently popularised by Ibn 'Arabi. See Muhyi-d-din Ibn 'Arabi), *The Wisdom of the Prophets* E.T. by Angela Culme-Seymour (Gloucestershire: Beshom Publications, 1975), p. 70.
15. Zamakhsharī identifies the sign which Jesus gave in response to his critics. It was his telling them what they ate and what they stored up in their houses.
16. According to the *Annals* of Ṭabarī, Shem was the ancestor of the Arabs, the Persians and the white-skinned peoples. Tabari, *De la création à David* (Paris: Sindbad, 1984), p. 107.
17. Apollonius of Tyana rescued a young woman from her bier and gave her an additional dowry. Philostratus, *Life of Apollonius* 4:45.
18. To distinguish it from ṣūras 2, 3, 29, 30 and 31 which also begin with these three mysterious letters.
19. *qad qāla Ibn abī Ḥātim*.
20. See Ibn Ḥajar *Tadhīb al-Tadhīb* (Beirut: Dār Ṣādir, 1968) vol. 8, p. 244, no. 448. Unfortunately Ibn Kathīr does not comment on the isnād. Mālik b. Ismā'īl was a well-known Kūfan scholar (see Dhahabī op. cit. vol. 3, p. 587, no. 7715). Muḥammad b. Ṭalḥa (d.167/784) is cited by both Bukhārī and Muslim (see Dhahabī op. cit. vol. 3, p. 424, no. 7008). I am not certain who is intended by Abū Bishr as there were at least seven scholars with this name (see Dhahabī op. cit. vol. 4, p. 495). Note that the isnād is *mu'an'an* (i.e. the means of transmission is not stipulated. It is simply *'an* 'on the authority of').

21. Cited by Rāzī in *Traité sur les noms divins* présenté, traduit et annoté par Maurice Gloton (Paris: Dervy-livres, 1986 and 1988), vol. 1, pp. 190f.
22. Ibn Kathīr op. cit. vol. 5, p. 404.
23. Ibid. vol. 7, pp 66f.
24. Ibid. This too is said to have taken place in pre-Islamic times for the Prophet begins the story with the words 'There was a man from among those who were before you'. Ibn Kathīr describes this tradition as *munkar jiddan*, i.e. of very weak authority.
25. Horst op. cit. p. 302.
26. Sezgin op. cit. pp. 32f.
27. According to Horst loc. cit. Aḥmad b. al-Mufaḍḍal was a Shī'īte and 'Amr – whom he identifies as 'Amr b. al-Hammād al-Kūfī – was a Rāfidite.
28. Cited in J.D.M. Derret, *The anastasis* (Warwickshire: Drinkwater, 1982) p. 25.
29. My attention was drawn to these passages by J. Jomier, 'Unité de Dieu, Chrétiens et coran selon Faḥr al-Dın al-Rāzī', *Islamochristiana*, 6, (1980), pp. 149–77.
30. Rāzī vol. 2, p. 464, lines 15–16.
31. Cited by Jomier op. cit. (1980), p. 158. (I have been unable to find this passage as I do not have access to the 32-volume Cairo edition of *Tafsīr Kabīr* used by Jomier. The reference he gives is vol. 7, p. 176.)
32. Ibid. p. 156 (Rāzī vol. 12, p. 61 of the 32-volume edition).
33. Rāzī vol. 2, p. 434, lines 18–20.
34. Ibn Kathir vol. 2, p. 41.

15 THE VIRGINAL CONCEPTION

1. Éphrem de Nisibe op. cit. p. 66.
2. Cassiani, De Incarnatione Christi, lib. 7 cap. 6, MG 50 col. 214. Cited by Th. O'Shaughnessy, *The Development of the Meaning of Spirit in the Koran* (Rome: 1953), p. 60.
3. Éphrem de Nisibe op. cit. p. 49.
4. Hennecke op. cit. vol. 1, p. 199.
5. The Qur'ān does not explicitly refer to the Messiah as an angel but see 3:45 and 4:172.
6. Our knowledge of these Jewish Christian sects is derived principally from brief allusions to them in the church fathers. The main texts are Epiphanius *Panarion* 30:16 and the so-called *Epistle of Barnabas* 18:2. They are quoted and discussed in J. Danielou, *The History of Early Christian Doctrine Before the Council of Nicaea*, vol. 1 (London: DLT, 1967), pp. 55ff.
7. Hippolytus, *Elenchos* 9:14 quoted by Danielou op. cit. p. 65.
8. Hennecke op. cit. vol. 1, p. 379.
9. Ibid. p. 494.
10. This section is taken from my article 'Jesus and Mary in the Qur'ān: some neglected affinities', *Religion*, XX (1990) pp. 161–75, and is reprinted with the permission of the Editor.

11. The various traditions are summarised in N. Abbott, *Aishah The Beloved Of Mohammed*, (London: Al-Saqi Books, 1985), pp. 44f. where references to the original sources are given. For Ḥafṣa's former marriage see W.M. Watt, *Muhammad at Medina*, (Oxford: OUP, 1956), p. 396. For 'Ā'isha's vaunting the fact that she was Muḥammad's only virgin bride, see N. Abbot op. cit. p. 65.
12. For the description of the mosque see Maxime Rodinson, *Mohammed*, E.T. (Harmondsworth: Penguin Books, 1971), pp. 149f.
13. For the change to virilocal marriage see W.M. Watt, op. cit., pp. 272–7. The information about 'Ā'isha is conveniently set out by W.M. Watt, ''Ā'isha bint Abī Bakr', *The Encyclopaedia of Islam*, New Edition, vol. 1, pp. 307f.
14. According to Muslim tradition followed by Nöldeke this passage was revealed at Mecca, i.e. before the *ḥijāb* was introduced for Muḥammad's wives.
15. For the accusation against 'Ā'isha and the incident which provoked it, see N. Abbott, op. cit. pp. 29–38.
16. The word «calumny» (*buhtān*) occurs six times in the Qur'ān. In the expression «a tremendous calumny» (*buhtān 'aẓīm*) it occurs only twice – at 4:156 in connection with Mary and at 24:16 in connection with 'Ā'isha who is not named.
17. Ṭabarī part 16, pp. 45–7. Zamakhsharī vol. 2, pp. 504f. Rāzī vol. 5, pp. 528–31. Bayḍāwī p. 404. Ibn Kathīr vol. 4, pp. 444–6.
18. 'Fakhr al-Dīn al-Rāzī and the Virginal Conception', *Islamochristiana*, 14, (1988), pp. 1–16.
19. It is not clear whether any of these views was ever attributed to an early authority.
20. Probably Abū Muslim b. Muḥammad b. Baḥr al-Isfāhānī (d.934).
21. Abū Ḥaywa's name does not occur in the list of seven systems which gained canonical status nor was he one of 'the three in addition to the seven' or of 'the four in addition to the ten' favoured by some scholars. His full name is Abū Ḥaywa Shūrayḥ b. Yazīd al-Ḥaḍramī (d.819). He was reader in Ḥims (Syria) and his readings were transmitted by his son. See Nöldeke op. cit. vol. 3, p. 173.
22. On the subject of miracles as irrefutable proofs of a prophet's veracity see L. Gardet and G.-C. Anawati *Dieu et la destinée de l'homme* (Paris: Vrin 1967), pp. 193–201. The belief that only men can be prophets is based on Qur'ān 12:109, 16:43 and 21:7.
23. Technical term for a miracle granted to a saint as distinct from a *mu'jiz* which is only granted to a prophet. This option was not open to 'Abd al-Jabbār (the Mu'tazilite cadi of Raiy d.1025) because he dismissed the miracle-working claims of saints as charlatanry – see Gardet and Anawati op. cit. p. 204.
24. Abū 'Amr (d.770) was reader in Basra. Rāzī confuses him with Ibn 'Āmir (d.776) of Damascus. According to Zamakhshari and Bayḍāwī this reading was also supported by Nāfi' (d.785), Ibn Kathīr (d.737) and Ya'qūb (d.820).
25. That is to say even if Gabriel were to be endowed with the power to bestow a son on Mary by creation there could be no question of his

sharing in God's negative attributes. By 'negative attributes Rāzī understands attributes of God such as Self-sufficient (*ghanī*), i.e. exempt from needs and Unique (*wahīd*), i.e. exempt from having others like Him. See Fakhr ad-Dīn ar-Rāzī *Traité sur les noms divins* t.1 presenté, traduit et annoté par Maurice Gloton (Paris: Dervy-Livres 1986), p. 92.

26. Ephrem de Nisibe, op. cit. p. 68.
27. Hennecke op. cit. vol. 1, p. 380. The mosaic is early fourteenth century but probably represents an ancient iconographic tradition. It is also worth noting that in Byzantine mosaics angels often appear as beardless (but winged) youths.

16 THE REPRESENTATION OF JESUS IN THE SHĪ'ITE COMMENTARIES

1. For a general introduction to Twelver Shī'ite exegesis see M. Ayoub, 'The Speaking Qur'ān and the Silent Qur'ān: A Study of the Principles and Development of Imāmī Shī'ī *tafsīr*' in Rippin op. cit., (1988), pp. 177–98.
2. M.H. Ṭabāṭabā'ī, *The Qur'an in Islam: Its Impact and Influence on the life of Muslims*, (London: Zahra, 1987), pp. 48f. gives the impression that this is because of the unsound asānīd and the evident contradictions in the traditions. A more telling reason is that the Companions failed at first to recognise 'Alī's claim to leadership and cannot therefore be immune from criticism as Sunnites maintain.
3. Abū al-Ḥasan 'Alī b. Ibrāhīm al-Qummī *Tafsīr al-Qur'ān* 2 vols (Najaf, 1386 AH).
4. Abū Ja'far Muḥammad b, Ḥasan al-Ṭūsī *Tibyān* 10 vols (Najaf, 1376–1387 AH).
5. Abū 'Alī al-Faḍl b. al-Ḥasan al-Ṭabarsī *Majma' al-Bayān fī Tafsīr al-Qur'ān*, 5 vols (Qumm, 1333 AH). See Musa O.A. Abdul, 'The Unnoticed *Mufassir*: Shaykh Ṭabarsī, *Islamic Quarterly* XV (1971), pp. 96–105 and 'The *Majma' al-Bayān* of Ṭabarsī', ibid., pp. 106–20.
6. Qummī vol. 1, pp. 157f on 4:159. Ṭūsī vol. 3, pp. 386f. on 4:159. Ṭūsī vol. 9, pp. 211f. on 43:61.
7. Abū al-Qāsim b. Muḥammad al-Balakhī (d.319/931), one of the teachers of the Baghdad branch of the Mu'tazilites.
8. Ibrāhīm Abū Isḥāq b. Muḥammad al-Surrī al-Zajjāj, grammarian and tutor of the children of Caliph al-Mu'taḍid.
9. Qummī vol. 1, p. 103 on 3:55. Ṭūsī vol. 2, p. 478 on 3:55, vol. 3, p. 382ff. on 4:157. Ṭabarsī vol. 1, pp. 448f. on 3:55.
10. This interpretation did not originate with al-Farrā'. It was known to him but he thought that it was not necessarily correct and that the meaning might be that God grasped Jesus from the earth without causing him to die. See Abū Zakariyyā Yaḥyā b. Ziyàd al-Farrā', *Ma'āni al-Qur'ān* part 1, p. 219.
11. See page 133 above.
12. Qummī vol. 1, p. 102 on 3:49, vol. 1, p. 190 on 5:110f. Ṭūsī vol. 2, p. 467f on 3:49, vol. 4, pp. 59f. on 5:110f. Ṭabarsī vol. 1, p. 445 on 3.49.

13. This is different from anything we find in the Sunni commentaries. It is similar to the thought of 'Abd-al-Jabbār who rejected the earlier Mu'tazilite view that the spirit was the life-principle. See Peeters op. cit., (1976), pp. 164f.
14. Qummī vol. 1, p. 102 on 3:42, vol. 2, p. 49 on 19:21f. Ṭūsī vol. 2, p. 406f. on 3:42, vol. 7, pp. 113 on 19:18. Ṭabarsī vol. 1, p. 440 on 3:42, vol. 3, p. 507 on 19:18.
15. See Momen op. cit. p. 161f. Qummī wrote after the Lesser Occultation but the details were probably not known in his day. I have failed to discover any similar reports about earlier figures revered by the Ghulāt sects.

17 THE REPRESENTATION OF JESUS IN THE ṢŪFĪ COMMENTARIES

1. Its contents are outlined in Arberry op. cit. (1950), pp. 74–79.
2. Abū al-Qāsim 'Abd al-Karīm al-Qushayrī, *Laṭā'if al-Ishārāt*, 6 vols, (Cairo: 1969–71). Arnaldez op. cit. (1988), pp. 29–64 summarises Qushayrī's comments on 2:253, 4:172, 5:110, 19:31 and 19:33.
3. See further Rashīd Ahmad, 'Abū al-Qāsim al-Qushairī as Theologian and Qur'anic Commentator', *Islamic Quarterly*, (13), 1969, pp. 16–69.
4. Despite the fact that all manuscripts of this work attribute it to Qāshānī, it is usually published under the name of Ibn 'Arabī. This is the case with the edition which I have used: Muḥyī al-Dīn Ibn 'Arabī, *Tafsīr al-Qur'ān al-Karīm*, 2 volumes (Beirut: Dār al-Andalus, 1978), henceforth referred to simply as Qāshānī. M. Vàlsān has published annotated French translations of a number of excerpts. For full details see my Bibliography.
5. Qāshānī vol. 1, p. 4.
6. For a detailed discussion see P. Lory, *Les Commentaires ésotériques du Coran d'après 'Abd ar-Razzâq al-Qâshânî* (Paris: Les Deux Océans, 1980), esp. pp. 44–82.
7. Qushayrī vol. 5, p. 372 on 43:61, vol. 1, p. 254 on 3:46.
8. Qashānī vol. 1, p. 191 on 3:56–8, vol. 1, p. 296 on 4:157, vol. 2, pp. 450f. on 43:61.
9. Qushayrī vol. 1, pp. 257f. on 3:55, vol. 2, p. 82 on 4:157.
10. Qāshānī vol. 1, pp. 189–91 on 3:55, vol. 1, p. 296 on 4:158f.
11. Qushayrī vol. 1, pp. 256f. on 3:49.
12. Qāshānī vol. 1, pp. 187f. on 3:49, p. 350 on 5:110, p. 447 on 7:104–41.
13. Qushayrī vol. 1, p. 254 on 3:42.
14. Qāshānī vol. 1, p. 180 on 3:34, p. 187 on 3:47, vol. 2, pp. 11–13 on 19:16f.
15. See Qāshānī vol. 1, p. 247.

Bibliography

BIBLIOGRAPHICAL AND REFERENCE WORKS

Anawati, G.C., 'Polémique, apologie et dialogue islamo-chrétiens. Positions classiques et positions contemporaines', *Euntes docete*, XXII, (1969), pp. 375–472.

Caspar, R. et al., 'Bibliographie du dialogue islamo-chrétien', *Islamochristiana*, 1, (1975), pp. 125–81; II (1976), pp. 187–249; III (1977), pp. 255–86.

EI² = *Encyclopaedia of Islam*, 2nd edn (Leiden: Brill, 1960–).

Kazimirski, A. *Dictionnaire Arabe-Français* (Paris: Maisonneuve, 1860).

Lane, E.W. *Arabic-English Lexicon* (London: Williams & Norgate, 1863).

WORKS IN ARABIC

al-A'shā, *Dīwān* (Beirut: al-Mu'assasa al-'Arabiya li 'l-Tibā'at wa 'l-Nashr, n.d.).

'Abd al-Bāqī, Muḥammad Fu'ād, *al-Mu'jam al-Mufris li 'l-Alfaz al-Qur'ān al-Karīm* (Beirut: Dār al-Fikr 1401 H/1981 CE).

'Abd al-Bāqī, Muḥammad Fu'ād (ed.) *Mu'jam Gharīb al-Qur'ān Mustakhrijan min Ṣaḥīḥ al-Bukhārī* (Beirut: Dār al-Ma'rifa, n.d.).

al-Bayḍāwī, 'Abd Allah b. 'Umar, *Anwār al-Tanzīl wa-Asrār al-Ta'wīl* (Beirut: Dār al-Jīl, 1329 H).

al-Bukhārī, *Ṣaḥīḥ*, 9 parts bound in 3 vols (Beirut: 'Ālam al-Kutub, n.d.).

al-Dhahabī, 'Abd Allah Muḥammad b. Aḥmad b. 'Uthmān, *Mizān al-I'tidāl fī Naqdi al-Rijāl*, 4 vols (Beirut: Dār al-Ma'rifa, 1382 H/1963 CE)

al-Ghazālī, Abū Ḥāmid Muḥammad b. Muḥammad, *al-Radd al-Jamīl li-Alhiyati 'Īsā bi-Ṣarīh al-Injil* (Istanbul: Waqf Iklas, 1988).

Ḥusayn, Ṭaha, *al-Ayyām*, vol. 2 (Cairo: Dār al-Ma'ārif, 1939).

Ibn 'Arabī, Muḥyī al-Dīn, *Tafsīr al-Qur'ān al-Karīm*, 2 vols (Beirut: Dār al-Andalus, 1978).

Ibn Ḥajar, Tadhīb al-Tadhīb (Beirut: Dār Ṣādir, 1968).

Ibn Hishām, *al-Sīratu al-Nabawiyya*, 4 vols (Beirut: Dār al-Iḥyā al-Turāth al-'Arabī, n.d.).

Ibn Kathīr, Abū al-Fidā' Isma'īl, *Tafsīr al-Qur'ān al-'Aẓīm*, 7 vols, (Beirut: Dar al-Andalus 1385 H).

Ibn Manẓur, *Lisān al-'Arab* 6 vols (Beirut: Dār al-Ma'ārif, n.d.).

al-Qāshānī, 'Abd al-Razzāq. See Ibn 'Arabī.

al-Qummī, Abū al-Ḥasan 'Alī b.Ibrāhīm, *Tafsīr al-Qur'ān*, 2 vols (Najaf, 1386 H).

al-Qushayrī, *Laṭā'if al-Ishārāt*, 6 vols, (Cairo: 1969–71).

al-Rāzī, Fakhr al-Dīn, *al-Tafsīr al-Kabīr*, 8 vols, (Beirut: Dār al-Fikr, 1398 H/1978 CE).

al-Suyūṭī, Jalāl-al-Dīn, *al-Itqān fī 'Ulūm al-Qur'ān*, 2 parts bound in 1 vol. (Beirut: Dar al-Fikr, 1399 H/1979 CE).

al-Ṭabarī, Abū Ja'far Muḥammad b. Jarīr, *Jāmi' al-Bayān fī Tafsīr al-Qur'ān*, 30 parts bound in 12 vols (Būlāq, 1324 H).

al-Ṭabarī, Abū Ja'far Muḥammad b. Jarīr, *Tarīkh al-Rusul wa 'l-Mulūk*, 10 vols (Cairo, 1960–69).

al-Ṭabarsī, Abū 'Alī al-Faḍl b. al-Ḥasan, *Majma' al-Bayān fī Tafsīr al-Qur'ān*, 5 vols (Qom, 1333 H).

al-Tibrīzī, al-Khāṭib, *Sharḥ al-Qaṣā'id al-'Ashar* (Beirut: Dār al-Afāq, al-Jadīda, 1980).

al-Ṭūsī, Abū Ja'far, *al-Tibyān fī Tafsīr al-Qur'ān*, 10 vols (Najaf, 1957–63).

al-Ya'qūbī, Aḥmad b. abī Ja'far b. Wahb b. Wāḍiḥ, *Tarikh*, 2 vols (Beirut: Dār Ṣādir, n.d.).

al-Zamakhsharī, Abū al-Qāsim Jār Allah Maḥmūd b. 'Umar, *al-Kashshāf 'an Ḥaqā'iq al-Tanzīl wa-'Uyūn al-Aqāwil fī Wujuh al-Ta'wīl*, 4 vols, (Beirut: Dār al-Fikr, n.d.).

Zuhayr b. Abī Sulmā, *Dīwān*, (Beirut: Dār Ṣādir, n.d.).

BOOKS AND ARTICLES IN EUROPEAN LANGUAGES

'Abd al-Tafāhum, 'The Qur'ān and Holy Communion', *Muslim World*, XL, (1959), 239–48.

Abbot, N., *Aishah the Beloved of Mohammed* (London: Al-Saqi, 1985).

Abdul, Musa O.A., 'The Unnoticed Mufassir: Shaykh Ṭabarsī', *Islamic Quarterly*, (15), 1971, pp. 96–105.

—— 'The Majma' al-bayān of Ṭabarsī', *Islamic Quarterly*, (15), 1971, pp. 106–20.

Agius, D.A., 'Some Bio-bibliographical notes on Abū 'l-Qāsim Maḥmud b. 'Umar al-Zamakhsharī', *al-Arabiyya* (*Journal of the American Association of Teachers of Arabic*), XV, (1982), pp. 108–30.

Ahmad, Rashīd, 'Abū al-Qāsim al-Qushairī as Theologian and Qur'anic Commentator', *Islamic Quarterly*, XIII, (1969), pp. 16–69.

Allouche, I.S., 'Un traité de polémique christiano-musulmane au IXe siècle', *Hespéris*, XXVI, (1939), pp. 123–53.

Anawati, G.C., ''Isā', *EI²*, vol. 4 pp. 85–90.

—— 'Fakhr al-Dīn al-Rāzī', *EI²*, vol. 2, pp. 751–5.

Andrae, T., *Les Origines de L'Islam et Le Christianisme*, (Paris: Adrien-Maisonneuve, 1955 – German original 1923–5).

Arberry, A.J., *The Doctrine of the Sūfīs* (Cambridge: CUP, 1935).

—— *Sufism* (London: George Allen & Unwin, 1950).

Arkoun, M., *La Pensée Arabe*, 2e édn (Paris: PUF, 1979).

—— *Lectures du Coran* (Paris: Maisonneuve & Larose, 1982).

Arnaldez, R., *Grammaire et théologie chez Ibn Hazm de Cordoue* (Paris, 1956).

—— 'Apories sur la prédestination et le libre arbitre dans le commentaire de Razi', *MIDEO*, VI, (1959–60), pp. 123–36.

—— 'L'oeuvre de Fakhr al-Dīn al-Rāzī commentateur du Coran et philosophe', *Cahiers de civilisation médiévale*, III (1960), pp. 307–23.

—— 'Trouvailles philosophiques dans le commentaire coranique de Fakhr al-Dīn al-Rāzī', *Études philosophiques et litteraires*, III, (1968), pp. 11–24.
—— 'Les chrétiens selon le commentaire coranique de Rāzī' in *Mélanges d'Islamologie dédiés à la memoire d'A. Abel* (Leiden: Brill, 1974), pp. 45–57.
—— *Jésus Fils de Marie Prophète de L'Islam* (Paris: Desclée, 1980).
—— *Jésus dans la Pensée Musulmane* (Paris: Desclée, 1988).
Atallah, W., 'L'Évangile selon Thomas et le coran', *Arabica*, XXIII (1976), pp. 309–11.
Ayoub, M., 'Towards an Islamic Christology, II: The Death of Jesus, Reality or Delusion', *Muslim World*, LXX, (1980), pp. 91–121.
—— 'The Speaking Qur'ān and the Silent Qur'ān: A Study of the Principles and Development of Imāmī Shī'ī tafsīr' in Rippin op. cit., 1988, pp. 178–93.
Beck, E., 'Les houris du Coran et Ephrem le Syrien', *MIDEO*, VI (1959–60), pp. 405–8.
Beeston, A.F.L., *Baidāwī's Commentary on Sūra 12 of the Qur'ān* (Oxford: OUP, 1963).
—— (ed.), *Arabic Literature to the End of the Umayyad Period* (Cambridge: CUP, 1983).
Bell, R., *The Origin of Islam in its Christian Environment* (London: Macmillan & Co., 1926).
Bell, R. & Watt, M., *Introduction to the Qur'an* (Edinburgh: EUP, 1970).
Berque, J., *Les dix grandes odes arabes de l'Anté-Islam* (Paris: Sindbad, 1979).
Blachère, R., *Introduction au Coran* (Paris: Maisonneuve & Larose, 1977).
—— *Histoire de la Littérature Arabe* (Paris: Adrien-Maisonneuve, 1964–1980).
—— *Le Coran (al-Qor'ān)* traduction (Paris: Maisonneuve & Larose, 1980).
Bowman, John, 'The Debt of Islam to Monophysite Syrian Christianity', *Nederlands Theologisch Tijdschrift*, XIX, (1964–65), pp. 177–201.
Burton, J. (ed.), *Abū 'Ubaid al-Qāsim b. Sallām's K. al-nāsikh wa-l-mansūkh* (Cambridge: Gibb Memorial Trust, 1987).
Charfi, Abdel Majīd, 'Christianity in the Qur'ān Commentary of Ṭabarī', *Islamochristiana*, VI, (1980), pp. 105–48.
Cragg, K., *Jesus and the Muslim* (London: George Allen & Unwin, 1985).
Cresswell, K.A.C., *A Short History of Early Muslim Architecture* (Harmondsworth: Penguin, 1958).
Crone, P. and Cook, M., *Hagarism* (Cambridge: CUP, 1977).
Culme-Seymour, A., *The Wisdom of the Prophets by Muhyi-d-din Ibn 'Arabi* English Translation (Gloucestershire: Beshom, 1975).
Daniel, N., *Islam and the West: the Making of an Image*, (Edinburgh: EUP, 1964).
Danielou, J., *The History of Early Christian Doctrine Before the Council of Nicaea*, vol. 1, (London: DLT, 1976).
Decret, F., *Mani et la tradition manichéene* (Paris: Seuil, 1974).
Denffer, Ahmad von, *Christians in the Qur'ān and Sunna*, I. F. Seminar Papers II (Leicester: Islamic Foundation, 1979).
—— *'Ulūm al-Qur'ān: An Introduction to the Sciences of the Qur'ān* (Leicester: Islamic Foundation, 1983).

Derret, J.D.M., *The anastasis* (Warwickshire: Drinkwater, 1982).
D'Souza, A., Jesus in Ibn 'Arabī's 'FUṢUṢ AL-ḤIKAM', *Islamochristiana*, VIII, (1982), pp. 185–200.
Elder, E.E., 'The Crucifixion in the Qur'ān', *Muslim World*, XIII (1923), pp. 242–58.
Éphrem de Nisibe, *Commentaire de l'Évangile Concordant ou Diatessaron*, Sources Chrétiennes No. 121 (Paris: Cerf, 1966).
Ferré, A., 'L'historien al-Ya'qūbī et les évangiles', *Islamochristiana*, III, (1977), pp. 65–83.
—— 'La vie de Jésus d'après les Annales de Ṭabarī', *Islamochristiana*, V, (1979), pp. 7–29.
Fitzgerald, M., 'The manner of revelation, the commentary of al-Rāzī on Qur'ān 42, 51–53', *Islamochristiana*, IV, (1978), pp. 113–25.
Gardet, L., *Dieu et la Destinée de l'homme* (Paris: Vrin, 1976).
Gaudel, J.-M. and Caspar, R., 'Textes de la tradition musulmane concernant le taḥrīf (falsification) des écritures', *Islamochristiana*, VI, (1980), pp. 61–104.
Gätje, H., *The Qur'ān and its Exegesis: Selected Texts with Classical and Modern Interpretations*, trans. and ed. A. Welch (London: Routledge & Kegan Paul, 1976).
Gilliot, C., *La sourate al-Baqara dans le commentaire de Ṭabarī*, unpublished doctoral thesis, (Université de Paris III, 1977).
—— 'Deux études sur le coran', *Arabica*, XXX, (1983), pp. 1–37.
—— 'Portrait «mythique» d'Ibn 'Abbās', *Arabica*, XXXII, (1985), pp. 127–84.
Goldfeld, I., 'The Tafsīr of Abdallah b. 'Abbās', *Der Islam*, 58/1, (1981), pp. 125–35.
Goldziher, I., 'Aus der Theologie des Fakhr al-Dīn al-Rāzī', *Der Islam*, III, (1912), pp. 213–47.
—— *Die Richtungen der islamischen Koranauslegung* (Leiden: Brill, 1920).
Gräf, E., 'Zu den christlichen Einflüsen im Koran', in *Festschrift J. Henniger* (Bonn: St Augustine, 1976), pp. 111–44.
Guillaume, A., *The Traditions of Islam* (Oxford, OUP, 1924).
—— *The life of Muhammad: a translation of Ibn Ishaq's Sirat Rasul Allah* (Oxford: OUP, 1945).
—— *Islam* 2nd edn (Harmondsworth: Penguin, 1956).
Hamidullah, M., *Six originaux des lettres diplomatiques du prophète de l'Islam* (Paris: Tougi, 1986).
Haveneth, A., *Les arabes chrétiens nomades au temps de Mohammed* (Louvain-la-Neuve: Cerfaux Lefort, 1988).
Hayek, M., *Le Christ de L'Islam* (Paris: Seuil, 1959).
Hennecke, E., *New Testament Apocrypha*, vol. 1 (London: SCM, 1973).
Horst, Heribert, 'Zur Uberlieferung im Korankommentar at-Tabaris' *Zeitschrift der Deutschen Morgenlandischen Gesellschaft*, CIII/Neue Folge, XXVIII, (1953), pp. 290–307.
Hussaim, J.M., *The Occultation of the Twelfth Imam* (London: Muhammadi Trust, 1982).
Hussein, Taha, *The Stream of Days: A Student at the Azhar* (London: Longmans, Green, 1948).

Ibn al-'Arabi, *The Bezels of Wisdom* E.T. by R.W.J. Austin (London: SPCK, 1988).
Ibrahim, Lutpi, 'Al-Bayḍāwī's life and works', *Islamic Studies*, XVIII, (1979), pp. 311–21.
—— 'Az-Zamakhsharī: His life and works', *Islamic Studies*, XIX, (1980), pp. 95–110.
—— 'The Concepts of *Iḥbāṭ* and *Takfīr* according to az-Zamakhsharī and al-Bayḍāwī', *Die Welt des Orient*, XI, (1980), pp. 117–21.
—— 'The Concept of Divine Justice according to al-Zamakhsharī and al-Bayḍāwī', *Hamdard Islamicus*, III/1, (1980), pp. 3–17.
—— 'The Relation of Reason and Revelation in the Theology of az-Zamakhsharī and al-Bayḍāwī', *Islamic Culture*, LIV, (1980), pp. 63–74.
—— 'The Place of Intercession in the Theology of al-Zamakhsharī and al-Bayḍāwī', *Hamdard Islamicus*, IV/3, (1981), p. 3–9.
—— 'A Comparative Study of the Views of az-Zamakhsharī and al-Bayḍāwī about the position of the grave sinner', *Islamic Studies*, XXI, (1982), pp. 55–73.
Irenaeus, Saint 'Adversus Haereses' E.T. in *Ante-Nicene Christian Library* vol. 5 (Edinburgh: T. & T. Clark, 1868).
Jafri, S.H.M., *The Origin and Development of Shi'a Islam* (London: Longman: 1979).
Jefferey, A., *Materials for the History of the Text of the Qur'ān* (Leiden: Brill, 1937).
—— *The Foreign Vocabulary of the Qur'ān* (Baroda: Oriental Institute, 1938).
Johns, A.H., 'Al-Rāzī's treatment of the Qur'anic episodes telling of Abraham and his guests. Qur'anic exegesis with a human face', *MIDEO*, XVII, (1986), pp. 81–113.
Jomier, J., 'Les mafatih al-ghayb de l'Imam Fakhr al-Din al-Razi: quelques dates, lieux, manuscrits', *MIDEO*, XIII, (1977), pp. 253–90.
—— 'Unité de Dieu, Chrétiens et coran selon Faḫr al-Dīn al-Rāzī', *Islamochristiana*, VI, (1980), pp. 149–77.
—— 'Qui a commenté l'ensemble des sourates al-'Ankabūt à Yāsīn (29–36) dans "Le tafsir al-kabīr" de l'Imām Fakhr al-Dīn al-Rāzī?', *Int. J. Middle East Studies*, XI, (1980), pp. 467–85.
—— 'Fakhr al-Dīn al-Rāzī et les commentaires du coran plus anciens', *MIDEO*, XV, (1982), pp. 145–72.
—— 'Jésus tel que Ghazālī le présente dans «al-Ihyā'»', *MIDEO*, XX, (1987), pp. 45–81.
Jourdan, F., *La tradition des sept dormants* (Paris: Maisonneuve et Larose, 1983).
Katsh, A.I. *Judaism and the Koran* (New York: Perpetua, 1962).
Kelly, J.N.D., *Early Christian Doctrines*, 3rd edn (Edinburgh: T. & T. Clark, 1965).
Kholeif, F., *A Study on Fakhr al-Dīn al-Rāzī and his Controversies in Transoxania*, 2nd edn (Beirut: Dar el-Machreq, 1984).
Khoury, A.-Th., *Les Théologiens Byzantins et L'Islam*, 2nd edn, (Louvain and Paris: Nauwelaerts, 1969).

Kraus, P., 'The 'Controversies' of Fakr al-Dīn Rāzī', *Islamic Culture*, XII, (1938), pp. 131–53.
Lammens, H., 'Les Chrétiens à la Mecque à la veille de l'hégire', *Bulletin de l'Institut Français d'Archéologie Orientale*, XIV, (1917), pp. 191–230.
Lazarus-Yafeh, H., 'Étude sur la polémique islamo-chrétienne: Qui était l'auteur de al-Radd al-ǧamīl li-Ilāhiyat 'Īsā bi-ṣarīḥ al-Inǧil attribué à al-Gazzālī?' in *Revue des Études Islamiques*, (1969), pp. 219–38.
Lecomte, G., *Le Traité des divergences du Hadīt d'Ibn Qutayba* (Damascus: Institut Français, 1962).
Ledit, Charles-J., *Mahomet, Israel et le Christ* (Paris: La Colombe, 1956).
Lory, Pierre, *Les Commentaires ésotériques du Coran d'après 'Abd ar-Razzâq al-Qâshânî* (Paris: Les Deux Océans, 1980).
Loth, O., 'Ṭabarī's Korancommentar', *Zeitschrift der Deutschen Morgenlandischen Gesellschaft*, LIII, (1881), pp. 588–628.
Luke, K., 'The Koranic Recension of Luke 1:34', *Indian Theological Studies*, XXII, (1985), pp. 381–99.
Lüling, G., *Über den Ur-Qur'ān* (Erlangen: H.Lüling, 1974).
Macdonald, D.B., *The Development of Muslim Theology, Jurisprudence and Constitutional Theory*, (London: Darf, 1985).
Maçoudi ('Alī b. Ḥusayn), *Les prairies d'or*, text and translation by C. Barbier de Meynard & Pavet de Courteille, 9 vols (Paris: Imprimerie Impériale, 1861–7).
Margoliouth, D.S., *Chrestomathia Baidawiana: The Commentary of el-Baidāwī on Sura III Translated and Explained for the Use of Students of Arabic* (London: Luzac, 1884).
McAuliffe, J.D., 'Qur'anic Hermeneutics: the Views of al-Ṭabarī and Ibn Kathīr' in Rippin, op. cit., 1988, pp. 46–62.
Marquet, Y., 'Les Ikhwān al-Ṣafā' et le christianisme', *Islamochristiana*, VIII, (1982), pp. 129–58.
Massignon, L., 'Le Christ dans les Évangiles selon Ghazālī', *Revue des Études Islamiques*, (1932), pp. 523–36.
—— 'La mubāhala', *Annuaire de l'École Pratique des Hautes Études, Section des Sciences Religieuses* (1943–1944), pp. 5–26.
—— *La Passion de Hallāj*, 4 vols, 2nd edn (Paris: Gallimard, 1975).
Masson, D., *Le coran et la révélation judéo-chrétienne: études comparées* (Paris: Maisonneuve, 1959).
Metzger, B.M., *The Early Versions of the New Testament* (Oxford: OUP, 1967).
Michaud, H., *Jésus selon le Coran* (Neuchatel: Delachaux et Niestlé, 1960).
Michel, T.F., *A Muslim Theologian's Response to Christianity: Ibn Taymiyya's al-Jawab al-Sahih* (New York: Caravan, 1984).
Mingana, A., *The Book of Religion and Empire By 'Ali Tabari* (Manchester and London, 1922).
Momen, M., *An Introduction to Shi'i Islam* (Yale: YUP, 1985).
Nader, A.N., *Le Système philosophique des Mu'tazil* (Beirut: Dar el-Machreq, 1984).
Netton, I., *Muslim Neoplatonists: an Introduction to the thought of the Brethren of Purity* (London: George Allen & Unwin, 1982).

Nicholson, R., *The Kashf al-Mahjūb the oldest Persian treatise on Sufism written by 'Alī b. 'Uthmān, al-Hujwīrī* (trans.) (London, 1911).
Nicholson, R., *The Mystics of Islam* (Routledge & Kegan Paul: London and Boston, 1963) – reissue of 1913 edition.
Nöldeke, T., *Geschichte des Qorans* reprint of 2nd edn (Hildesheim: Georg Olm, 1981).
O'Shaughnessy, Th., *The Development of the Meaning of Spirit in the Koran* (Rome, 1953).
Paret, R., *Der Koran, Übersetzung*, 2nd edn (Stuttgart: Kohlhammer, 1980).
—— *Der Koran, Kommentar und Konkordanz* (Stuttgart: Kolhammer, 1980).
Parrinder, G., *Jesus in the Qurān* (London: Faber & Faber, 1965).
Peeters, P., *Évangiles Apocryphes* vol. 1 (Paris: Librairie Alphonse Picard et fils, 1914).
Peters, J.R.T.M., *God's Created Speech* (Leiden: Brill, 1976).
Philostratus, *Life of Appolonius* (Harmondsworth: Penguin, 1970).
Powers, D.S., 'The Exegetical Genre: *nāsikh al-Qur'ān wa mansūkhuhu*', in Rippin op. cit. (1988), pp. 117–38.
Provera, M.E., *Il vangelo arabo dell'infanzia: secundo il ms. laurenziano orientale (n.387)* (Jerusalem: Franciscan Printing Press, 1973).
Putman, H., *L'Église et l'Islam sous Timothée I 780–823* (Beirut: Dar el-Machreq, 1986).
Rabbath, E., *L'Orient Chrétien à la veille de l'Islam* (Beirut: Librairie Orientale, 1980).
Rabbin, Chaim, *Qumran Studies* (Oxford: OUP, 1957).
Race, A., *Christians and Religious Pluralism* (London: SCM, 1983).
Raïsänen, H., *Das koranische Jesusbild* (Helsinki, 1971).
Al-Rāzī, F. ad-Dīn, *Traité sur les noms divins* traduit et annoté par M. Gloton, 2 vols (Paris: Dervy-livres, 1986 and 1988).
Rippin, A., 'The exegetical genre *asbāb al-nuzūl*: a bibliographical and terminological survey', *Bulletin of the School of Oriental and African Studies*, XLVIII/1, (1985), pp. 1–15.
Rippin, A. (ed.), *Approaches to the History of the Interpretation of the Qur'ān* (Oxford: OUP, 1988).
Robinson, J.M. (ed.), *The Nag Hammadi Library In English* (Leiden: Brill, 1977).
Robinson, Neal, 'The Qur'ān as the Word of God', in Linzey, A. and Wexler, P. (ed.) *Heaven and Earth: Essex Essays in Theology and Ethics* (Worthing: Churchman, 1986), pp. 38–54.
—— 'Fakr al-Dīn al-Rāzī and the virginal conception', *Islamochristiana*, XIV, (1988), pp. 1–16.
—— 'Creating Birds from Clay: a miracle of Jesus in the Qur'ān and Classical Muslim Exegesis,' *Muslim World*, LXXIX/1, (1989), pp. 1–13.
—— 'Jesus and Mary in the Qur'ān: Some Neglected Affinities', *Religion*, XX, (1990).
Robson, J., 'Al-Djarḥ wa 'l-Ta'dīl', *EI²*, vol. 2, p. 462.
—— 'Ḥadīth', *EI²*, vol. 3., pp. 23–8.
Rodinson, M., *Mohammed* (Harmondsworth: Penguin, 1971).

Roncaglia, M.P., 'Éléments Ebionites et Elkésaïtes dans le Coran', *Proche-Orient Chrétien*, XXI, (1971), pp. 101–25.
Sahas, J.D., *John of Damascus on Islam*, (Leiden: Brill, 1972).
Samir, K., 'Le commentaire de Ṭabarī sur coran 2/62 et la question du salut des non-musulmans', *Annali dell'Istituto Orientale di Napoli* NS, XXX, (1980), 555–617.
Schedl, C., *Baupläne des Wortes* (Vienna: Herder, 1974).
—— *Muhammad und Jesus* (Vienna: Herder, 1978).
Schimmel, A., *Mystical Dimensions of Islam* (Chapel Hill: University of North Carolina Press, 1975).
Scholem, G., 'Sepher Yeẓirah', *Encyclopaedia Judaica*, vol. 16, pp. 782–8.
Sed, N., *La mystique cosmologique juive* (Paris: Mouton, 1981).
Sezgin, F., *Geschichte des Arabischen Schrifttums*, vol. 1, (Leiden: Brill, 1967).
Ṣiddiqi, A.Ḥ., *Ṣaḥiḥ Muslim Rendered Into English* 4 vols, (New Delhi: Kitab Bhavan, 1977).
Smith, M., *The Way of the Mystics* (London: Sheldon Press, 1976).
Sourdel, D., 'Une Profession de foi de l'historien al-Ṭabarī', *Revue des Études Islamiques* (1968), part 2, pp. 178–99.
Stern, S.M., 'Quotations from Apocryphal Gospels in 'Abd al-Jabbār', *Journal of Theological Studies*, NS. XVIII, (1967), pp. 34–57.
—— ''Abd al-Jabbār's Account of how Christ's Religion was Falsified by the Adoption of Roman Customs', *Journal of Theological Studies*, NS. XIX, (1968), pp. 28–185.
Ṭabāṭabā'ī, M.H., *The Qur'ān in Islam*, (London: Zahra, 1987).
al-Ṭabarī, Abū Ja'far Muḥammad b. Jarīr *Commentaire du Coran*, Godé, P., (abridged trans.) (Paris, 1983–).
—— *The Commentary on the Qur'ān*, Cooper, J. (abridged trans.) (Oxford: OUP, 1987–).
Trimingham, J.S., *Christianity among the Arabs in Pre-Islamic Times* (London and New York: Longman, 1979).
Vālsan, M., 'Un commentaire ésotérique du coran: les Ta'wīlātu-l-Qur'ān d'Abdu-r-Razzāq al-Qāchānī', *Études Traditionnelles*, (1963), pp. 73–80 (= annotated translation of Qāshānī's preface.)
—— 'Commentaire de la Fātihah' *Et. Trad.*, (1963), pp. 81–94.
—— 'Les lettres isolées' *Et. Trad.*, (1963–4), pp. 256–62.
—— 'Les trois sourates finales', *Et. Trad.*, (1969), pp. 159–71.
—— 'La sourate 96' *Et. Trad.*, (1969), pp. 255–64.
—— 'La Sourate 56' *Et. Trad.*, (1972), pp. 255–74.
—— 'La Sourate 24' *Et. Trad.*, (1973), pp. 97–114.
—— 'Sourate Ya Sin', *Et. Trad.*, (1975), pp. 122–38.
Watt, W.M., *Muhammad at Mecca* (Oxford: OUP, 1953).
—— *Muhammad at Medina* (Oxford: OUP, 1956).
—— ''Ā'isha bint Abī Bakr', *EI*[2] vol. 1, pp. 307f.
Wolfson, H.A., 'The Muslim Attributes and the Christian Trinity', *Harvard Theological Review*, XLIX/1, (1956), pp. 1–18.
Wright, A., *A Grammar of the Arabic Language*, 3rd edn, 2 vols (Cambridge: CUP, 1896 and 1898).

Zaehner, R.C., *At Sundry Times: An Essay In Comparative Religions*, (London: Faber & Faber, 1958).

Zahniser, A.H.M., 'The Forms of Tawaffā in the Qur'ān: a contribution to Christian-Muslim Dialogue', *Muslim World*, LXXIX/1, (1989), pp. 14–24.

Indexes

INDEX OF QUR'ANIC ĀYAS

The āyas which are mentioned only on pp. 3–7, 27–30 and 117f are not indexed.

INDEX OF REFERENCES TO THE BIBLE AND NT APOCRYPHA

INDEX OF PERSONS

The Arabic definite article al- and the contracted form 'l are ignored. Thus al-Qummī is listed after Qatāda. The terms ibn (abbreviated to b.) and abū (abbreviated to a.) are ignored when they occur in the middle of a name, e.g. Wahb b. Munabbih, but are indexed when at the beginning, e.g. Ibn Isḥāq.

SUBJECT INDEX